The
Holy Vedas
For All

P D Mishra

Books For All
Delhi-110052

Distributed by
D.K. Publishers Distributors (P) Ltd.
4834/24, Ansari Road, Darya Ganj,
New Delhi-110002
Phones: 3278584, 3278368, 3261465,
e-mail: dkpd@del3.vsnl.net.in
visit us at: www.dkpd.com

First Published 2002

ISBN 81-7386-252-4

Published by
Books For All
(an imprint of Low Price Publications)
A-6, Nimri Commercial Centre,
Near Ashok Vihar Phase-IV,
Delhi-110052
Phones: 7401672, 7452453
e-mail: lpp@nde.vsnl.net.in
visit us at: www.lppindia.com

Printed at
D K Fine Art Press P Ltd.
Delhi-110052

PRINTED IN INDIA

Dedication

मे पितु वस्यां असि– मे माता च समा । ऋग्. 8.1.6

**(Lord, you are Greater than my father but equal
to my Mother!**

To My Mother Gaura Devi

Acknowledgement

I acknowledge with profound gratitude my sincerest debt to following Sages, authors, publishers, scholars, well wishers and friends-

Sriyut Sri Aurobindo, Shri Pad Damodar Satwalekar, Rishi Dayanand Saraswati, Bharat Ratna P.V. Kane, Ralph T.H. Griffith, Arthur Anthony Macdonell, F. Max Muller, M. Winternitz, Swami Satyaprakash Saraswati, Pandit Satyakam Vidyalankar, Maharshi Mahesh Yogi, Shri R.L. Kashyap, Shri M.P. Pandit, Shri Rishi Kumar Mishra, Dr. Braj Bihari Chaubey, Dr. Raghubir Vedalankar, Shri Tarinish Jha, Shri Prabhakar Narayan Kavthekar, Dr. Tony Neder, Shri Jaidev Vidyalankar, Dr. Sudhikant Bharadwaj, Dr. Kapil Dwivedi, Dr. Pravesh Saxena, Bibek Debroy and Dipavali Debroy;

Swadhyay Mandala Pardi, Gita Press Gorakhpur, Shri Aurobindo Ashram Pondicherry, D.K. Publishers Delhi, Rashtriya Sanskrit Sansthan Delhi, Rupa & Co. New Delhi, Pustak Mahal Delhi, Vedic Sahitya Sadan Hoshiyarpur, Hariyana Sahitya Akademi, Chandigarh;

Shri Prabhu Dayal Agnihotri, Shri Vidya Niwas Mishra, Dr. Ramkrishna Saraf, Shri Vishnu Kant Shastri, Bhaskaracharya Tripathi, Shri Durga Charan Shukla, Shri Krishna Kishor Dwivedi, Shri Ganga Ramji Shastri, Shri Anadi Lal Tiwari, Shri Abahya Awasthi and Shri Ishnarayan Joshi;

Shri N.B. Lohani, Dr. Mohan Gupta, Shri Ram Rasayni, Shri Ramdeo Mishra.

Contents

Vedic Call for the Revival of Pure Knowledge

Vedas are the most ancient storehouse of all knowledge. As the very name of the texts suggests, *Veda* stands for the process of knowing as well as the knowledge itself. Although the books come to us as written documents now, but according to the Indian belief cherished down the ages, the truth imbibed in them is a pure knowledge form perceived by the seers (*rishis*) in the state of deep *Smâdhi* (realization.) There are thus no writers mentioned but only the names of the *'drastâ'* (seers) appearing for every verse or the *mantra*, as the case may be. Modern western interpreters of *Vedas* who often termed them as the pastoral poetry did not probably had that deep insight which according to *Nirukta* by *Yâska* written earlier than 2nd BC is the problem faced by a blind man colliding against a pillar which is at all not responsible for this loss of sight. There are a number of Indian commentaries beginning with *Brâhmanas, Sâyana* and *Yâska* till modern times notably by, *Dayânanda Saraswatî, Shri Aurobindo* and *Sâtavalekar.* However, the direct message and a common appeal to the masses through *Vedas* still need to be stressed and highlighted.

Indians are fond of claiming that the *Vedas* are *Apaurusheya,* which means that they are not man made; they have their origin in the Divine. Some interpret this statement to mean that since they have appeared as revelation of truth like other scriptures such as Bible or Koran, they should also be called so. They are also called *Shruti,* as they were being remembered by heart after in turn heard from the masters and later on compiled by *Veda*

Vyâsa in the present form. The text and the texture of the books are incredibly so intact and superb that there is no question of any loss of the actual meaning. The only limit is our capability of comprehension. The further explorations in this vast field of this knowledge therefore, must go on. It is possible only when the gates of this storehouse are wide open. There is no point in keeping the 'secrets of *Vedas*' confined to a chosen few. There is no reason why that direct and yet great knowledge should not be available to everyone.

This is only a modest attempt in this direction. I have no claims as to be an interpreter of any secret knowledge of *Vedas*. I have simply proposed a direct and easy meaning available to be followed so that a further probe may well continue by those who can strive for it. I am of the firm opinion that the natural poetry, the original quest of mankind and a common cause of celestial human values propounded in the *Vedas* must be followed and appreciated. Generally western as well as Indian commentators have either much simplified or mystified the meaning of the *Vedas* in their respective approaches. The natural and direct meaning has thus remained throughout obscured and the natural appeal of *Vedas* often missed in that course.

A direct and the vibrant truth interwoven underneath all *Vedas* is undoubtedly superb which continues to be a mystery in spite of the fact that so many voluminous treatises and commentaries have already been written on them. It is indeed the mystery of the world and the riddle of life represented in entirety in the creation and the texture of the *Vedas*. Therefore the exploration process of *Vedas* much like our life and the universe can hardly come to an end. And yet the urge and the utility should also at the sometime not diminish. The *Atharva Veda* rightly makes this declaration-

पश्य देवस्य काव्यम् न ममार न जीर्यति । अथर्व. *10-8-32*

(Behold, it is a divine composition; it will never cease or diminish)

The basic difference between other philosophies and sciences as compared to the Vedic one is this that whereas the former touch upon just one or the other part of the truth, the later represents human consciousness in a complete epic form of direct experience aiming at human emancipation for all time to come.

Indeed our entire quest for eternal peace and bliss in the present world and beyond has been reflected here and finds a fundamental expression in about twenty thousand verses (hymns) of *Vedas*. The infallible knowledge revealed to the ancient seers was to make human beings aware of their innate divinity so that they come to realize their true nature and attain happiness here and after without any fail.

Bhopal   P.D.Mishra

1

A Brief Introduction to Vedas

The term *Vedas* encompasses four parts of the Vedic literature, i.e., *Samhitâs* such as *Rigveda, Yajurveda, Sâmaveda* and *Atharvaveda; Brâhmans* such as *Aitreya* and *Shatpatha;* the *Âranyakas* such as *Brahdâranyaka* and the *Upanishads* such as *Chhândogya, Mundaka, Kathopnishad* etc. There is a further supplementary part of *Vedas* known as *Vedânga* (limb of *Vedas*), which have been termed as *Shikshâ* (Education), *Kalpa* (Ritual prescriptions), *Vyâkarana* (Grammar), *Nirukta* (Mode of Expression, etymology) and *Chhanda* (Metre).

Another term used for *Vedas* is '*Shruti*'. It is the subtle sound concept exemplified through this name. The subtlest sound lies at the origin of all creation. Indian philosophy describes it as '*Parâ-Vâk*', the meta-sound. Ancient seers heard this voice in a state of deep Smâdhi therefore it came to be called as '*Shruti*'. When they gave it a form of their expression, it came to be known as '*Richâ*', a stanza of a hymn. The composer was called to be a '*Rishi*', the seer. The mode of this expression was called '*Chhanda*', the metre and the content of the verse is '*Devatâ*', the deity. A combination of these three is the '*Samhitâ*' part of the *Vedas*, which is at the basis of the huge classic known as Vedic literature.

The contents of *Vedas* as *Apourusheya* creation are naturally at times abstract and esoteric. Their dissemination and assimilation was therefore necessary. It was also necessary for *Vedas* to be partitioned and divided into various group in accordance with their contents, texture and implications. The sage who divided these solemn texts was *Vedavyasa*, the term *Vyasa* literally meaning division. It is *Vedavyasa* therefore who is credited to have divided Vedic knowledge into categories like *Rigveda, Yajurveda, Sâmaveda* and *Atharvaveda*.

There are two schools of thought classifying Vedic literature. The first and the foremost school believe that the four *Rig, Yaju, Sâm* and *Atharva Vedas* were perceived in their vision by seer *Agni, Vâyu, Âditya* and *Angirâ* respectively. According to them, only the original four basic Classics were passed on under a Divine dispensation. The other school is however of the opinion that all four major works i.e., the *Samhitâ*, the *Brâhmans*, the *Âranyakas* and the *Upanishads* are equally divine and they have all got to be studied together.

Interpretations

Vedas have been interpreted ascribing them a meaning, which is spiritual, scriptural, divine, ritualistic, sound based, grammarian, allegorical, historical and symbolical. These are as a matter of fact, the Indian systems of the study of Vedic literature. Modern European scholars naturally were inclined to accept *Vedas* as an attempt of the primal men towards self-expression, which incidentally also represents a basic urge of human kind in his long journey towards evolution and fulfilment.

Historically speaking, the earliest interpreter was *Yâska* whose *Nirukta* written about 700 BC is the first and foremost treatise on the *Vedas*. *Sâyana* of 14th Century AD forms another landmark of this history whose primary object of writing commentaries was to explain and elaborate the ritualistic aspect of the *Vedas* for the performance of *Yajna* (sacrifices). Another name is that of *Mahidhar* worth mentioning among ancient schools.

Among modern noticeable Indian commentators, the names to be mentioned with regards are *Swâmi Dayananda Sarswati, Shri Aurobindo* and *Shripad Damodar Sâtavalekar*. *Swami Dayânanda* was a revolutionary thinker working with a missionary zeal. He is largely responsible for reviving the original Vedic appeal as a testimony of the final truth and their (Vedas) new role in the emancipation of Hindu society. *Shri Aurobindo* in his great philosophical treatise 'Secret of the *Veda*' discards both the extremes of either calling the Vedic poetry a 'pastoral poetry' or a 'ritualistic order' in the lines of western writers and *Sâyana* respectively. Because he himself was a great philosopher of a deep insight, he has written long and detailed essays giving symbolical meanings of natural powers like Sun, *Agni, Indra, Varuna, Vâyu* etc. as well as cows, horses, herbs and other elements of nature and the world. According to him for instance, *Agni* stands for Will Power, *Indra* for the Divine Mind, *Vâyu* for Life Energies, *'go'* (cow) for Light of Knowledge and *Sûrya* for Light and force and so on so forth. According to Shri M.P. Pandit, an Aurobindonian philosopher of high repute, 'The hymns (*Vedas*) speak of the material prosperity of the society, the dynamic development of the heroes, the mental development of the seers who could see beyond time and space. They speak more of the spiritual ascent of man towards the world of undying Light and the part played by the various gods assisting him on the way opening closed doors on new horizons breaking down obstructions with their shining weapon' (From preface to *Rigveda Samhitâ*)

The elaborate commentaries of all the *Vedas* provided by *Shri Sâtavalekar* are rooted deep in their underlining utility of the books for the society as well as the Nation. Thus the terms like *'Parmbrahma'* (Almighty God) stands for The President of the World, *Parmatma* for the Vice President, *Agni* for the Education Minister, *Indra* for the Defence Minister, *Rudra* for the Commander in chief, *Marut* for the soldiers and likewise.

Among modern European interpreters, Arthur Anthony McDonnell is to be first remembered who had the following widely accepted and popular notion to forward-

'The higher Gods of the *Rigveda* are almost entirely personification of natural phenomena such as Sun, Dawn, Fire, Wind.'

The historical and the newly evolved linguistic theory of Indo-European languages had a particular bearing in their interpretations of the *Vedas*. The comparative study of Indo-European languages was to subsequently play a leading role in this field. Some other names worth mentioning in this regard are

Vedic Hymns by H. Oldenberg (1897), A history of Indian Literature by M. Winternitz (1927), The *Rigveda* by K.F. Geldner (1907), The Hymns of *Rigveda* by R.T.H. Griffith (1963), *Rigveda* Brâhmans by A.B. Keith (1920) and A History of Sanskrit Literature by F. Max Muller (1926).

Period

While ascertaining the time of the composition of this earliest piece of these writings, we face following three basic questions i.e. whether all verses of *Rigveda* were completed in one particular time? Whether the seers of these verses were the virtual writers? And when actually *Veda*s were compiled in the present form?

The internal evidences gathered from *Rigveda* suggest that different verses as well as the books of *Veda*s were completed in different times. The language, the metre, the texture and the category of seers specifically indicate it. The very next *mantra* of the first verse of the first book of *Rigveda* talks about the earlier seers who were worshiping *Agni*.

Therefore while Indian belief goes for the timeless origin of these sacred books, Western researchers basically had the historical perspective governing their approach. It is worthwhile to consider some of these important findings about the approximate timings of these writings.

Max Muller, the author of 'The History of Sanskrit Literature' is naturally the first among all work mentioning in this regard. According to him *Veda*s were written in about 1000 BC. He has reached this conclusion based on the historical evidence of *Buddha* taking birth in about 500 BC. The supporters of this belief were further prepared to take the time to 1200 BC at the most. But this has been much criticized later on as it had no scientific basis and it was by and large an arbitrary thesis.

It is quite surprising that in spite of this theory being under serious attack by western and eastern thinkers alike, it has been alluring a number of writers and commentators. Even Keith, Gonda and McDonnell feel that this contention is also well worth proved because the *Âryans* may not have moved from Iran to

India before 1300 BC. A further serious probe on the subject was based on astronomical calculations derived from the internal evidences of the *Vedas* themselves. This is more in fitness of things since not only the observations but also the rituals prescribed were performed after the calculations of the auspicious timings for them. *Lokmanya Bal Gangadhar Tilak* in India and Herman Jacoby in Europe thus concluded that during the period of *Brâhmans* being written vernal equinox fell in *Kritikâ* star and the time calculations were made beginning with that point of time. On the earlier period of *Vedas* on the other hand, the vernal equinox existed in the *Mrigshira* star. *Rigveda* as well as many other ancient books contain evidence of astronomical significance like the position of Sun in the Zodiac on the two equinoxes, vernal or spring equinox and autumn equinox. Again several *Shulbha Sûtras* declare that a pole star is visible. Since a visible pole star occurs only at certain epochs, it is indicative of a range of dates of that event. Astrologically calculating thus, the period of *Brâhmans* is estimated to be about 2500 BC and that of *Vedas* about 4500 BC. *Tilak* is further in favour of taking back the time to 6000 BC.

Archaeological discoveries about the similarities of *Âryan* and *Mitanni* as well as *Hittite* cultures have provided another dimension to this concept. There is a strange similarity in the names and descriptions of gods like *Miter, Varuna, and Indra* etc. The question arises how these *Âryan* gods have made their entry into *Mitanni* race in Asia Minor? This evidence clearly supports the view that *Âryan* were present in Asia Minor in the 2nd BC. What probably we can state with emphasis is the fact that *Jains* and *Buddhists* accept the existence of Vedic literature long before them. Even independent of all other estimation, this particular aspect clearly points out that *Vedas* were written about 2500 to 3000 BC.

Rigveda repeatedly refers to ancient sages and modern sages in 1.1.2. The age associated with these ancient sages can be called as the high Rig Vedic period which is declared to be 3100 B.C.E or early. The period 3700-3800 B.C.E is the closing of the Rig Vedic age, especially the *Mandals* seven and third associated with the sages *Vashishtha* and *Vishwâmitra*. The *Shulabha Sûtra* texts-*Baudhâyana, Ashwalâyana* etc can be dated 3100-2000 B.C. 1900 B.C.E is the dying up of *Saraswatî* river and the end of Vedic age. The Vedic civilization ended, as indicated by the Harappa ruins for ecological reasons- draughts and desertification. There was no invasion by any one as such.

A comparative analysis of Vedic mathematics and the mathematics of Old-Babylonia (1700 BC) and the Egyptian Middle Kingdom (2000 to 1800 BC) shows that the layer of the (post-Vedic) *Sûtra* literature containing the works of *Baudhâyana, Asvalâyana, Apastambha* and *Kâtyayana* (and possibly others) must have been in existence well before 200 BC. Combining this with astrological data lends support to the traditional date 3100 BC for the closing of the Vedic Age and the *Mahâbhrata* war. This is also suggestive of the fact that *Rigveda* belongs to an earlier layer of civilization prior to the beginning of the ancient world's great civilization –Egypt, Sumeria, the Saraswatî-Indus and China.

Rigveda: its Subject Matter and Ten Books

Philosophically speaking, the subject matter of *Rigveda* can be summarized in following four key- points

1.   There is a truth higher and deeper than the truth of the outer existence. There is an immortality towards which the human soul has to rise.

2.   There is an inferior truth of this world because it is mixed with much falsehood. But the highest is the world of Truth and Light.

3.   In the vast journey of this world, human life is a battlefield of the *Devâs* and *Asuras,* the light and the darkness. We have to invoke the gods for assistance for this purpose with the power of *Mantra.*

4.   At the summit of all teachings of *Rigveda* is the pronouncement that there is just 'One Reality.' Thus the basic keynote of immense significance is the all integrated exposition of this truth everywhere. He pervades all existence, both living and non-living.

There is no conception of hell as such and there is no divide seen between the spiritual and the worldly life in it. All persons, men, women, married couples, householders, wandering mendicants, any one are free to tread the path of immortality. It has more than forty hymns about aspects of every day life such as marriage, the householder's life, the celibate student, wandering ascetic, the various professions, health, sickness and death. It deals extensively with the cause of suffering, the presence of evil forces, their origin and their influence on human life.

In the Rig Vedic theme, the knowledge is like a vast net in which various topics are intimately connected. Moreover, every dominant aspect of human personality is intimately connected with the corresponding one in the cosmos. All the realms of mental operations in a man like thinking, imagining, meditating and so on are associated with the cosmic world at times. It is suggestive of the truth that every human action has also a cosmic dimension. Thus there is a dominant contribution of *Devâs* in practically all-human actions. There is in this manner a visible collaboration possible between men and *Devâs*.

Rigveda has two broad divisions of ten *Mandals* and eight *Ashtakas*. *Manadals* consist of *Sûktas* in varying numbers. As regards the *Ashtaka* division, each *Ashtaka* is divided in 8 chapters and the chapters in turn into *Vargas*, quarters.

In the appendix of *Rigveda* there are 36 *Khil Sûktas* included. The contents of these hymns seem to be at the root of many mythological stories and characters. There are mentions of later characters like *Garuda, Astîka, Janmejaya, Narmada, and Shri etc*. *Rigveda Samhitâ* literally stands for the collection or compilation of 'Mantras' or 'Richâs' of hymns or verses composed in various metres in various contexts. It consists of ten 'Mandals' (Books). These *Mandals* contain hymns of various orders composed by *Rishis*, seers in different 'Chhandas', metres. *Rigveda* consists of 1,028 hymns in all. This number includes 11 hymns of 8th *Mandala*, which are said to be later additions. These hymns contain about 10600 mantras (stanzas), which nearly provide an average ten for each verse, the shortest with just one and the longest containing as many as fifty-eight stanzas. The Vedic seers, as a matter of fact, were so exact and conscious about their compositions that they had even calculated the number of words and the letters themselves, which are 153826 and 432000 respectively.

From the second to the seventh book of *Rigveda*, the character and content of the text is homogeneous in the sense that the richas belong to a particular and distinct family and the gods are also grouped accordingly. This part is believed to be the oldest one. The richas of these *Mandals* are namely *Gritsmada, Vishwâmitra, Vâmadeva, Atri, Bhâradwâja* and *Vasishtha* in the stated order. Other Books namely first, eighth and tenth have been written and compiled by a number of *richas* of various orders. Ninth Book on the other hand is very distinct in the sense that all the hymns of it are addressed to one deity, *Soma* in one metre alone. It has also been thus concluded that the hymns of this Book have been selected and taken out from other Books from the point of view of the content.

The tenth Book is supposed to be the last addition in the work. The subject matter, the language and the style of it are the clear indications of this faith. Its placement in the end and the comparability of the number of hymns with Book one (191 in both cases), are clear evidences for this effect. Its *richas* are common figuring in other Books as well. However, the most important aspect of this Book are its philosophical overtones (*Nâsadiya, Hiranyagarbha* and *Viswakarmâ* hymns for instance) and the conversational poetry introduced in hymns like 'Saramâ-Pani' and 'Urvashî-Pururava' which were to form the basis of all Indian philosophy and great mythological Indian literature.

2

Outer Frame Of Rigveda

Rishi, the seer, *Devatâ*, the deity and *Chhanda*, the metre form the basic intrinsic framework of *Rigveda*. Traditionally believed in India, the combination of these three makes the hymn a perfect whole. It is supposed to be compressed with a far deeper meaning and knowledge, which an ordinary mind may not even comprehend. The combination in itself is unique and any effort of changing it will only dislodge us from following the true meaning. Because the Vedic composition is a record of direct spiritual experience, this frame is best suited for it. The seer passes through the experience, the deity is the experience and the metre the process of the experience. There is every chance for the person following this path to undergo the same divine experience. But more often than not, the speaker is the *Rishi* and the deity addressed to, the *Devatâ*. In *Sûktas* (hymns) like *Saramâ-Pani, Urvashî-Purûrava, Nadi, Mandûk* etc. this becomes very clear. This fact again proves it very evidently that the trinity of the knower, the knowledge and the process of knowing is all interwoven.

Gods

Gods in Rigveda are generally great and mighty. They wield a command on various forces of nature and regulate their order for the greater good of mankind. They are also capable of driving away the potent evil powers of demons posing a threat to peace loving human beings. They are always rewarding to the honest, righteous and obedient people.

The Vedic gods are eager to help a person and manifest their power in him. According to Vedic seers, each god is a conscious being associated with particular type of power. The relationship of human beings can be as intimate as that of a father and son, friend or spouse. As these gods generally represent various facets and phenomena of nature, their identification with the natural forces brings them closer to the material powers. They are fond of distinct objects of worship, adoration, prayer, awe and fear. They rarely share tender human feelings and emotions. This always keeps them at an arm length away from human beings and the complete identification and surrender of later devotional poetry is seldom visible. It is a kind of dual existence, which the seers of *Rigveda* are very conscious. They must acknowledge the existence of these gods as they are definitely closer to natural forces and shall form a bridge between the two distinct entities for the benefit of mankind. This is again a philosophy quite farther from the later developed *Adwait Darshan*, non-duality of *Sanatan Hindu* thought. Therefore whether from the mystic viewpoint of India or the western view of the content, the gods of *Rigveda* have got to be properly understood. In any case, as has been said, those who have best followed the 'divine' element in them can better follow *Vedas*.

The earliest of the commentators, *Yâska* has classified these gods into three categories i.e., belonging to heaven, air and earth. The celestial gods are *Daus, Varuna, Mitra, Sûrya, Savitra, Pûsan,* the *Aswins* and the goddess *Ushâ,* Dawn and *Râtri,* night. The atmospheric gods are *Indra, Apama, Napat, Rudra,* the *Maruts, Vâyu, Parjanya,* and *Âpas,* the waters. The terrestrial deities are *Prithivî, Agni* and Soma.

There are a few abstract deities such as *Prajapati, Brahaspati, Twastr* and also *Shradha, Anumati* (favour of gods), *Aramati,* Devotion and *Sunrta,* 'Bounty' etc. *Aditi* among these is one who is throughout celebrated as she occupies a unique position in her personification. She is the mother of gods, *Âdityas,* literally just not the opposite of *Diti,* the mother of demons, but also a giver of all riches and happiness to mankind.

Goddesses play an important part in *Rigveda*. *Ushâ, Sarswati, Vâk, Prithvi* and *Râtri* need a definite mention about them. Some divine mistresses such as *Agnayi* (wife of *Agni*), *Indrâni* (wife of *Indra*) and *Varunâni* (wife of *Varuna*) also draw our attention at times.

Another striking feature of gods in *Rigveda* is the Dual Divinities. There are in fact pairs of such deities whose names are combined as compounds such as *Mitra-Varuna, Dyava-Prithvi* and *Ashwini Kumâras*. There is similarly a category of group-deities such as *Maruts, Âdityas, Bhaga, Daxa, Ribhus* and *Viswe-Devâs*.

The personification of natural forces and the objects of nature as gods is a common characteristic of the Rig Vedic approach of godhead. Therefore rivers and mountains are often addressed as divinities what to speak about plants, sacrificial tools or weapons.

The total number of objects addressed and identified, as gods are about two hundred in numbers. Some names are even synonymous such as *Vat* and *Vâyu, Savita* and *Sûrya* etc. Animals such as *Ashwa* and *Go*, birds such as *Suparn* and *Shyen*, war materials such as *Rath* (chariot), *Dundibhi* (bugle), *Dhanush* (arrow) and *Varm* (armour), abstract feelings such as *Man* (mind), *Gyân* (knowledge), *Daxinâ* (alms), *Shraddhâ* (reverence) and inanimate objects like *Aksh* (die), and *Anna* (food grain) are all the divine personifications in *Rigveda*. Some details about the important gods of *Rigveda* are given below.

Agni

Agni is one of the most important gods of earth. After *Indra, Agni* occupies the second place in order of significance in it. About two hundred *Sûktas* have been dedicated exclusively to this god for the purpose of invocation. *Agni* is normally representing the physical fire in most of the places but his form has been also described. His teeth are golden (7.58.5). His tongue finds a mention at a number of places. He accepts the oblation through it only. He has been compared with a bull (5.3.12) and has got horns (5.1.8). He has also been compared with a horse (6.12.6), which helps people attain gods. Further, he is compared with birds (7.15.4), with a hawk (7.15.4) and so on.

Wood and oblations are his food and the purified butter his drink. He is also invited at times for the *Soma* drinking ceremony along with gods. He is shining as bright as Sun and removes darkness in the night. He attacks forests at times and like a barber removes the forestation from the earth. His flames are worth comparison with the waves of the Sea. His voice is wind like and he roars like a lion and a cloud. His chariot shines like gold pulled by two or three horses.

Agni has been informed to be present in all medicines. He has been suggested being the navel of the Earth. Likewise he is also told to be present in the Sea. He has three heads, three tongues, and three bodies (3.20.2)

Agni is quite close to human beings as compared to other gods. He has been repeatedly addressed as the lord of the house. He resides in every house and is a regular and the common guest of every one. He is the father of mankind but at times he is also addressed as the brother, the son and the mother of the devotees. He is the messenger, the forerunner and the priest. In the Vedic ritual, there are three types of priests, *adhwaryu,* the controller of the path, *hotra,* the caller and *udgâta, the singer. Agni* is the performer of all these three functions. He is the director of all *Yajnas,* calling different gods for manifestation and finally empowering human beings to be the singers in praise of divine powers.

He is always working for the betterment of human beings. He protects his devotees from the enemies and crushes evil doers. He is the giver of all riches and causes rains in deserts.

Agni is undoubtedly a universally acknowledged god of India and Iran. He was believed to be an Omnipotent Purifying Power and therefore in Italy, Greece and India, *Agni* was offered oblation for his pleasure.

Soma

Soma has been identified as *Homa* of Parsees. Like *Yajnya* with *Soma* in India, Parsi priests were also performing Soma rite. The opinions of both the *Brâhmans* and Parsees on the effect of drinking Soma (Homa) juice are nearly the same. Like Vedic exposition, Parsees also believed that Homa is a plant and a great angel. Any one, who has drunk the Homa juice, becomes united with the angel, and after his death an inhabitant of the paradise. According to the Vedic seers, likewise, *Soma* juice has pre-eminently the power of uniting the sacrifice on this earth with the celestial king *Soma*, and makes him thus one of his subjects, and consequently an associate of the gods, and an inhabitant of the celestial world.

About 120 *Sûktas* have been dedicated to *Soma*. He is thus next to *Agni* in order of reference. His physical form is developed far less as compared to *Indra* and *Varuna* since the herbal content of his being were predominating the thoughts of the Vedic seers. He has got sharp and fierce weapons, which he holds in his hand (9.61.30). He is the charioteer of *Indra's* chariot. He appears during sacrifices and accepts oblations.

Soma is generally identified with the divine elixir, which is sweet, refreshing, and is enjoyed in a mood of festivity. The extraction of this drink involves the process of squeezing it from the herbs after crushing them on stones. It is offered to *Agni* and the priests also take it to attain the mood of godly worship. It is mixed with water and milk and sweetened further for drinking purposes. He also exercises some control over waters and causes rains from heaven.

The sound of *Soma* has been compared with a bull. He is himself like bull amidst the riches signified by cows (9.16.6, 9.72.4). He is thus the lord of the cows.

His colour is yellow and shines like Sun. He covers himself by the rays of the Sun. He fights against the forces of darkness and after defeating them causes light.

Gods love drinking *Soma* as it makes them happy and immortal. It has also got many nutritious values. It cures many illnesses. It gives eyes to the blind and feet to the lame persons. He is the bodyguard of human beings and increases longevity in their life. He makes voice vibrant and is *Vâchaspati* (9.26.4) in this respect. He is the origin of all verses, the greatest of all poets, and the seer among saints, the soul of the sacrifice and the Creator *Brahma* among gods.

The greatest contribution of *Soma* lies in the fact that he is an effective intoxicant for *Indra* in heaven to fight against the demons all the time. He prepared *Indra* to give challenge to the fiercest of all demons *Vrittra*. He is himself acclaimed as a warrior for his close association with *Indra* in this manner. He is always victorious, he is invincible, he is first among commanders and at the same time he is also modest. He is the giver of all earthly riches, food, animals, horses etc. to his devotees.

Soma is the infant of heaven (9.38.5), the nectar of gods (9.51.2). He is the lord of heaven, he is all pervading and his abode is the highest heaven. *Rigveda* describes (4.26.27) in detail how the falcon carried *Soma* for *Indra*. Because it is the most superior kind of medicine, it is mentioned as the king of all herbs.

Soma has also been identified with Moon, but the essence and the liquid character of it is the most acclaimed identity. *Rigveda* and Avesta both mention about the grinding process of the herb and that the colour of it is yellow. Both of them also talk about the mixing of milk in it and quality of increasing vitality and longevity is also equally present at both the places.

Brahaspati

This god has been invoked in 11 *Sûktas* independently and in two *Sûktas* along with *Indra*. The physical form of *Brahaspati* is not quite developed. There are only such indications available that he has seven mouths, seven rays, low tongue, sharp horns, blue back, golden form, pious and distinct audible voice. He has got a sharp arrow and a bow with a string of *rit*. He moves out in a chariot destroying demons. His presence is always fatherly for gods and he is a priest like *Agni*. Sacrifices are never complete without him. He is the singer of *Shâstras* (10.36.5) and his verses are reaching the heaven. He also sings in company and therefore he is mentioned as the leader of devotional singers. He is successful in recovering his cow flock from the captivity of *Panis* in this manner only. He destroys darkness attaining *Ushâs,* and *Agni*. *Indra* invites him quite often and he drinks *Soma* in his company.

He is helpful to his devotees. He helps virtuous people at the time of troubles and bestows riches on them. He also increases longevity of human beings and cures their illnesses.

Brahaspati is exclusively an Indian god. He is originally a priest, a scholar and the exponent of the cult of devotion.

Indra

About one fourth part of *Rigveda* (*Indra* has been invoked in 250 *Sûktas*) is dedicated to *Indra* alone. As a matter of fact, *Indra* is the first representative Indian god according to Vedic structure. Beginning with natural forces like rain or thunder, he has come to be gradually developed as the most powerful and commanding deity responsible for the maintenance of order in nature and the world. His physical features are fairly developed as compared to other gods. His arms are long, healthy and strong. He is attractive like Sun in his shining effulgence. He is *Vajra-Bâhu*. *Twashtâ* made this weapon. He some times keeps the bow and arrow also.

He moves in a golden chariot, which is pulled by two green horses. *Indra* is very fond of *Soma*. He indeed committed theft for drinking *Soma* (3.48.4). This drink keeps him fit for the performance of his duty of maintaining order and destroying demon *Vrittra*. One of the verses of *Rigveda* is a monologue in which *Indra* after drinking *Soma* is full of praise for his valour and wisdom.

Immediately after his birth, *Indra* makes the universe shine in his effulgence and helps move the wheel of the Sun. The earth, the heaven and the mountains tremble on his appearance. *Agni* and *Pûshan* are his brothers. *Indrani* is his wife. *Maruds* are his very good friends who accompany him during wars. He is also closely associated with *Varuna, Soma, Brahaspati, Pûshan* and *Vishnu.*

Indra is described to be as big as a giant in his appearance. The heaven and earth are smaller than he is. If earth attains a size ten times larger than the present, it could equal up his form (1.52.11). He is invincible, indestructible and always young. The whole earth and the heaven shake as he uses *Vajra* (thunder bolt) to destroy *Vrittra.* This demon was hiding in the waters and he had stopped rainfall. He ultimately got released rains, rivers and cows from the clutches of this demon. He also stops the movement of the earth and the mountain and makes them stable. He had to cut off the wings of the mountains as they used to fly according to their wishes in the beginning. He is also responsible for keeping the earth and heaven apart.

Those who clamour for victory, respectfully invoke *Indra* as a warrior god. He is the protector of *Âryans* and the destroyer of *Dasyus.* He is very kind, helpful to his devotees and the righteous people. He showers happiness and riches on his subjects. Prayers are frequently made for this god to give cows, horses and other richness.

In one of the stories of *Rigveda Indra* helps *Turvash* and *Yadu* cross rivers. He helps *Brahaspati* recover his cows from *Pani* deputing *Saramâ* as an emissary. He helped king *Sudâsa* in a fierce battle of *Dâshragya* after he was pleased by the invocations of the priest *Tritsu* for it. He ultimately got the enemies drowned in the river *Parushni.*

Avesta makes a mention of *Indra* twice. He is a demon and not a god in it. His form is also not quite settled in it. Thus *Indra* as a warrior god is common, but his other qualities, form and the person are well developed in Vedic literature.

According to Aurobindonian school of interpretation, 'Indra aims to manifest in man the higher knowledge, the knowledge of the different planes, the knowledge of gods, methods of obtaining their grace, the methods of not exposing oneself to hostile forces, etc.'

Rudra

There are only three complete and one partially allocated *Sûktas* for *Rudra* in *Rigveda*. There is then just a mention of his name in one other *Sûkta* dedicated to *Soma*. His hands remove sufferings and have curing touch for mankind. His arms are strong, his lips beautiful and his colour brown. His form is bewildering for the onlooker. His electric sword travels right down the earth after rising in the sky (7.46.3) He has got bow and arrows. He moves out in the company of *Maruts* who is his father.

Rudra comes to be referred as *Tryambaka* (7.59.12) which a later name of Lord *Shiva*. At occasions *Rudra* is also fierce and fiery. He has been therefore prayed not to affect his devotees, their parents, their kith and kin, animals, horses etc. adversely in anger. He should rather direct his anger in the direction of the enemies of his devotees. He should be just helpful and kind to the human beings. He should remove their illness and obstacles. He has immense potency for removing illnesses, as he is the source of many medicines. His very arm is full of nectar.

The source of the physical origin of *Rudra* in the forces of nature is not quite distinct and definable. Later on he certainly becomes the synonym of *Shiva*. From the angle of the linguistic root origin, the word *Rudra* has his origin in *Rud*, which means to weep, or one who can cause to weep.

Parjanya

Parjanya has been prayed in three *Sûktas* of *Rigveda*. As the word *Parjanya* means, this force of nature stands for clouds bringing rains. He has been addressed as *Vrishabha*, a bull who roars. He rides in a rainy chariot and opens floodgates of waters all around. He roars like a lion at such time. He has been prayed to cause rains and also to put a halt when the rains are sufficient.

The rain god quenching the thirst of the desert, causing darkness on earth, watering plants and destroying evil forces- all these details find vivid descriptions.

Earth has been referred to be this god's wife. It also finds mention as the father of *Soma* at one place. *Maruts* are also invoked along with *Parjanya*. *Maruts* have been requested to invoke *Parjanya* through prayers. He has also been compared with *Indra,* as both are important for causing rains.

Âpah

There are four *Sûktas* and few *Mantras* in praise of *Âpah* in *Rigveda*. The personification of this god is rather incomplete. They have been referred to as mother, a woman and goddesses attending sacrifices to bless. They follow the tracks set by gods. *Indra* digs the path by his *Vajra* for them. They are the perfect law abider lots. They are constantly treading their path set towards great Ocean. Wherever there are gods residing and where ever *Mitra Varuna* lives, they are invariably to be found. They are close to the Sun and the Sun is always near them. *Varuna* moves right deep inside them.

Âpah cause fire like a mother. They have great herbal contents. They increase longevity of human life. They are also associated with honey at times. They mix some honey in their milk like mothers. When mixed with purified butter, it becomes a favourite drink of *Indra*. *Soma* enjoys the company of *Âpah* in the manner young boys do with the young girls. *Âpah* also move towards *Soma* the way a beloved follows the lover.

Varuna

Varuna's significance in context of the number of *Sûktas* dedicated to him is comparable with that of *Marudgana*. However his physical form is less developed as compared to his moral aspects. He comes particularly to be referred along with *Mitra* and *Aryama*. His face is that of *Agni* and *Sûrya* like in the case of

Mitra is his eye.[1] *Varuna* has great far sight and he is thousand eyed. (7.34.10) He sits on the grass during sacrifice along with *Mitra* and *Aryamâ* and enjoys *Soma*. Among his accomplishments, his chariot and chains are particularly worth mentioning. The golden abode of *Mitra* and *Varuna* is in heaven. He supervises the deeds of every one while sitting in his high home. It is indeed quite high and is standing on about thousand pillars. It has also got thousand doors. Even the Sun keeps reporting the deeds performed on earth to *Varuna* as he pays a visit to him. (7.60.1,3)

Varuna keeps employed quite a few detectives as well. He is also at places as alone as *Yama*, the god of death is. But he is also a king, not only of human beings, but also of gods. He is Lord of many lords and sovereign power (2.27.100). Strikingly *Varuna* has also been addressed as *Asura* many times, which in case of *Agni* and *Indra* has been used just severally.

Varuna has prepared the path of Sun along with *Mitra* and *Aryamâ*. Because of the determination of this god, the Moon moves in the night shining and the bright stars get lost during daylight. He keeps the day and night properly divided and is the regulator of the six seasons and twelve months.

He is the lord of Oceans and keeps the rivers flowing in order. He is the lord of rivers as is *Mitra*. He has all the information of the boats far flung in Ocean. He also gets associated with the rains. He sprinkles water in earth, heaven and in the space.

He is a strict disciplinarian. If the law and order is broken and unrighteous deeds done, he is very angry and punishes all such offenders with pluribus. He has got chains, which put these people in bondages, unbreakable. He is in possession of number of medicinal herbs, which can even bring back a person from the clutches of death. He is the giver of immortality.

---

1   चक्षुर्मित्रस्य वरुणस्याग्ने: 1-115-1

Vishnu

Vishnu in *Rigveda* occupies comparatively a less important place than many other gods. There are only five *Sûktas* available invoking or praising him. His personification is however distinct as he is referred to as young and of broad form. His three *pada-* steps find a mention as he measures up all three worlds by them. Only two of his steps are visible for living human beings as the third one move far beyond them. This highest abode of *Vishnu* is the desired place of virtuous people and gods. Cows with long horns easily and happily move around in it. These three steps are in fact indicative of the path of the Sun. According to McDonnell, these steps stand for heaven, earth and space. He has been frequently identified with *Sûrya* for his movement and the effulgence. No wonder therefore, that one of the names of the Sun in India is *Sûryanârâyana*. He has also performed feats with *Indra* for expanding earth and the heaven. *Indra* appears in some *Sûktas* as his close associate. It is *Indra's* might that helps *Vishnu* take big three steps and he was certainly helping *Indra* in his great adventure of killing *Vrittra*. Before vanquishing *Vrittra*, *Indra* states, 'Vishnu, my friend! Take longer steps.' (4.18.11) *Vishnu* also helped *Indra* destroy the ninety fort of *Shambar* and defeated the companions of *Varchin*. He is a natural ally of *Indra* and keeps cows in a flock along with him. They seem also to be sharing one other's habit at a time. Thus *Indra* might well be equipped with the power of transgressing three steps and *Vishnu*, enjoying *Soma*. They also share the responsibility of creating Sun, Dawn and *Agni*.

Vishnu has got many forms. For instance, he is stated to be hiding his real form, as during war he is totally different. He is the protector of the wombs. He is absolutely pure, generous and all embracing. He is emanating earth, heaven and great space. He has set the whole universe on proper pillars to stay on.

Pûshan

Pûshan finds a mention in eight *Sûktas* of *Rigveda*. The form of this god is abstract and the personification process of his being is perhaps incomplete. There is a mention of his feet and his right arm (6.54.10). His hair is curly and he has got a beard. He has got a sharp spear. His chariot also finds a description and he himself is a very good charioteer. Goats pull his chariot. He is the very soul of all animate or inanimate beings. He loves his sister *Ushâ* quite a lot. Gods married him with *Sûrya* who was in his love. He used to float in the space ship for meeting *Sûrya*. He obeys the commands of *Savita*. He helps the dead forefathers reach their right place in their journey upward. He is a skilled guide for his devotees as he is also the supervisor of the grand high ways. *Pûshan* has been also requested to remove thieves and foxes from the way. He has all the knowledge where the hidden money lies. He even protects domestic animals from harm and helps them reach home when they have lost their way.

He has been prayed as an associate of *Indra* and *Soma*. *Indra* also finds a mention as the brother of *Pûshan*. He has also been invoked along with *Bhaga* and *Vishnu*. *Pûshan*, literally though standing for the nourisher, does not seem to be representing any particular natural force like many other gods.

Savita

Savita finds mention in eleven full and many other *Sûktas* of *Rigveda*. He is a god of effulgence. His eyes tongue and hand are all full of light. He has a golden chariot of golden horses. He makes the heaven, the earth and the space shine. He comes following *Ushâs*. His path in sky is free from dust or mud. He is a strict disciplinarian and the air and water obey his orders. He has controlled and kept the earth in its orbit in a pillarless void space in a superior technical device. In one of the *Mantras*, *Savita* has been prayed to enlighten his devotee's intellect in righteous path. *Savita* and *Sûrya* are nearly identical in most of the places. At other places they become distinct and he becomes the inspirer of Sun. He also declares human beings to be pure when produced before *Sûrya*.

Savita has relationship with morning and evening both. He keeps all awake whether human beings with two feet or animal with four. He is restful to the travellers. The night comes to join at his command.

Ushâs

Ushâ has been invoked in as many as twenty *Sûktas*. She is the goddess of dawn. Her personification is not distinct, but this natural phenomenon is quite vivid before the Vedic seer. The poetic beauty of the description of *Ushâ* is unexcelled in any ancient literature of the world. She comes like a damsel covering her body with white cloths. After appearing in the east, she uncovers her beautiful form gradually. It is as if she takes bath in the tub of light and removes darkness from the earth. She wakes up quite early and inspires birds; animals and human beings get up soon. She unlocks the gates of heaven and removes all darkness of dream and reality.

Red horses draw the chariot of Ushâ. She opens up the gate for *Sûrya* to move out. Sun follows her the way a lover follows his beloved (1.115.2). She is the wife of Sun and the sister of *Bhaga*. She is also the sister of night. She kindles up fire. *Agni* also moves up to meet her. *Ashwini Kumârs* are the friend of *Ushâ*. She awakens them and they move along with her.

She bestows upon her devotee's prosperity, offspring, security and long life. She brings reputation to poets and fame to brave people. Her devotees pray that she should be as kind and loving to them as the mother to his children is.

Ashwini Kumâr

The pair of these two gods finds mention in about fifty *Sûktas* of *Rigveda*. There are a number of stories and myths associated with these gods. This factor brings further mystery around them.

Their physical form and the identity as a force of nature are not distinct. They are closely associated with honey as compared to other gods. They have a skin pot, which is full of honey. They are also fond of taking *Soma*. Apart from horses, swan and hawks also pull their chariot.

There are a number of stories about their feats. They brought wife for *Vimada* in their chariot. They saved *Bhujyu*, the son of *Tugra* who was getting drowned in the sea. They took him away in their boat from the sea having no island in it. This boat was quite mysterious as it was invincible and could also fly in the air. They gave *Aghâshwa* the white horse. When *Atri* fell in a pit after getting burns, they made him cool with ice and saved. When *Gautama* was thirsty, they turned the well upside down and quenched his thirst. They turned the old and aged *Chyavan* into an attractive young man using alchemy. They gave sight back to *Rijrâshwa*. They joined the severed leg of *Vishpalâ* in the battlefield. They put the head of a horse in the body of *Ddhyang*, the son of *Atharvan* from which mouth he revealed that *Twashtâ* is the origin of honey. Some persons as well as animals associated with *Ashwini Kumârs* are *Vimad, Bhujyu, Aghashwa, Atri, Gautama, Vandana, Atharwan, Bhadrimati, Rjrâshwa, Bhâradwâja, Vartika, Brka, Rasabha, Vrashabha, and Shishumara*. They got married with *Sûrya*, the daughter of Sun. *Sûrya* is seen off after marriage in their three-wheeled chariot.

Saraswatî

Rigveda mentions many times a mighty river *Sarawati* in the northern India, which stretched from the mountains to the ocean but has dried since. The extensive archaeological excavation conducted in India after 1950 at more than hundred sites confirms the existence of this river. *Sarawati* in the later *Puranas* is the goddess of learning and fine arts with her icons displaying a *vina* in her hands. According to commentator *Sâyana Saraswatî* is a river in some verses and a speech in others. Wilson and Griffith are of similar opinion though they prefer to call it a river-goddess. According to Shri R. L. Kashyap, an Aurobindonian commentator, however, '*Saraswatî* is a power of inspiration descending from the supreme plane of Truth which manifests to the *rishis* as inspired learning.'

Metres

Rigveda is a metrical composition. The knowledge of these metres has always been treated to be a prerequisite of Vedic learning. There are seven kinds of metres used in *Rigveda* which can also be divided in three different categories-*Gâyatrî* and *Ushnik*, consisting of three lines (*pada*), *Anushtup, Brihti, Trishtup* and *Jagatiî*, consisting of four lines and *Pankti*, consisting of five lines each. The line forming an important metrical unit normally consists of eight, eleven or twelve syllables. The most common metres of *Rigveda*, however, are the *Trishtubh* (4/11 syllables), the *Gâyatri* (3/8) and the *Jagatiî* (4/12) nearly covering two third of it. The classification of the total number of stanzas in all seven metres is as follows-

Gâyatri	2467
Ushnik	341
Anushtup	855
Trishtup	4253
Brihti	181
Jagatiî	1358
Pankti	312

Usually a hymn of *Rigveda* consists of stanzas of the same metre, but there are numerous exceptions. In all cases the Rig Vedic metres are the foundation of Classical Sanskrit metres having a quantitative rhythm throughout in it.

Seers

There are different *Rishis* perceiving *mantras* in all the ten *Mandals* of the *Rigveda*. It is an extra sensory perception, as a matter of fact, in their case as they were great thinkers, meditators and the mystics of their times. The number of these seers in case of the first eight and ten *Mandala* is more whereas the representative seer of rest of the seven Books is one. Thus *Madhuchhandâ, Gautama, Agastya, Bhrigu, Ushnâ,*

Kutsa, Atharva, Shunahshep, Brahaspati etc. are the important seers of the first eight and ten *Mandala. Gritsmada* is the seer of the second. Because of his singular contribution for the making of this *Mandala*, it has been named as *'Gârtsmada Mandala'*. Third Mandala has been perceived by seer *Vishwâmitra* that is also therefore known as *'Vaishwamitra Mandala'*. *Vâmadeva* is the seer of the fourth, *Atri* of fifth, *Bhâradwâja* of sixth and *Vasishtha* of the seventh. Similarly seer *Kanva* perceived the eighth and *Angirâ* the ninth *Mandala*.

The total number of the seers of *Rigveda* is 403. Some of the seers figure individually whereas quite a few fall in their long family tradition. The number of the seers of the individual category is 88 whereas those belonging to one or the other family are 315.

Sapta Rishis, seven seers, namely; *Gotama, Bhâradwâja, Vishwâmitra, Jamdagni, Kashyapa, Vashishtha* and *Atri* are the origin of all later developed various clans and dynasties. All these seven are the common seers of hymn 107 of the ninth and 137 of the tenth *Mandala*. It has been said that 'the seven seers go to *Soma* in a sacrifice.'(9.92.2) In *Mandala* 10 (27.15) it is stated that 'the seven seers like *Vishwâmitra etc.* were born out of the body of *Indra*, the Chief of all subjects.' Out of these seven, although *Kashyapa, Gotama* and *Jamadagni* are not accredited with a particular *Mandala* like the other four, but some hymns are duly composed by them and they find mentions in a number of *Mantras*. The deeper researches into the origin of the first few *Rishi Kulas* suggests that they are just four namely, *Angirâs, Bhârgava, Kashyapa* and *Âtreya. Angirâs* in this case include *Gotam* and *Bhâradwaja, Bhârgavas* cover *Vishwâmitra* and *Jamdagni, and Vashishtha* comes under the fold of *Kashyapa. Atri* alone remains independent

Prajâpati, the original chief of all subjects, first created three sons- *Bhrigu, Angirâ* and *Atri* by performing sacrifice. *Bhrigu* had one of his sons called *Richika. Richika*, the father of *Jamadagni* also became the source of the origin of *Vishwâmitra* as the wife of king *Gâdhi*, (*Vishwâmitra's* father), also ate the milk dish prepared by him. *Vishwâmitra* thus owes his origin to the *Bhârgavas* clan only.

Angirâ had two sons, *Utathya* and *Brahaspati*. *Bhâradwâja* was the son of *Brahaspati*. *Deerghtama* was the son of *Utathya* and *Kakshiwân* his grandson who are all important Vedic seers. Further *Kanwas* also have their origin in this dynasty, as the father of *Kanwa* was *Ghora Angirâs*. So is the case with *Gotama* who was the son of *Rahugana*, one other inheritor of this tradition.

Like wise, *Vashishtha* is the grandson of *Kshyapa* whose tradition runs like this- *Marichi, Kashyapa, MaitraVaruna, Vashishtha, Shakti, Parashara* etc.

Composers of stanzas were just not the simple poets in the modern sense of the term. They have been called *Mantra Drashtâ Kavi,* the seers who could look far beyond their place and time. They have also been called *Vipra,* as they were highly illumined in knowledge. According to the Indian belief, they gave expression to the divine revelations of which they were the deserving instruments. *Mantra 5* of the hymn 43 of *Mandala 3* defines a *Rishi* to be an extra sensory perceiver. They were fully aware of the present and future event (1.25.11). They believed in the service of mankind which they have advocated everywhere. They had utmost regard for the guest and the gods. They were full of appreciation for the learned and the giver of donations. They used to criticize lazy, violent and also the people having envy with righteous people and gods. They were great admirers of *Yajna,* the sacrifice that they believed to be a live link between human beings and the gods. Above all, they were the firm exponents of truth that they believed to be the original strength through which the heaven and earth exist and all the forces of nature operate in the manner prescribed in the cosmic design of things.

A realization of Truth can be conveyed to others through the medium of words only. This medium can be made further effective if its pattern has been evolved through a well-developed structure of words, metre. As a matter of fact, the separation of the word and knowledge can exist unto the initial stage of expression only and at the stage of *Pashyanti,* extra sensory perception, the two get merged. Because Vedic utterances about Truth, gods are realizations of this sort, they form an integral whole in a unit of hymn or stanza by effectively merging the seer, the realized god through the medium of the specific metre.

The god, the seer and the metre have deep intrinsic relationship and value. It is indeed through an effective merger of these three that the formation of a stanza or *mantra* and a hymn or *Sûkta* becomes complete. It has been therefore stressed time and again that the proper identification and appreciation of the seer, the, metre and the god can only help a person understand the true meaning of Vedas.

This scheme of giving manifestation the pure knowledge through a specific design is as complicated and perfect as human physiology. This makes it as live and pure as any living organism is. Dr. Tony Neder, a follower of Maharshi Mahesh Yogi has done lot of research on the subject and has come to conclude that the composition of Veda in syllables and gaps has special arrangement. "The centre of the gap is the unmenifest point of pure intelligence into which one syllable dissolves and from which the next syllable emerges. In the process of transformation of one syllable into the next is the liveliness of the dynamism of Veda, pure knowledge. In the middle of the gap is the silent state of Veda... This unmenifest state of Veda is the abstract structure of Veda. It is the level of intelligence – creative intelligence- which is fully awake within itself. It is that self-referral level of intelligence which is the Samhita of *Rishi, Devata* and *Chhanda.*" (From Maharishi's Commentary on Rk Veda as quoted by Dr. Tony Neder)?

Indian age-old tradition of first taking a vow, *Viniyoga,* before starting an act of worship makes it evidently clear. It can also be stated that when the chanter of the Vedic *mantra* remembers the seer, for instance, he establishes a spiritual link with the ancient seeker and while trying to board in the distinct chariot of words, he is sure to be piloted to the destination of pure knowledge.

Language

Long before *Pânini*, the grammarian, at the end of the fourth century BC stereotyped Classical Sanskrit, *Veda*s were written. The language of *Vedas* undoubtedly has a greater variety of forms than the Sanskrit. Its case forms in nominal and pronominal inflexion as well as particles and genders are more numerous. The vowels as well as the consonants of it have got some very distinctive features. The vowels here have got musical rhythms depending on the pitch of the voice underlined throughout. As against *Hraswa* and *Dîrgha* two vowels of Sanskrit, the Vedic Sanskrit has one *Plut* vowel, which is longer than the long one- *Dîrgha*.The pronunciation of aspirated -: and the nasal voice is distinct. Similarly it has some more consonants covered in it and the use as well as pronunciation at times differs quite a lot.

The Vedic language is predominantly verbal in form therefore very rich and fluent throughout. It also uses subjunctive quite frequently and has as many as twelve subjunctives as compared to only one now surviving in Sanskrit. According to the great grammarian *Pânini*, whenever a stanza begins with a verbal form, it has a stressed vowel and while figuring in end, it is unstressed. It is indicative of the fact that whenever it is stressed, the thing of comparison is more important than the thing compared and vices versa

The *Sandhi* on the other hand represents a less complicated stage as against Sanskrit. After *e* and *o*, for instance, *a* is nearly always pronounced in *Rigveda* whereas in Sanskrit it is invariably dropped. The union of words is also not that hard pressed. The word and noun forms of *Rigveda* are also at times quite different. The forms pronouns in *Rigveda* are far more in number than the Sanskrit. It is also fond of using nouns and pronouns like adverbs at occasions. That is why persons only conversant with Sanskrit find it difficult to follow the correct meaning of it.

The stresses have got utmost significance here. The meanings of the *Mantras* can only be best understood if these stresses are properly borne into mind. It has three kinds of stresses- *Udâtta*, *Anudâtta* and *Swarit*. The various parts of a verse stanza are also so arranged that they only convey the desired meaning. It has been said that the arrangement of the parts of the stanzas is well planed so that they are always pregnant with deep meaning. It is also not proper to rearrange words in *'Anvayay'* like Sanskrit and derive the meaning from it. Here every part has to be studied independent of the other and a final meaning deduced accordingly.

Some words of Vedic Sanskrit have definitely undergone changes. The word *'Errata'* here, for instance, meaning misery and enmity stands for just enemy in Sanskrit. *'Ari'* standing for God in *Veda* becomes enemy in Sanskrit. Similarly *'Vadh'* standing for a weapon, becomes killing in Sanskrit.

Objects Outlining

What were the objectives before the Vedic seers when they were composing the hymns of *Rigveda*? This question is very difficult to answer, as the very composition is only a matter of speculation and research. Whether the hymns are the revelations, compositions or the inspired poems, the objects outlining is so comprehensive that the sphere of *Rigveda* is a world, an encyclopaedia of its own kind. It practically covers all aspects of social, political, family, phenomenal, religious and personal life of people of just not that time, but for all time to come. Even the most difficult questions of philosophy and science as well as many riddles of life here and after have been answered and sorted out. The cosmic origin, the life and death, the real object of human life, literary merits, medicine, history, geography, astronomy, astrology and the travel in space or waters are all dealt and defined in this Classic. The most important part of the treatment of the subject is the secularism with which the seers of *Rigveda* have dealt them. The seeds of mythology becoming all so important in later *Puranic* literature are to be best found in *Rigveda*. *Indra, Vishnu, Sûrya, Rudra, Brahaspati, Viswâmitra, Vashistha, Urvashî, Shri, Vâk, Saraswatî, Yama, Yami, Garuda* and kings like *Purûravâ, Dâshrâgya* etc. find very important roles in the stories of *Râmâyana, Mahâbhârata* and *Purânas*. The valour and triumph of *Indra* and other gods as well as the cravings of human beings for victory against all enemies is the basic instinct, which later on develops into the fiercest of wars of the *Purânic* literature.

The Rig Vedic *Rishi* has a special interest and style when he deals with the riddle of life or the Universe. He is fond of using very abstract and at times quite unintelligible symbols in describing the Creator of this Universe. In the 58 hymn of the 4th Book of *Rigveda* the Creator of this world is described to be having four horns. The seer goes a long way telling that this 'Mahâdeva has four horns, three legs, two heads, seven hands, is bound at three points, speaks very loudly possessing human beings on earth.'[2] *Nâsadiya, Purush, Viswakarmâ* and *Hiranyagarbha* hymns try at length to solve these riddles. The Rishi is indeed very honest when towards the end of *Nâsadiya Sûkta* (10/129) he first imagines that the One who created this universe must surely know the origin of it. But as if by way of introspection and not hiding his genuine doubt, he questions, 'supposing that even if He Himself doesn't know, then?'[3] The Hymn comes to an end at this point. There is definitely ample space to believe that it is the sheer doubt of an ordinary human being expressed and this is the limitation of a man's imagination. and understanding only and never any extent set for the Infinite Being worth human expression.

There are ample geographical and historical data compiled from *Rigveda*. It is the most ancient and accurate record of the social and occupational life of people of that period. Social customs, rituals, celebrations, garments, dresses, eating habits, marriages, travels, cattle, war, worship, sports, amusements, singing, dancing, agriculture etc. are all the objects and the topics of these hymns. However, this superb poetry is more of a connecting link, a bridge for working on line with the other world much richer and meaningful.

---

2 चत्वारि शृंगा त्रयो अस्य पादा हे शीर्षे सप्त हस्तासो अस्य
   त्रिधा बद्धो बृषभो रोरवीति महा देवो मर्त्या आ विवेश । ऋग्-4&58&3
3 इयं विसृष्टिर्यत आबभूव यदि वा दधे यदि वा न
   यो अस्याध्यक्ष:परमे व्योमन्त्सो अंग वेद यदि वा न वेद । ऋग्. 10&129&7

3

Contents Of Rigveda

Rigveda stands literally for a compiled code of *Richâs*, hymns. *Richâs* are also called *Mantras*. Both of these terms signify the ancient seer's secrets of verbal communication with a higher and a far superior existence called *Devatâ*. It is further not a simple compilation but a direct perception of truth, which is worth sharing by true seekers in their quest of knowledge. The word *Veda* thus attains a meaning of a collective wisdom and experience of all information and knowledge in man's effort towards greater goal of self-realization. Some important topics and subject matters of *Rigveda* are as follows.

Invocation

The first impression gained after a study of *Vedic* hymns is that of a worshipper trying to offer prayers to a superior power known as *Devatâ* to have mercy and provide assistance in worldly gains. His appearance in a subtle or material form will certainly help human being attain his objectives. This Power can be visualized and felt in many forms and facets as *Veda* propounds in depth how purposefully well ordained transformation of the Unmanifest to the manifest form became possible. Theism of *Veda*, putting it in other words, is thus the core note of Vedic concept. The hymns are generally invocations of gods who are mainly personified powers of nature. It is in this manner, essentially a polytheistic religion that only sometimes seems to be assuming a pantheistic colour in last few hymns of the classic. The gods are invoked to accompany the oblation of *Soma* juice and the fire sacrifices of melted butter. These gods are believed to have had a beginning but every one did not come to being at one time. There are occasional references in *Rigveda* of earlier gods and certain deities are described as the offspring of others. Some of them have attained the state of immortality as they drank *Soma* and others after receiving it as a gift from *Agni* and *Savitr*.

The mode of invocation of these gods is essentially the rite of sacrifice called *Yajna*. Since the favourite food of gods is also that of human beings consisting of milk, butter, grain, and the flesh of sheep, goats, and cattle, it is offered to them in sacrifice. It is conveyed to them in heaven by gods of fire. They also at times come in their cars to partake it on the strew of grass prepared for their reception. Their most favourite drink is the exhilarating juice of *Soma* plant about which the Vedic seers are always very keen. The abode of gods is also that heaven which is the third and highest step of *Vishnu* where cheered by draughts of *Soma* they live a life of eternal bliss. Gods have been described as great and mighty. They govern and regulate the order of nature and are capable of thwarting the evil designs of demons. Human happiness largely depends on the fulfilment of desires on earth and these gods certainly help achieving this goal. Riches in the form of servants, cows, horses etc. and prosperity, fame, victory over enemies and a general well being of every one in the society are some such desires, which are sought to be fulfilled by godly assistance. It is specifically to be noted that unlike mythological characterization of gods, in *Rigveda*, whereas they have brilliance, benevolence and wisdom in common, their physical and attributive distinction is very vague. Invoking deities in pairs like Mitra-Varuna, Dyava-Prithvi and AshwiniKumârs etc indeed further intensifies this vagueness. Although in such cases both gods share similar characteristics and thus the identification of one with the other is quite simple. This identifying mark can indeed be extended to that important Rig Vedic philosophy where various deities become different forms of a single divine being. This indeed represents the pantheism of *Rigveda* that becomes characteristic of later Indian thought in the form of the *Vedanta* philosophy.

Among the category of abstract gods invoked, the most important is *Prajapati,* the Lord of creatures. Similarly *Vishwakarmâ* and *Hiranyagarbha* are also equally important in the sense that the philosophical notes of hymns composed in their invocations are as a matter of fact the origin of all perennial philosophies, which come to be known and accepted till date.

At least in two places gods have been described as old, young and babies but it has been also asserted that no god is young or old and that all are great. It is well underlining in this context that two gods, namely valiant *Indra* and righteous *Varuna* are those gods to whom maximum number of hymns are dedicated in the invocation process.

Supreme Reality in *Rigveda* is not just a philosophical abstraction, but also a manifestation and experiences of truth, which a man should invoke and evoke for the fulfilment of his ultimate goal of life. It is an invocation and a concept of dynamic reality-Theism. It is our concern for every moment. 'All effulgence behind God's creation is His effulgence; the mighty force behind nature's force is His force. He is light behind light; terror behind the terror, the sweetness behind everything that is sweet and incessant activity behind all actions'[1] *Rigveda* admires this force, invokes these bounties of nature and moves far ahead to the Unmanifest Reality and the eternal source of enlightenment and bliss. *Rigveda* invokes this Lord in terms of many attributes and functions and helps us achieve a personal relationship- 'Two birds, which are closely associated and intimate friends, perch on the same tree. Of them one (the lower self) tastes of its fruits; the other (the Supreme Lord) shines resplendently without tasting.'[2]

Prayer

Rigveda faithfully represents all basic human characteristics and aspirations necessary for human evolution and growth. There

---

1   Swami Satya Prakash Saraswati in Foreword to *'The Holy Vedas'* by Pandit Satyakam Vidyalankar

2   द्वा सुपर्णा सयुजा सखाया समानं वृक्षं परि षस्वजाते
    तयोरन्य: पिप्लं स्वाद्वत्तरशन्यो अभि चाकशीति । ऋग् 1-164-20

is always a will, a force and motion within the reach of every human being but at times he starts finding himself some short of means for achieving the target he sets. He starts looking on such occasions for some external and superior help. Definitely if such help comes from a higher power who is also close to his own self, it is indeed more welcome. The attributes of gods are in this context identifiable as well as worth modelling with those of human aspirations. Therefore a man tries to get nearer to the grace of god through a universal language of heart. Every prayer has its origin here only.

The prayer content is so much dominating in *Rigveda* that it has been sometimes termed as a book of prayers only. But the term in this particular context has to be well understood. It is simply not a religion. It is a dialogue, a drama and a process of scientific evolution and growth. And the pursuit is also far superior, as the objective behind this is the attainment of lasting peace and fulfilment in this life as well as beyond it.

Since the Vedic concept of God is essentially ethical, Vedic verses uphold moral values. According to Swami Satyaprakash Sarswati, God in Vedic verses 'is the Truth personified, Activity personified, Purity personified, Love personified and Bliss personified.'[3] Human beings therefore crave to imbibe His qualities in them. The prayer naturally is the best medium of its expression. The most prominent note of these prayers is the commonality of attributes of all kind of gods worshipped or prayed. In the 5th *Mandala, Sûkta 3* and *mantra 1, Agni* is described as *'Varuna by birth, Mitra after getting awakened. Thou the son of Power, all the gods pivot round you; you are Indra for the provider of oblivion.'*[4] In 1.164.46 again it is said *'they call him Indra, Mitra, Varuna, Agni, and he is heaven nobly-winged Garutman. To what is one, sages give many a titles; they call it Agni, Yama, Mâtrisvân.'*[5] This instance about *Aditi* from Rig. 1.89.10 should well illustrate this point-

---

3 Swami Satyaprakash Sarsvati in his foreword to *'The HolyVedas'* by Pandit Satyakam Vidyalankar

4 त्वमग्ने वरुणो जायसे यत् त्वं मित्रो भवसि यत् · समिद्ध:
  त्वे विश्वे सहसस्पुत्रा देवास्त्वमिन्द्रो दाशुषे मर्त्याय । ऋग्. 5-3-1

5 इन्द्रं मित्रां वरुणमग्निमाहु रथो दिव्य: स सुपर्णो गरुत्मान
  एकं सद् विप्र बहुधा वंदन्त्यग्निं यमं मातरिश्वानमाहु: ।ऋग्. 1-164-46

'Aditi, is the heaven, Aditi is mid air, Aditi is the Mother and the sire and the son. Aditi is all gods, Aditi five classed men, Aditi all that hath been born and shall be born.' [6]

Rigveda begins with the glorification of gods primarily as a force of nature but generally ends with their sublimation as an All Powerful One. While praising *Indra, Sûrya* and *Varuna* have been described as his subordinates. *Indra, Mitra, Varuna, Aryama* and *Rudra* cannot transgress the authority of *Savita* (Rig. 2.38.9).

Rig Vedic hymns generally end with a prayer after the invocation. The very first hymn in *Mandala* one in its last 9 stanza prays *Agni ' be to us easy of approach, even as a father to his son: Agni, be with us for our weal.'* The Vedic seer who is overwhelmed by the affluence of the brilliant presence of Sun has this prayer to offer in the end of this hymn-

' This day, O Gods, while Sûrya is ascending, deliver us from trouble and dishonour. This prayer of our may Varuna grant, and Mitra, and Aditi, and Sindhu, Earth and Heaven.' [8]

Vedic prayers are not to be misunderstood to have been made for the fulfilment of individual material gains. The social consciousness of these seers is evident all over and they are simply aiming at attaining general well being through the divine assistance. In *Vishwedeva Sûktas* (1.89, 90) the collective approach for the whole group of gods is all obvious.

' Gods! may we', the seer prays *'with our ears listen to what is good, and with our eyes see what is good, ye Holy Ones. With our limbs and bodies firm may we extolling you attain the term of life appointed by Gods. A hundred autumns stand before us, O ye Gods within whose space ye bring our bodies to decay. Within whose*

---

6 अदितिर्द्यौरदितिरन्तरिक्षमदितिर्माता स पिता स पुत्रा:
   विश्वेदेवा अदिति: पंच जना अदितिर्जातमदितिर्जनित्वम् ।ऋग्. 1-89-10

7 स न: पिता सूनवेऽग्ने सूपायनो भव । सचस्वा न: स्वस्तयं ।। ऋग् .1-1-9

8 अद्या देवा उदिता सूर्यस्य निरहंस: पिृता निरवद्यात्
   तनबाने मित्रो वरुणो मामहन्तामदिति: सिन्धु: पृथिवी उत द्यो: । ऋग् .1-115-6

space our sons become fathers in turn. Break ye not in the midst our course of fleeting life.' [9] *(1.89.8-9)*

Personification

Natural forces such as rains, thunder, air, water, Sun; earth, space, dawn, rivers, wealth, wisdom and time are all personified in *Rigveda*. They are, however, treated like gods. Their appearance may have some human similarities, but it is more like an image than a reality. Their physical limbs generally signify their natural attributes. There are descriptions available about their face, mouth, eyes, hair, shoulders, chest, stomach, arms, fingers etc. Heads, chest and arms, for instance, have been described in case of *Indra* and *Marudgana*. *Indra* has been generally spoken as *Vajrabâhu* (having *Vajra* in hand) or *Vajrahasta*. The arms of the Sun are his rays and his eyes are his actual physical forms. The tongue of fire and its flames represent its limbs. The stomach of *Indra* is also often talked about, as it is indicative of his addiction for *Soma*.

Some gods have been described in ornaments and dresses. *Ushâ* bears beautiful and charming dresses. Gods also put on armour around their body and the head and they ride in the shining horse driven chariots. The chariot of *Pushâ* is driven by goats and of *Marudgans* by deers etc.

These gods have a special taste and choice for divine nectar *Soma*. They come for receiving sacrificial offerings. Although they are living in heaven or the abode of *Vishnu,* they are appearing on earth for supporting righteous human beings. Traditionally gods have come to be described as living on earth, in heaven or space. But the most common feature to be attributed is the aspect of personification as discussed.

Gods like *Indra* and *Agni* are supraphysical powers and the powers in nature like rain, wind and so on are aspects of their

---

9 भद्रं कर्णेभिः शृणुयाम देवा भद्रं पश्येमाक्षभिर्यजत्राः
थरैरंगैस्तुष्टवांसस्तनूभिव्यशेम देवतिं यदायुः
शतमिन्न शारदो अन्ति देवा यत्रा नश्चक्रा जरसै तनूनाम्
पुत्रासो यत्रा पितरो भवन्ति मा नो मध्या रीरिषतायुगन्तो । ऋग् .1-89-8,9

powers. Since the seer had established a relationship with one or more of such cosmic powers, he could appeal to these deities so that the physical powers of nature act so as to be beneficial to the human beings. For instance, god *Indra* was to be appealed to release rains in times of draught and to stop the downpour in times of excessive rainfall.

Poetry

Rigveda is rich in poetic values and literary accomplishments. The deep state of meditation, the inner contentment and the appreciation and gratefulness of gods have all gone into the making of it an eternal epic of human aspirations. The well thought arrangement and the relationship of the seer; the god and the metre make it complete and the meaningful whole. The poetry of it might appear sometimes to be 'the spontaneous overflow of powerful feelings' but it is also at the same times great 'thoughts recollected in tranquillity'. There are some interpreters of this classic classifying the hymns into categories like, songs, drama, comedies and long poems. As a matter of fact, various elements of poetry have got to be sought never in such order in it as they are scattered all over. As the gods have been generally personified representing natural forces, the hymns written for praising them are quite rich and noble in beautiful imagery. The hymns addressed to dawn are highly poetical and can be well compared with the best poetry of the world. *Ushâ* (7. 76. 3) has long waited for the Sun to arise like a beloved and not just a housewife.[10] Similarly hymns to *Indra* are rich in graphic power; to *Maruts* depict with vigorous imagery the phenomena of thunder and lightening. The hymn to *Parjanya* (5.83) paints vividly the Devâstating effect of the rain and storm. *'Lift up the mighty vessel,'* it reads *'pour down water, and let liberated streams run forward. Saturate both the earth and heaven with fatness, and for the cows let there be drink abundant'. 5.83.8).*[11]

---

10 तानीदहानि बहुलान्यासन् या प्राचीनमुदिता सूर्यस्य
   यत: परि जार इवाचरन्त्युषो ददृक्षे न पुनर्यतीव । ऋग् .7-76-3
Italics quoted with gratitude from RALPH T.H. Griffith's English rendering of the Vedic stanzas from the *Hymns of the Rigveda*.

11 महान्तं कोशमुदचा नि षिंच स्यन्दन्तां कुल्या विषिता: पुरस्तात्
   घृतेन द्यावापृथिवी व्युन्धि सुप्रमाणं भवत्वघ्न्याभ्य: । ऋग् .5-83-8

Similarly the Gambler's lament in *'Aksh Sûkta'* (10.34) is an interesting specimen of pathetic as well as comedian poetry. The funeral hymns (10.18) solemnly pictures the departure of dear ones and the images connected with such a pathetic sight in the following lines-

'Rise, come unto the world of life, o woman: come, he is lifeless by whose side thou liest.

Wifehood with this thy husband was thy portion, who took thy hand and wooed thee as a lover.' (10.18.8)[12]

Rigveda is a high-class poetry since it displays high-class symbolism. A symbol always attempts to describe an experience beyond the realm of senses. It is auditory as well as visual. Here are four classes of symbols in *Rigveda*. Firstly the gods like *Agni, Indra* and goddesses like *Saraswatî; Saramâ, Mahi* etc represent distinct type of divine powers. In the second category fall the evil forces like *Vrittra, Vala, and Shushna etc.* The third class of symbols consists of common noun like *go, ashwa, nadi* etc. Lastly is the class of the names associated with the sages and seers like *Kanva* and *Kutsa*. Sri Aurobindo and Sri Kapil Shastri whose commendable task requires expansion have done the unravelling of the symbolism behind each word of these seekers of the truth.

Dramatic Dialogues

The mythological dialogues between *Saramâ* and *Pani* (10.108), *Yama* and *Yami*, (10.10), *Vishwâmitra* and rivers *Vyâs* and *Satlaj* (3.33) and *Urvashî-Pururava* (10.95) are the best specimens of dramatic poetry of *Rigveda*.

The hymn of *Saramâ- Panis* is a colloquy between *Saramâ and* the messenger of *Indra* and the *Panis* who had carried off the cows of *Brahspati*. *Saramâ* and *Panis* are alternatively object (*Devatâ*) and subject (*Rishi*). The *Panis* begin with addressing *Saramâ* who has unwittingly found her way to the rocky stronghold in which the stolen cows are kept. *Panis* try to allure *Saramâ* by first offering her a share in the stolen property and then proposing her to become their sister on which *Saramâ* has this to react-

---

12 उदीर्ष्व नार्यभि जीवलोकं गतासुमेतमुप शेष एहि
हस्तग्राभस्य दिधिषोस्तवेदं पत्युर्जनित्वमभि सं बभूथ । ऋग्. 10-18-8

'Brotherhood, sisterhood, I know not either: the dread Angirâs and Indra know them. They seemed to long for kine when I departed. Hence into distance, be ye gone, O Panis.'[13]

Hymn 33 of the Book 3 is again a dialogue between *Vishwâmitra* and river *Vipâsa* and *Shutudri* who are also regarded to be *Rishis* or seers of the stanzas ascribed to them. According to *Sâyana, Viswâmitra,* the *Purohit* or family priest of the king *Sudâsa, having* obtained wealth by means of his office, came along with it near these rivers. In order to make these rivers provide him a safe passage, he lauds them with first three verses. The rivers, though seemingly reluctant in the beginning, provide him a passage in the following manner-

'Yea, we will listen to thy words, O singer. With wain and car from far away thou comest

Low like a nursing mother, will I bend me, and yield me as a maiden to her lover.' (3.33.10)[14]

Hymn 95th of the tenth Book is again a dialogue between *Pururava* and *Urvashî* who are severely the speaker, the *Rishi* and addressee, the *Devatâ.* This dialogue contains the root of a legend related in *Shatpath Brâhman* and appearing again in *Mahâbhârata* and other *Purânas* forming further the plot of the well-known drama, *Vikramorvashi* of *Kâlidâsa.*

The romance of poetry is at its peak when *Pururava's* dejected declaration that his bed would be 'the destruction's bosom and there let fierce rapacious wolves devour him', *Urvashî* cries-

'Nay, do not die, Pururava, nor vanish: not let the evil omened wolves devour thee.

*With women there can be no lasting friendship: hearts of hyenas are the hearts of the women.' ***

---

13 नाहं वेद भ्रातृत्वं नो स्वसृत्वमिन्द्रो द्विंगिरश्च घोरा:
गोकामा मे अच्छदयन् यदायमपात इत पणयो वरीय: ऋग् .10-108-10
14 आ ते कारो शृणवामा वचांसि ययाथ दूरादनसा रथेन
नी ते नंसै पीप्यानेव योषा मयायेव कन्या शश्वचै ते। ऋग् . 3-33-10
* English renderings are quoted from *Hymns of the Rigveda* by Ralph T.H. Griffith published by Munshiram Manoharlal

Hymn 10 in the Book 10 known, as *'Yama Yami Sûkta'* is another specimen of a very good poetry. The contents of this verse beautifully combine the attributes of a good poem and morality. An oft-quoted remark of the great commentator Winternitz is an apt point to be remembered at this stage, which warns that *'Rigveda* is everything except a book on morality.' This has both, the positive as well as a negative connotation. Negatively while it can mean to be a book defying the concept of morality as such whereas, positively it suggests that in matters of higher philosophy or deep poetry, the common concept of morality have not got any place. Therefore when in this hymn under reference *Yami* proposes her brother 'then let thy soul and mine be knit together, and as a loving husband take thy consort', *Yama* naturally turns down the offer and states 'I will not fold mine arms about thy body: they call it sin when one comes near his sister.' Following remark from Griffith's 'Hymn of the *Rigveda'* may certainly be not out of place here- ' As the Hebrew conception closely connected the parents of mankind by making the woman formed from a portion of the body of the man, so by the Indian tradition they are placed in the relationship of twins. This thought is laid by the hymn in question in the mouth of *Yami* herself, when she is made to say- *Even in the womb the Creator made us for husband and wife.'* [15]

Philosophy

Ancient Indian seers were drawing many inspirations from their observation of Nature, Natural Forces, God, God's Creation, the world and the purpose of life on earth as such. Their deep study and observation of the world, the life on earth and the forces beyond human control made them believe in a much higher Power, Who, was the Creator of all and knew the Reality of its coming into being-

'Whose eye controls this world in highest heaven, he verily knows it...' 10.129.7 [16]

---

15 पुरूरवो मामृथा मा प्र पप्तो मा त्वा वृकासे अशिवास उ क्षन्
न वै स्त्रौणानि सख्यानि सन्ति सालावृकाणां हृदयान्येता । ऋग् . 10-95-15

16 यो अस्याध्यक्ष: परमे व्योमन् त्सो अंग वेद यदि वा न वेद । ऋग् . 10-129-7

Rigveda demonstrates that the world is the source book of all studies. Exploring mysteries of the complex world and the vital disciplines of life and death was a definite challenge before the ancient seekers of truth in India. Surely their search raises the reader 'from Creation to the Creator, from the Sun to the Sun that shines behind the Sun, to the fire that glows behind the mundane fire...to the Light that enlightens the entire light familiar to us.'[17]

Purush Sûkta (10.90) is the first scientific and logical explanation and an exposition of the theory of evolution, which came to be so known and understood much later by the modern world. The English rendering of the sixth stanza of this hymn is quoted with gratitude from 'The Holy *Vedas*' of Shri Satyakam Vidyalankar to bring home this notion-

'With the coming into being of the dynamic universe

The adaptation of the primordial matter was made in the primeval activities

Thus began the changes in the atomic composition of the matter.

In this colossal cosmic sacrifice, substances to sustain life were produced

As well as vegetation, grains, fruit, flowers and therapeutic substances that increase both energy and life span.

This made it possible for animal life to thrive.' (Rig.10.90.6)

The seers of *Rigveda* viewed a human being as a symbol of the Supreme Divine. This is the natural meaning of the *Purush Sûkta*. It is indicative of the truth that each human being's structure mirrors that of the cosmos. Similarly, the individual mind has also a corresponding relationship with the cosmic one. It demonstrates in no uncertain terms that the structure of a human being replicates that of the macrocosm.

The difference between a human being and the Divine, however, remains this that the cosmic worlds associated with the Divine are perfect whereas there is a sheath in human being corresponding to every world. Each human being is at a different stage of development.

---

17 Swami Satyaprakash Sarswati in his foreword to the *'Holy Vedas'* wrote by Pandit Satyakam Vidyalankar.

The goal stated in *Rigveda* is the attainment of immortality or perfection in all aspects. Immortality is not mere freedom from death and living in aging body for ever. The decay of our physical and mental powers is the characteristic mortality imminent. The gods are thus simply helping human beings attain perfection in all directions.

Science

Rig Vedic seer did not draw distinctions between science and spirituality, physics and metaphysics or good and evil. Their approach of truth is based on plurality therefore the so-called theism of *Rigveda* is essentially polytheistic. There is thus an ample scope for the scientific scrutiny and analysis in it. In lower stages of study like ours, the disciplines of knowledge may be separate. For instance, botany here is not physics, hearing is not seeing and so on and so forth. Therefore in order to understand the true nature of this science, the above character requires to be borne into the mind. However, in present terms of the case, there are following few facets of this branch of knowledge to be described.

A. Medical Science- there are a number of healing techniques such as acupuncture, acupressure, naturopathy, and homeopathy talked about these days of which seeds may be discovered in *Rigveda*. There are quite a few mantras in hymns of *Rigveda* regarding diseases, their cure and the herbs available for it. There was treatment given through the prescribed use of water also. The divine doctors *Ashwni Kumârs* are the famous characters of *Rigveda*. In the 85th hymn of the Tenth book there is an epic description of the marriage of *Aswini Kumârs* with *Sûrya* where the seer does not forget to mention the name of the infectious disease tuberculosis for which the lord of *Yajna* are stated to be taking care when necessary.

'Consumptions, from her people, which follow the bride's resplendent train

Let holy gods again bear them to the place from which they came.'[18]

---

18 ये वध्वश्चन्तु वहतुं यक्ष्मा यन्ति जनादनु
पुनस्तान यज्ञिया देवा नयन्तु यत आगताः । ऋग् . 10-85-31

There are a number of references available outlining their miraculous power of healing. They're giving sight to the blind (1.117.17), restoring youth to the old (1.117.13) and so on.

B. Geography- *Rigveda* provides a detail description of Ocean, rivers and mountain with an historical accuracy and correct geographical sense. It talks about *Vyâs* and *Shatlaj* rivers in particular and about *Sapt Sindhava* in general for pointing out towards the name of the rivers *Sindhu, Vitastâ, Parushni, Vipâsha, Shatudri, Asikni* and *Saraswatî*. Mountain *Munjwân* finds a special mention in it as it contained famous *Soma* medicinal herb.

C. Astronomy and Astrology- Âryans living in Vedic era were definitely aware of the movement of the planets and the stars. In the 35th hymn of Book one of *Rigveda*, the rise, the course and the effect of the Sun on Moon and Earth has been described. Even the movement and the course of earth have been described in the 149th hymn of the Tenth book. It has been repeatedly said that the gravitational pull of the Sun holds on the earth and makes it move on its course. Seven horses of the Sun are indicative of seven colours of light. It also makes a mention of different seasons and twelve astrological signs. These seers were also aware of the solar eclipse and the north and southward courses of the Sun.

D. Boats and Planes- Âryans were aware of the use and the manufacturing of boats and airplanes. The 5th mantra of the 116th hymn of the First book talks about a boat, which is driven by hundred oars. In the 2nd mantra of the 34th hymn of the 2nd Book there is a mention of the chariot of *Ashwini Kumârs, which* was an airplane of three wheels! [19]

Sacrifice

According to the Rigvedic theme of existence, a human being performs skilful actions only with the assistance of gods surely available to him. Even the very act of the composition of hymns of the *Vedas* is nothing but the transcription of the revelations through memory with the same divine aid of all knowing

---

19 अनारम्भणे तदवीरयेथा मनास्थाने अग्रभणे समुद्रे
यदश्विना उहथुर्भुज्युमस्तं शतारित्रां नावमातस्थिवांसम् । ऋग् . 1-116-5

gods in appropriate metres. Sacrifice, the rite as well as the act of this knowledge known as *Yajna,* is the testimony of this collaboration between gods and human beings. This thought finds its finest culmination in the theme of *Bhagwat Gîta* in which sacrifices of *tapa,* penance, *Gyân,* knowledge and *swadhyaya,* self-study has been mentioned. According to Indian philosophy, in this manner, the whole creation, its sustenance right up to the breathing activity of living beings is the performances of *Yajnas.*

Agni produces altogether an entirely new object when a thing is blended into it. Other chemical of physical mixture produce just a transient by product where a particular blending in fire called *Yajna* is virtually the process of acculturation bringing about refinement, *Samskara.* This is, in this way, a process of purification on the physical level and also the education, training, making sacred and the regeneration process at the subtler level.

The sacrificial rite is not just dramatized as a cosmic play of creation in the *Purush Sûkta* alone, the *Brâhmans* and the commentary of *Sayana* stand basically for this aspect of *Veda*s which according to them is the representative character of the Book. There came thus the terms *hota, adhwaryu, udgâta* and *Brahmâ* standing for the *Rig Veda, Yajur Veda, Sâm Veda* and *Atharva Veda* respectively.

Adhwaryu, for instance, is derived from *adhwa,* path and *raw* to move. The term naturally came to be associated with the rite of sacrifice as one of the principal priests in it is called *Adhwaryu.* The function of this priest is to direct the rite in tune with the meaning assigned to *adhwara.* Just as merchants go in their boats to distant places for bringing valuable treasures, *Veda* points out, similarly a person performing *Yajna* wins heavenly treasures on earth.

Shri R. L. Kashyap in his 'Introductory Essay on *Rigveda'* goes on to elaborate that the *Yajna* also stands for a 'constant battle between the helpful powers of nature, the *Devâs* and the deterrents like *Vrittra* and *Vala.* The performer of the sacrifice invokes the righteous forces so that he wins the battle against these fierce adversaries tempting mankind towards hatred, jealous and greed. The ritual begins with the invocation of *Agni* by lighting the physical fire...the fire is nourished by *ghee*, which symbolizes mental clarity. The *Soma* herb, which stands for the bliss released in all actions, is also offered to *Agni'.*

As regards four priests, the *hota* calls *Devâs* to come and participate in the *Yajna. Adhwryu* lays down various steps in the successful performance of it. *Udgata* chants the *mantras* in the suitable metres. *Brahma* presides over the entire rite and makes sure that the *Yajna* is performed in the strictest prescribed manner. *Rigveda* also talks about *Agni* performing all these roles. It also states about the four-faced creator-god in hymn 58 of *Mandala* 4 by whom every human being is possessed intimately.

Society

The famous *Purush Sûkta* (10.90.12) talks about the four *Varnas- Brahmin, Kshatriya, Vaishya* and *Shûdra*. They virtually stood for the various limbs of the one organic whole.[20] The whole life span was divided into four *Ashramas*, resorts, *Brahmcharya* (studies in celibacy), *Grahastha* (household), *Vanprastha* (forest recluse) and *Sanyâsa* (renunciation). Marriage formed an important part of the household stage, which marked a complete harmony of relationship among various kith and kins. The bride occupied a special place of high command in that system of society-

'Over thy husband's father and thy husband's mother bear full sway

Over the sister of thy lord, over his brothers, rule supreme.' [21]

Woman thus occupied a very respectful position in the Rig Vedic age. *Ushâ, Sûrya, Vâk, Prithivî, Shree* etc. were the various commanding forces of nature.

There are descriptions of thieves, servants and soldiers. About houses, *Rigveda* makes a mention of one for *Vishnu 'where oxen of high horns would move easily and freely.'*[22] *(1.154.6).* their food consisted of milk, butter, ghee, rice and grains. Whether they ate meat or not is disputed but there are mentions of animal

---

20 ब्राह्मणो अस्य मुखमासीद्वाहूराजन्य: कृत:
उरू तदस्य यद्वैश्य: पद्भ्यां शूद्रो अजायत । ऋग् . 10-90-12

21 सम्राज्ञी श्वशुरे भव सम्राज्ञी श्वश्रुवां भव
ननान्दरि सम्राज्ञी भव सम्राज्ञी अधि देवृषु । ऋग् .10-85-46'

22 ता वां वास्तून्युश्मसि गमध्यै यत्रा गावो भूरि शृंगा अयास: ।

sacrifices. Among their drinks, *Soma* has a very distinct and prominent place. Whether it was an herb, an intoxicant or just a symbol of divine elixir is not clear.

They bore woollen as well as cotton cloths. There are mentions of deer skins and the wooden wrappers used. The cloths borne were of upper and lower kinds. These people, particularly women, were fond of ornaments. They were also dressing up their hair fashionably. Music, dance and social sports like horse riding and gambling also formed a part of the social life of the age. Agriculture, dairy development, mineral works and trade through road and sea transport formed important parts of the economic activity.

Nation

The concept of a Nation and the nationalism was well concretised at that time. In the sixth mantra of the 66th hymn of the fifth Book of *Rigveda*, the protection of the national territories is stressed. In hymn 33 of the Book 3 there is a repeated reference to *Bhâratas* (those living in *Bhârata*, India). *Vishwâmitra* and the rivers do not just agree to make a shift bridge for the seer alone to cross. *Vishwâmitra* has following request to make to the rivers-

'Soon as the Bhâratas have fared across thee, the warrior band, urged on and sped by Indra,

Then let your streams flow on in rapid motion.'[23]

The concept of a Nation and the national unity develops further in *Yajur Veda* and *Atharva Veda*. Earth has been invoked in stanzas 22 to 25 of chapter 9 of *Yajur Veda* and hymn 1 of chapter 12 of *Atharvaveda* in a very vibrant style. As a matter of fact, the whole world was just like one Nation for the Vedic seers. This attains its culmination in the famous *Prithvi Sûkta* of *Atharva Veda* where the earth has been described to be a natural abode of every human being irrespective of the faith he professes, the language he speaks and the part of the land he resides. In all cases the earth is like a simple thousand-breast cow to offer milk without any discrimination.[24]

---

23 अतारिषुर्भरता गव्यव: स मभक्त विप्र: सुमतिं नदीनाम्
  प्र पिन्वध्वमिषयन्ती: सुराधा आ वृक्षण: पृणध्वं यात शीभम् । ऋग् . 3-33-12
24 जनं बिभ्रती बहुधा विवाचसं
  नानाधर्माणं पृथिवी यथौकसम्
  सहस्रं धारा द्रविणस्य मे दुहां
  धु वेव धेनुरनपस्फुरन्ती ।अथर्व .12-45

Humanity

Rigveda is a sacred heritage of not only India, but also the whole mankind. The *Dharma*, a social order advocated in it is based on high moral and ethical principles, which have been held high in all ages by every society. For instance *Shraddhâ*, faith, *Tapa*, austerity, *Dayâ*, pity, *Dâna*, generosity, and peace *Shânti* are the preconditions of all good living. According to *Rigveda* a man is a social organism. He should be caring and serving just not only human beings, but every living being on earth.

The Rigvedic seer is very broad minded when he prays *Viswedeva* (plurality of gods) *'May powers auspicious come to us from every side, never deceived, unhindered and victorious.'* (Rig. 1.189.1)[25]

The following ancient mantras of Book 10 hymn 191 can never be out of date for a world to live in eternal peace and prosperity-

'Assemble speak together: let your minds be all of one accord

As ancient gods unanimous sit down to their appointed share.

The place is common, common the assembly, common the mind, so be their thought united.

A common purpose do I lay before you, and worship with your general oblation

One and the same be your resolve, and be your minds of one accord

United be the thoughts of all that all may happily agree.'

(Rig.10.191.2, 3.4) [26]

---

25 आ नो भद्रज्ञ: क्रतवो यन्तु विश्वतो-
ऽदब्धासो अपरीतास उदि्भिद: ।
26 संगच्छध्वं सं वदध्वं सं वो मनांसि जानताम्
देवा भागं यथा पूर्वे संजनाना उपासते ।
समानो मंत्रा: समिति समानी
समानं मन: सह चित्त मेषाम् ।
समानं मन्त्रामभि मन्त्रये
व: समाने न वो हविमा जुहोमि ।
समानी व आकूति: समाना हृदयानि व:
समानमस्तु वो मनो यथा व: सुसहासति ।

4

Myths And Parables In Stories

There are a number of myths in *Rigveda*, which form the basis of *Purânic* history in later India. In some cases there are just a few references of some important event or adventure and at places simply a mention of names. It is thus very difficult to take these stories to a logical conclusion for want of many missing links. However, the parables, the past and the future logistics of most of the references and tales require serious attention for understanding the true meaning of this aspect of *Rigveda*. A brief account of some of the important myths is given below.

Saramâ and Pani

Panis were the people coming from across the borders of ancient India. They undertook trading with the exchange of *Panya*, money. They were sometimes engaged in stealing and also fought with local inhabitants with sharp weapons. In the tenth Book of *Rigveda* the dialogue between *Saramâ*, an emissary of *Indra* and *Panis*, throw enough light about them. *Indra* had deputed *Saramâ* to persuade *Panis* to release *Brahaspati's* cows or else they would be facing mighty *Indra* in the fierce battle. *Panis* first try to bribe *Saramâ* offering a share in the property. They afterwards seek to impress her emotionally telling that she is just like a sister for them. She should no longer be afraid of *Indra* because they will take care of her safety. *Saramâ* had taken the form of a bitch. Dogs are still very widely used for detective purposes. The initiative from the side of *Indra* is also well in support of long Indian tradition. Much later during the eve of the great *Mahabharata* war, Krishna became the messenger of peace of *Pandavas*. Thus this story has got seeds of many old and new cult and traditions.

Vrittra

Vrittra was the first and the foremost enemy of *Indra*. Whether he was a historical or a force of nature is debatable. He is however distinctly passed on to Indian mythology to become an important archenemy of *Indra* much later as well. *Danu* was *Vrittra's* mother and *Twashta* his father. *Vrittra* is at places referred to as a snake. Snake is equally an original demon force in many world mythologies. *Indra* kills *Vrittra* with his favourite weapon *Vrittra*. It may also stand for the electricity extracting water from the clouds. *Indra* had virtually incarnated for the destruction this great evil power. (8.18.5, 10.55) According to the *Nirukta* interpreter, *Vrittra* was a historical person whereas most of the western interpreters suppose him to be a natural force who had withheld rainfall.

Shunah Shape

In verse 24 of the first *Mandala,* the story of *Shunah Shape* finds a mention. He was to be sacrificed in a ritual. There is a series of prayers made at this occasion. *Shunah Shape* is not just saved but the seer *Vishwâmitra* patronizes him as a seer of his tradition. This story has been dealt in great detail in the *Shatpath Brâhman* written as an interpretation of this *Veda.*

Vashishtha and Vishwâmitra

In the 53rd *Sûkta* of the third Book and the 33rd *Sûkta* of the seventh Book, the story of these two important Vedic seers appears. They later on become important characters of many mythological stories and *Puranic* history. Their rivalry and the patronage they offered to various kings of *Ayodhya* is the subject matter of many important Indian classics of ancient as well as modern times. There are references to the relationship between *Indra* and king *Sudâsa* available in their context also.

Trayaruna and Vrishjan

Sûkta 2 of the fifth Book has following interesting story to narrate. *Vrishjan,* the priest of king *Tryaruna* was driving the cart of the king. A boy playing on the ground jumps up on the wheel of the cart and gets killed. The priest told the king that he (the king) is the killer as he was the owner of the cart. The king on the other hand held that the driver of the cart was responsible. The matter was further referred to *Ikshwâku*, the Emperor, who ruled out that the driver, who should exercise the control, was in fact responsible for the death.

Saraswatî and Vadhyaswa

Sûkta 61st of the *Mandala* 6th makes a mention of *Saraswatî* granting a son called *Divodâsa* to the seer *Vadhyaswa*. *Saraswatî*, the goddess is also a river in it. She is referred to have assisted gods in the destruction of *Asuras*. It has been stressed that *Saraswatî* should have been perceptible at the time of *Indra's* battle with *Vrittra*. She helps *Âryans* regain the land *Asuras* had snatched from them. She is the giver of food grain and all riches. She also helped other rivers to be full of water. The seers desire to reside near the waters of this river only.

The present *Saraswatî* is not visible but there are evidences of *Saraswatî* having ample water at the time when the *Rigveda* was written. *Panis* were living across this river *Rasa* (another name of *Saraswatî*). They had therefore to ask 'how did you *Saramâ* cross the flooded waters of the river *Rasa*?' (10.108.1)

In the 33rd *Sûkta* of the Book 3, sage *Vishwâmitra* makes a request to the river *Vyâs* and *Satlaj* to make way for him through the water on his way back from south. This is fairly in order of the request made to *Saraswatî* elsewhere.

Vishnu and Trivikrama

Rig Vedic reference of *Vishnu* measuring the whole universe in three steps contains many seeds of many successive mythological stories. The story of the incarnation of *Vishnu* in the form of *Vamana* has its origin here only. Western interpreters of *Vedas* consider *Vishnu* to be another name of the Sun. They have thus interpreted his three steps to be the light of the Sun covering earth, heaven and the space.

Vishnu is all pervading. He has some convert connection and almost an identity with *Rudra*. *Rudra* is the fierce and violent godhead. Vishnu's constant friendliness to man and his helping gods is at times shadowed by an aspect of formidable violence, - 'like a terrible lion ranging in evil and difficult places'- which is spoken of in terms more ordinarily appropriate to *Rudra*. *Rudra* is the father of the vehemently- battling *Maruts*. *Rudra* is the deity ascending in the cosmos and *Vishnu* a god helping and evoking the powers of ascent.

European scholars have made us believe for long that the *Purânic* theme about the greatness of *Vishnu* and *Shiva* are a later development and that these gods occupy a less significant place in Vedas as compared to *Indra* and *Agni*. It was also much propagated till very recently that *Shiva* is a conception borrowed from the Dravidians and he represents a partial conquest of the Vedic religion by the indigenous culture it had invaded.

As a matter of fact, the importance of the Vedic gods has not to be measured by the number of hymns devoted to them or by the extent to which they are invoked in the thoughts of *Rishis* but by the functions they perform. Although much larger hymns are addressed to *Agni* and *Indra*, but they are not greater than *Vishnu* or *Rudra*. They perform functions in the internal and external world, which are far more important. The *Maruts*, for instance, who are the children of *Rudra,* are certainly not divinities superior to their fierce and mighty father. Thus *Vishnu* is significantly providing the conditions of the Vedic work and assisting it from behind the more present and active gods. He may be less close in appearance but certainly more dominant in the deeper sense and meaning of it.

When *Indra* is about to slay *Vrittra,* he first prays *Vishnu,* his friend and comrade in the great struggle (1.22.19) 'O *Vishnu,* pace out in thy movement with an utter wideness.' The Supreme step of *Vishnu* is his highest seat, *parmam padam.* This is the goal of Vedic journey. He thus naturally becomes the precursor of the *Puranic Narayana,* the preserver and the lord of love. Whose, *Vishnu, Rudra, Brâhmanaspati, Agni, Indra, Vâyu, Mitra, Varuna* are all different forms

To the Vedic *Rishi* there must be one universal God of and various cosmic aspects. Each of them is in himself the whole God and contains all the other gods.

In hymn 154 of *Mandala*1, the seer *Deerghatama* celebrates the greatness of *Vishnu* for his 'three strides'. This mention may generally take us to the mythological figure of dwarf incarnation that snatched away heaven, earth and *Pâtala* from the titan king *Bali*. However, it is the triple principle beyond heaven, the supreme stride of the all-pervading deity who becomes important. He is supporting in his strides the earth, the material, the mid-world of vital force and heaven, and the state of fulfilment and delight. We can very well seek the origin of *'Sat chit Ananada'* in these strides.

King Sudâsa (Dasrâgya)

This has a reference to the 83rd verse of the Book 7th. The king *Sudâsa* figures in it in the reference of the great battle called *Dâsragya*. This is historically very important. He fought with ten kings in the battle and won it ultimately. *Indra* and *Varuna* extended their support to him, as he was the supporter of the cause of *Yajna* performed to please gods.

Dâsragya, in a way, was the First World War. It had a far-reaching effect in the Vedic society of that time. Even the seer *Vasishistha* helped *Sudâsa* in this battle by killing an enemy called *Bheda*. It is important to note that although *Sudâsa* was just a man of the world, but there are prayers made for him like a god. According to McDonnell and Keith, *Vishwâmitra* must have served *Sudâsa* as his priest who, however turned hostile to him and helped his ten enemy kings. The reason assigned to this behaviour of the saint was his age-old rivalry with seer *Vashistha* that finds further elaborations in the mythological and the *Purânic* literature. This story reaches its climax when *Vishwâmitra* incited the sons of *Sudâsa* to kill *Shakti*, the son of *Vashistha*.

Nahushâ

In the 2nd *Mantra* of *Sûkta* 95 of *the Mandala* 7 the king called *Nahushâ* prays *Saraswatî* who provides water and riches for him to be lasting for many thousand years. The story surrounding this name got developed further in the *Puranas* when this king once becomes the ruler of heaven by some virtues. He, however, falls from it because he desires to marry the wife of *Indra, Shachi*, who manages to escape with the help of the seven sages who ultimately cursed *Nahush* to become a snake to be subsequently transformed by *Lord Krishna* after many thousand years.

Urvashî and Pururava

In *Sûkta 75 of 10th Mandala*, the dramatic dialogue between *Urvashî*, the beauty queen from heaven and the king *Purûravâ* finds a long record of notice. Earlier the name *Purûravâ* finds a mention in the fourth mantra of the 31st verse of the first Book already. The dialogue commences from the stage the two lovers have to part company on account of the king's not being able to keep his promises. *Purûravâ* has desperate pleadings before *Urvashî* to stay on but she ultimately declines.

Devâpi and Shâtanu

Devâpi and *Shântanu* are two brothers. They were the rulers of *Kuru Pradesh*. *Devâpi* among them was the eldest but *Shântanu* managed to get the throne. The later Vedic part of literature records that this created unprecedented drought conditions in the state. It also brought leprosy to the usurper. *Rigveda* tells us that *Shântanu* thereafter performed a sacrifice to cure his ailing brother. (10.98.11)

Nâchiket

The conversation between *Nachiketâ* and *Yama* on the reality and theory of life after death is the famous story of *Kathopnishad*, the later part of *Vedas* known as *Vedânta*. The form and personality of *Nachiketâ* is not so developed in *Rigveda*. His mention in the 135 stanza of the tenth Book is however a conclusive proof of its origin in the Rigvedic era.

Ârya

There are references in *Rigveda* (1.33.4, 76.3, 8.70) that some classes of people were opposed to the culture of Âryan race. They were not performing sacrifices, were generally black skinned and they had withheld the flow of waters. (2.12.2) As regards the theory of the arrival of Âryans from west, the same is generally evolved and developed by the western historians. The Indian view, on the other hand, claims that Âryans crossed Indian borders at times and spread over Indian customs and culture far in the west in Iran and other countries. In an excavation completed in 1907 in Bogajkoi in Asia Miner, the names of Vedic deities like *Indra, Mitra, Varuna, Nasatyau* etc. have been found. This pertains to a period belonging to 1400 BC. Even four hundred years behind that, the names of the princes of Babylon were Surias and Maryatas which are so close to *Sûrya* and *Marut* of Vedic period.

According to *Maharishi Aurobindo, Agni* is symbolically standing for the Divine Will-Force. According to him as explained in detail in the book 'On The *Veda*, ' By (this) conscious force of the Godhead the worlds have been created and are governed from within by that hidden and inner control; *Agni* is the form, the fire the forceful heat and flaming will of this Divinity. As a flaming Force of knowledge he descends to build up the worlds and seated within them, a secret deity initiates movement and action.'

According to the modern exhaustive commentator of *Vedas Shri Satavalekar, Indra* is the Defence Minister of the World Government of *Vedas*. He is always defeating the enemies of the Nation with many other gods who are either friendly or subordinate to him in his adventures.

According to *Yogiraj Aurobindo, Indra* is the 'thought force' of mankind. According to his interpretation 'On the *Veda*', "*Madhuchhandâ*, son of *Vishwâmitra* invokes the *Soma*-offering *Indra*, the Master of luminous Mind, for increase in the Light. The symbols of the hymn are those of a collective sacrifice. Its subject is the growth of power and delight in *Indra* by the drinking of the *Soma*, the wine of immortality, and the consequent illumination of the human being so that the obstructions of his inner knowledge are removed and he attains the utmost splendours of the liberated mind."

Shri Aurobindo in his famous commentary on *Vedas* describes the spiritual symbolism of these deities in the following manner-

'The *Ashwins* like other gods descend from the Truth consciousness, the *Ritam*; they are born or manifested from Heaven, from *dyau*, the pure Mind; their movement pervades all the worlds, - the effect of their action ranges from the body through the vital being and the thought to the sperconscient Truth. It commences indeed from the ocean, from the vague of the being as it emerges out of the subconscient and they conduct the soul over the flood of these waters and prevent its foundering on its voyage.'

5
Ten Books Of Rigveda

Mandala One

The first *Mandala* contains 191 *Sûktas*, hymns with 2006 *mantras* or stanzas in all. The highest number of stanzas is dedicated to *Indra* and the seer perceiving the maximum of them is *Deerghatama Audathya*. The maximum hymns are ascribed to the seer *Agastya Maitra Varuni*. The seers and the hymns in the progressive order of the first *Mandala* are as follows-

	Seer	Hymns	Total
1.	Mdhuchhanda	1-10	10
2.	Jeta Madhuchhandâsa	11	1
3.	Medhatithi Kanva	12-23	12
4.	Shunah Shape Ajigarta	24-30	7
5.	Hiranyastoop Angirâsa	31-35	5
6.	Kanva Ghaur	36-43	8
7.	Praskanva Kanva	44-50	7
8.	Savya Angirâsa	51-57	7
9.	Nodha Gautama	58-64	7
10.	Parashar Shaktya	65-73	9
11.	Gotama Rahugana	74-93	20
12.	Kutsa Angirâsa	94-98	5
		105	1
		106-115	10

13.	Kashyapa Marichâ	99	1
14.	Rijarshwa Ambrish	100	1
15.	Kakshiwan Dairghatamas Ashija	116-126	11
16.	Paruchchhepa Devodasi	127-139	139
17.	Deerghatama Audachya	140-164	25
18.	Indra, Maruta, Agastya	165	1
19.	Agastya Maitra Varuni	166-178	13
20.	Lopamudra	179	1
	Agastya Maitra Varuni	180-91	12
	Total		191

As regards the *Mantras* or stanzas allocation to these seers, *Deerghatama Audachya, Maitra Varunai Agastya, Kutsa Angirâsa and Gautam Rahugana* are the *rishis* of 242, 220, 212 and 204 stanzas respectively in order of the highest number. The important break up, however, is that of the *mantra* allocation to the gods of the *Rigveda* which, in this *Mandala* in respect of a few important gods and in order of their significance is as follows –

Gods	Stanzas
Indra	469
Agni	407
Ashwini Kumâr	213
Vishwe Devatâ	152
Maruta	135
Ushâ	84
Sûrya	39

Other important gods who have been invoked and praised in numerous stanzas are *Varuna, Soma, Vishnu, Rudra, Pushâ, Savita, Vâyu, Brahaspati, Âpah, Saraswatî* and in one each *Vâk, Indu, Twashta* and *Prithivî* etc. Further gods in pair such as *Mitra-Varuna, Dyava-Prithivî, Indra-Varuna, Agni-Maruta, Indra-Vishnu* etc. have also been prayed in number of stanzas.

It is difficult to be answered in this first *Mandala*, which is the basic unit of the theme, the seer, the god, the hymn or the stanza? *Mandala* 2 to 9 have symmetry, as there is a coherence of seers or the gods in them, but the first and the tenth *Mandals* are clear exceptions. It is therefore, sometimes argued that these two are the later compilation of the Vedic contents. The seer of the first Book is often described as *Shatarchin* indicating that each seer of this Book has been normally attributed hundred hymns. Similarly the seers of the tenth Book are in general described as *Kshudra Sûkta* or *Maha Sûkta* as they are either composing small or larger hymns. It is also important to mention that the subject matter of one verse is also not sometimes the same and the seers and the gods can exchange for themselves while appearing and reappearing in it at time and again. This perhaps requires a deeper and mystic approach towards the understanding of it in the line of Shri Aurobindo who was doing an extraordinary work in the 'Secret of *Vedas*'. In order to bring home to the common reader the general contents of this *Madala*, various attributes of some important gods who form the basic texture of this part are discussed below.

Agni

Agni of *Rigveda* is the first and foremost Power of eminence. He is firstly not only the presiding deity of the rite sacrifice, but also an instrument of it. He has been called *'Purohita'* that stands for the fore- runner of all other gods. He is the store- house of all riches and also a donor of -*'dansheel'*. Agni is *'Kavikritu'* which stands for the force performing action with knowledge. He has been called *Angirâ* and as *Angirâs* He resides in human body nourishing and enriching it by digesting the food as *'Jathrâgni'*.

This deity is like the loving father of human kind residing always very close to him. He is thus the guide, the protector and the benefactor of human beings.

Agni is then the ambassador of gods. He has the power of removing all kind of illness and diseases without himself getting affected by any. He increases the longevity of human beings. He is called *'Vaishwânara'* as a resident of body responsible for the digestion of all kind of food consumed by human beings. [1] He is the uniting force of all other numerous gods residing in human body. There are contrary forces like water cooling down fire and the fire drying it up. The clouds hide out the Sun and the Sun makes them rain. Agni acts as the synthesizer of these conflicting powers.

Long before the concept of the 'brotherhood of mankind and the fatherhood of God' came to be universally acknowledged, *Rigveda* declared –'*Agni* is our father and we are all brothers'[2]

Agni according to *Rigveda* has three births. Firstly, he is born out of great Ocean in form of '*Badwânala*', the great fire. He is another form of fire as the Sun in '*Dyuloka*', the space. Lastly, he appears as electricity in clouds.

Indra

As stated earlier, there are 469 *Mantras* written in this *Mandala* in praise of *Indra*.

He is the controller of all riches, the performer of hundred sacrifices' *Shatkritu*' (48) and his glories are without any end '*Akshit Ootih*'. (49) He is the lord of all obstacles and lives in the company of brave people. He awards wisdom to the ignorant and charms to the ugly ones. He is always protecting one who is a donator with his arms. His actions performed for the welfare of human beings are spread over like the rays of the Sun.

He protected *Angirâ's* cows. He helped *Atri* get out of the prison. He offered many riches to *Vimad*, saved *Vavasana* in the battlefield. He destroyed the cities of demon *Pipru*. He is always destroying the forts of *Dasyus* in the interest of *Âryans*. He is a strict disciplinarian and is thus punishing the divine lawbreakers in the interest of law abiders. He is a great promoter of good deeds like *Yajna*, sacrifice, therefore is called '*Sukritu*'. He also nourishes mankind, therefore called '*Sambhutkritu*'

---

1 इत: जात: वैश्वानर: इदं वि चष्टे (1085)

   अहं वैश्वानरो भूत्वा प्राणिनां देहमाश्रित:

   प्राणापानसमायुक्त: पचाप्यन्नं चतुर्विधम् । गीता अध्याय 15-14

2 न: पिता, वयं जामय: (360)

Rigveda talks at length about the art of *Indra*'s warfare. He keeps on wielding his weapon *Vajra* in the battlefield like a mountain. He destroys his enemies through strategic designs. He can heroically surround the surrounding enemy. No one succeeded any time in measuring the strength of *Indra* in any war. All the animate and inanimate objects tremble at his thunder. Above all, *Indra* is fighting battles for the welfare of others. He therefore commands the respect of every one.

Ashwini Kumar

These twins hold the post of Health Ministers in the Government of the Universe of the *Vedas*. They were initially not entitled to share drink *Soma* with gods, but when they helped seer *Chyavan* attain sight and young age at the request of *Sukanya*, the daughter of king *Sharyâti*, they attained this high state of honour. One of these two brothers is proficient in surgery and the other one in medicine. They are said to be equipped with necessary equipment and tools for the health care.

Verse 1.157.6 tells that they transformed the old man into a young person by '*Kaya kalpa*'. *Mantra* 10 of hymn 116 of this *Mandala* vividly describes how after grafting skin in the old body of *Chyavan*, they made him so handsome that he became the husband of attractive wives.[3] In stanza 13 of the hymn 117 again they are described to have transformed old seer into a young man by skin grafting the way a snake takes out its skin grown old. They also made another man *Vandana* handsome in the similar fashion (1.119.7) and even granted them eyes for seeing. *Shyava* had got three deep cuts in his body for which they made him walk soon (1.117.24). They granted eyes to *Rijrashwa* who was blinded by his father (1.116.16-17) and also made the praying poet see on desiring.

The instances of their surgical wonders are many. The daughter of king *Khela* Called *Vishpalâ* had gone to fight in a battle. She lost one of her legs in the fight. They put an iron rod

---

3   जुजुरुषो नासत्योत वव्रिं प्रामुंचतं द्रापिमिव च्यवानात् ।
प्रातिरतं जहितस्यायुर्दस्नादित् पतिमकृणुतं कनीनाम् ।।

after operation and made her walk normally.[4] *Ashwini Kumârs* also cured wounded *Rebha* in the prison (1.112.5) and made a barren cow yield milk (1.112.3).

They are reported to be flying in their chariot in the sky as there were birds driving it. (1.118.4). There is another mention in stanza 10 of the hymn 120 that their chariot is driven without horses. They are also said to be the master of a technique of making the boat, which could swim in the water and fly in the air as well. They particularly helped *Bhujyu*, the son of *Tugra* who got strangled in a desert battle in this manner.[5] This chariot went on moving incessantly for three days and three nights in the air. Far away from the sea of water in the long desert, *Bhjyu* was thus taken home rescued by them (1.116.4). There was further one such occasion when from the deep sea of immeasurable depth, *Bhujyu* was rescued by a boat of hundred bamboo and taken home safe near his father (1.116.5).

Ushâ

Hymns dedicated to *Ushâ* are highly poetic and full of natural beauty. They evidently demonstrate how objective and delicate were the observations of those seers of past who after fully absorbing the abundant beauty of nature also vividly personified the picturesque aspect of it. This 'thing of beauty' for them was definitely 'a joy for ever'. The cosmic role of dawn is simply not paving way for the Sun to rise but it stands to define and demonstrate human relationship with nature as well as the intricacies of man and woman relationship on earth.

Ushâ is the awakening force. It leads the universe from 'darkness to light'. It announces the victory of light over darkness.[6]

4　चरित्रं हि वेरिवाच्छेदि पर्णमाजा खेलस्य परितक्म्यायाम् ।
　　सद्यो जंघमायसीं विश्पलायै धने हिते सर्तवे प्रत्यधत्तम् । 1-116-15
5　तमू हथुः नौभिरात्मन्वतीभिः अंतरिक्षप्रदि्भिरपोदकाभिः । 1-116-3
6　ज्योतिः कृणोति सूनरी 1-48-8
　　ज्योतिः विश्वस्मै भुवनाय कृण्वती
　　उष: तम: वि आव: 1-92-4

This goddess dawn causes stir in all sorts of animals. Those who have legs, they start moving. Birds rise up to fly leaving their nests.[7]

Similarly human beings get involved in their daily routine and start working. She indeed is the vitalizing and energizing force of nature. She is the virtual giver of glories and splendour to mankind.[8]

The Vedic seer invokes this daughter of *Dyau* to grant all sorts of riches and splendour to human beings on earth. They should have sufficient number of cows, horses children and servants.[9]

Ushâ is described as 'following effectively the path of the Truth'; *ritasya pantham anveti sadhu (1.24.3)* Dawn is sometimes described as *ritavary,* full of Truth, sometimes as *sunrtavari,* pleasant and true speech. She comes uttering her true and happy words. As she has been described as the leader of the radiant herds and the leader of the days, so she is described as the luminous leader of happy truths. 1.48.2 significantly thus points out 'dawns with their radiance (herds), their swiftness (horses), rightly knowing all things'.

Dawn is constantly represented in this Book as awakening to vision, perception, and right movement. 'The goddess', says *Gotama Raghugana,* 'fronts and looks upon all the worlds, the eyes of vision shines with an utter wideness; awakening all life for movement she discovers speech for all that thinks' (1.92.9). Shri Aurobindo in this context must surely be quoted to bring home the deeper meaning of this particular deity as expounded by him in his 'On the *Veda.*' According to him, thus, ' the dawn is the inner dawn which brings to man all the varied fullness of his

---

7 सूनरी उषा आयाति, पद्वत् ईयते,
   पक्षिण: उत्पातयति 1-48-5
8 विश्वं जीवं चरसे बोधयन्ती
   विश्वस्य हि प्राणनं जीवनं
   त्वे वि यदुच्छसि सूनरी 1-48-10
9 स अस्मासु धा गोमदश्वावदुक्थ्यं
   उषो वाजं सुवीर्यम् 1-48-12

widest being, force, consciousness, joy; it is radiant with its illuminations, it is accompanied by all possible powers and energies, it gives man the full force of vitality so that he can enjoy the infinite delight of that vaster existence.'

Rishis of this Mandala

These *Rishis* were simply not the composers or the authors in the modern sense of the term as they were no longer telling stories or writing treatises on selected topics. As the common experience goes, in a state of trance, the chronology and the sequence of events is difficult for establishment, but the richness of this experience is undisputedly far superior. Vedic seers used to be in direct touch with the cosmic source of all knowledge and a comprehensive vision of the visible world and the worlds beyond was occurring to them in their deep state of *Samâdhi,* meditation which found expression in a superbly designed metres and words. It is that height and richness which often leaves much for a reader to interpret and understand. It has been easier to elaborate the individual and the dynastic and clan characters of these seers on the basis of mythology by the interpreters in general, but their basic attributes may thus be misunderstood as according to the original Vedic designs, they are distinct and their original context would well suggest their identity. The details relating to them are therefore confined here to the original text which may seem to be incomplete but if an inference is to be drawn any further, the suggestion lies in the fact that one should stick to the original as possible for the correct identity.

Manu is the forefather of all human beings (1-60-3) He is referred to as a King, a royal seer and the head of all the subjects at different places. He heard about heaven from *Agni* (1.31.4) In 1.45.1 even the gods are mentioned to be the sons of *Manu.* Summarily in 1.80.16, he is the 'fore father' of all living creatures. He performed a number of sacrifices along with *Atharva* and *Dadhichi. Dadhichi* finds a mention as 'an ancient seer' along with *Manu* and *Angirâ.*

Gotama Rahugana is the author of a quite large number of hymns (1.74-93). His name finds mention in 1.62.13 and 78.2,5.

His relationship with *Angirâs* is also talked about repeatedly (1.62.1, 71.2)

Agastya is the seer of a number of hymns and stanzas (1.165.13-15,166-169,170.2, 5,171-178,179.3-4,180-191) of the first Book. There is a conversation between *Agastya* and *Lopamudra*, his wife in (1.179).

Bhrigu is the worshipper of fire. (1.58.6, 127.7) His first inventing fire finds a mention in *Rigveda* in a number of places. He brought the fire right into the navel of the earth (1.143)

Kutsa, the son of *Angirâ* is the seer of 1.94-98 and 101-105 hymns. *Indra* was helping him at the time of need. He once fell into a well from which *Indra* saved him (1.106.6). Likewise *Indra* was also in need of his support to demonstrate his valour. (1.174.5)

Kanva, the son of *Ghora* is the seer of the hymn 36 to 43 of this Book. In the 10th and 11th stanzas of the 36th hymns, there is the mention of this seer as 'deer to the guests' 1.112.5 talks about *Kanva* having been thrown into a dense darkness from which *Ashwini Kumâras* saved them. (1.112.5, 1.118.7) In 1.139.9 *Kanva* has been mentioned as 'an ancient sage of great longevity.'

Important Key-notes from Mandala One

1.   *Agni,* be to us easy of approach, even as a father to his son.

2.   Manifold are the riches granted by *Indra*

3.   Persons desiring godhead should worship gods.

4.   May human beings achieve that knowledge without which wise men do not succeed performing *Yajna.*

5.   Gods do not have enmity with any one.

6.   Truth loving *Ribhus* restored back young age to their parents.

7.   We bow down before *Agni,* who knows everything and is the performer of the *Yajna* rite.

8.   *Agni* is brilliant, young and bright faced.

9.   The motherland, the mother tongue and the mother culture are always comforting.

10.   Oh Earth, you be our happy abode without any thorns and make us comfortable.

11.   Wise men always see the highest abode of *Vishnu* in affluence like that the astral form.

12.   *Mitra-Varuna* is the proper guide for the right path and they keep it shine for the same.

13.   Water is the storehouse of nectar, medicines. You must be enthusiastic to shower praise for such water, gods!

14.   Whatever impurity I have, whatever wrong action I did, whatever lie I may have told, let the water take away all these ills from me and make me pure.

15.   The branches of this Sun are cast downward and the root up in *Dyuloka*. (Its) rays are spread over in the earth and space.

16.   All these stars settled in high sky appear shining during night. Especially Moon appears when it is night. The laws of *Varuna* are absolute.

17.   *Agni*! You first appeared as seer *Angirâ*. You later became the god of gods and their benefactor.

18.   This all pervading fire is the source of knowledge.

19.   *Agni!* You conferred sound in *Akash* for the welfare of mankind.

20.   O unenviable *Agni,* you among all gods always keep awake.

21.   The person abiding by natural laws and having a bright son attains all prosperity.

22.   In a house where meals full of taste are kept ready for guests and sacrifices are performed for the good of all creatures, that house is like a heaven on earth.

23.   *Indra* killed the dragon (*Vrittra*), and then released great streams making way for rivers through mountains.

24.   You both, *Ashwin,* are easily available for wise people.

25.   This god *Savita,* discarding all evils come from a distant place.

26.   Truth loving great men earns reputation all around with their glory touching sky.

27.   One who makes donations earns riches.

28.   Brave and wise men should be praised in high spirits.

29.   Men with arms win freedom.

30.   He who worships his motherland like his own mother becomes immortal.

31.   One, who gives valued alms to the performer of sacrifice, earns undiminished reputation.

32.	A person moving on the path of truth finds an easy road without thorns.

33.	A person harming, nay, abusing others and aspiring to attain divinity should not talk to me.

34.	Let us make all contented with fair resolutions.

35.	No one should aspire to talk ill.

36.	One should not confront the person who has accomplished all four achievements; i.e. *Dharma*, *Artha*, *Kama* and *Moksha*.

37.	O God, take us out of sin leading towards prosperity.

38.	Keep away from my path the sinful, the cruel and unworthy of service ruling over us.

39.	I have all praise for the protector.

40.	Virtuous people are always to be worshipped.

41.	Those wise people who get up at the time of dawn and are self- realized deserve to be called gods.

42.	The path of truth is the right path for getting out of sorrows.

43.	This dawn like a wise woman keeps the world (house) in order.

44.	Oh Sun, arising today, take away my cardiac, tuberculosis and jaundice diseases.

45.	Whose spies are spread over all around, please that *Indra* by prayers.

46.	*Indra* destroys the unfaithful for the sake of the faithful ones.

47.	This (*Indra*) helps patriots destroy the enemy of the nation.

48.	*Indra!* You are the manifested form of earth.

49.	His (Indra's) expansion is unmeasured by heaven and earth.

50.	Land and rivers could not touch that end.

51.	He alone is the Creator of this world.

52.   He manifests himself in the potentials of mankind.

53.   High heaven has all praise for your bravery.

54.   Rivers are flowing because of your order.

55.   Our ancestors achieved knowledge with the help of this *Indra*.

56.   He killed the exploiter for protecting the virtuous.

57.   Let us live happily hundred years of vitality.

58.   Gods followed the path of truthfulness and transformed earth into heaven for happiness.

59.   Like a good housewife at home, (*Agni*) makes us comfortable.

60.   A seeker of knowledge does find riches.

61.   *Agni* is the embodiment of all divine elements.

62.   May the subjects of the nation be rich, glorious, contented without cravings and laborious doing sacrifices to please gods and human beings.

63.   *Agni,* you have extra-celestial perceptions. Pray, let us not lose the grace of our forefathers.

64.   Old age ruins our charms, O *Agni,* you therefore ruin this before it appears.

65.   The seekers of truth do reach the state of enlightenment.

66.   The seekers of truth do find the path of glory for certain.

67.   The passenger on the path of truth is the saviour of every one from sins.

68.   The person having well wishing friends lives happily in this world.

69.   An unenviable husband and devoted wife keep the world in order.

70.   Wise persons making donations should live long.

71.   We should be preaching for those who are prepared to hear.

72. Gods should be worshipped for the purification of the mind.

73. A man should become wise and perform actions with others efficiently.

74. *Agni* is the charioteer of the body chariot.

75. No one is born as great as you are and ever shall be so.

76. *Indra* bestows his virtuous powers upon the performer of sacrifice.

77. One, who worships these gods well, lives long.

78. You are keeping arms on your body to win and live in comfort and not for harming others.

79. May our actions performed for the general well-being, remain unsurpassed, undefeated and be always directed for the higher pursuits.

80. The simple and straightforward intellect on the path of truth does only good to others.

81. May we always live in the company of gods.

82. May gods let us live for long towards a complete life on earth.

83. We invoke that god for our protection, which is the lord of all animate and inanimate beings and is the source of all knowledge.

84. That lord of glories, *Indra*, all knowing *PUshâ*, seated on a constant moving chariot, *Tarkshya*, and *Brahaspati* be good to us.

85. May we hear good speech from our ears.

86. May we see good objects from our eyes.

87. With a stable and healthy body parts, may we be worshiping gods whole life.

88. Hundred years is the passage of our life.

89. Let the chain of our life not break in between.

90. May learned *Mitra*, *Varuna* and *Aryama* lead us on the path truth straight.

91.   For the persons following the path of simple truth, the air and the water in the river carries honey along it.

92   *Soma* is a wonderful herb for the longevity of our life.

93.   We shall not die till we live in consonance with *Soma*.

94.   One ray of Sun is many for others.

95.   So that we have a longer life span, we should make our intellect and actions one pointed.

96.   All foods are settled by it in the stomachs of living beings.

97.   May *Agni* redeem us from all sins.

98.   That one *(Indra)* alone is the lord of all actions of the universe.

99.   The space, the earth, the waters , the Sun and the rivers- all operate under the absolute law of this *Indra*.

100.   That controlling everyone is simultaneously present in all actions.

101.   The Sun and the Moon are moving to spread the true knowledge.

102.   He is without an enemy right from his birth.

103.   We are demanding from you the means you have for man's well being, his real comfort and the removal of sufferings.

104.   The strength of forefathers may have a congenial presence in the descendents.

105.   The mortal human being can attain immortality and divinity, both.

106.   The night and the dawn, the two sisters have one way and it is without any end.

107.   May everyone in the village be healthy and without any disease and the two and four legged animals live in peace.

108.   Manifold are the riches granted by *Indra* . The Sun is the effulgence and the unique eye of gods.

109.   *Sûrya* is the soul of all animate and inanimate worlds.

110.   This woman *Ushâ* never breaks the rule Supreme and appears on the appointed space in time.

111.   Worldly joys should increase longevity.

112.   He (*Indra*) is capable of destroying all his enemies together but his enemies cannot kill him even when all joined.

113.   He rules over the law-breakers for the sake of the believers.

114.   *Indra!* You are sure to attain the final abode of truth.

115.   *Ushâ* weaves on beautiful cloths.

116.   Cows with nectar like milk give all kind of riches.

117.   Wise men enjoy worldly bliss with their strength.

118.   A good ruler receives praises from his subjects.

119.   The brightness of a man with a charming face spreads all over.

120.   A wise man of firm resolute completes the task of his determination in advance, not later; he keeps himself away from the ridicule.

121.   That which is true need be proclaimed.

122.   One who is the sustainer of all worlds, that *Vishnu* is praised for his valour.

123.   He (*Vishnu*) is the friend of industrious people.

124.   In that sublime seat of *Vishnu* exists the stream of nectar.

125.   The non-violent parents should be pleased with prayers.

126.   Wise, valiant and powerful people attain divinity.

127.   Whatever said should always be in a sweet and loving voice.

128.   Whatever we wish to achieve should be accomplished through deeds.

129.   Man should become brave by his own bravery.

130.   Gods do not help one who pretends tiredness.

131.   He (*Agni*) is aware of all our actions.

132.   Let us keep ourselves away from the sins of mischief.

133.   May we pray God each day!

134.   May we cross all the barriers of the world moving on the path of goodness.

135.   May this earth and the cities on it become broad and beautiful for us.

136.   Persons not worshiping fire earn diseases.

1.   अग्ने! सूनवे पिता इव न: स्वस्तये आ सचस्व (मँत्र सं 7)

2.   इन्द्रस्य रातय: पूर्वी: (मँत्र सं 105)

3.   देवयते देवान् यज (मँत्र सं 158)

4.   विश्ववेदसं अस्य यज्ञस्य सुकृतृ अग्निं वृणीमहे (मँत्र सं 153)

5.   विश्वे देवासो अद्रुह: (मँत्र सं 188)

6.   सत्यमंत्रा: ऋजूयव: ऋभव: पितरा पुन: युवाना अकृत (मँत्र सं 198)

7.   पुरुप्रियं अग्निं विश्पतिं सदा हवन्ते (मँत्र सं 111)

8.   अग्नि: कवि: युवा जुह्वास्य: (मँत्र सं 116)

9.   इला सरस्वती मही तिस्र: देवी: मयोभुव: (मँत्र सं 131)

10.   पृथिवि ! स्योना अनृक्षरा निवेशनी भव, सप्रथ: शर्म न यच्छ (मँत्र सं 223)

11.   विष्णो: यत् परमं पदं दिवि आततं चक्षु: इव सूरय: सदा पश्यन्ति (मँत्र सं 228)

12.   ता मित्रावरुणा ऋतेन ऋतावृधौ ऋतस्य ज्योतिष: पती (मँत्र सं 234)

13.   अप्सु अन्त: अमृतं अप्सु भेषजं, उत अपां प्रशस्तये देवा: वाजिन:भवत: (मँत्र सं 248)

14.   मयि यत् किं च दुरितं यत् वा अहं...अनतं इदं आप: प्र वहत (मँत्र सं 251)

15.   नीचीन: स्थु: एषां बुध्न: उपरि, अस्मे अन्त: केतव: निहिता: स्यु: (मँत्र सं 260)

16.   अमी ऋक्षा: उच्चा निहितास: ये नक्तं ददृश्रे, विचाकशत् चन्द्रमा नक्तं एति, वरुणस्य व्रतानि अदब्धानि (मँत्र सं 263)

17. अग्ने! त्वं प्रथम: अंगिरा ऋषि: अभव:, देवानां देव: शिव: सखा अभव:(मैत्र सं 351)

18. विभु: विश्वस्मै भुवनाय मेधि-र: (मैत्र सं 352)

19. अग्ने! त्वं मनवे द्यां अवाशय: (मैत्र सं 354)

20. अनवद्य! देव:देवेषु जागृवि (मैत्र सं 359)

21. व्रतपां सुवीरं सहस्रिण: राय: यन्ति (मैत्र सं 360)

22. स्वादुक्षद्मा वसतौ स्योनकृत् य: जीवयाजं यजते स दिव: उपमा (मैत्र सं 365)

23. अहिं अहन्, अनु अप: ततर्द, पर्वतानां वक्षणा प्र अभिनत् (मैत्र सं 369)

24. मनीषिभि: अभ्यायं सेन्या भवतं (मैत्र सं 399)

25. सविता देव: विश्वा दुरिता अपबाधमान:परावत: आ याति (मैत्र सं 413)

26. मह: सत: अर्चय: विचरन्ति, भनव: दिवि स्पृशन्ति (मैत्र सं 424)

27. य: मर्त्य: ददाश स विश्वं धनं जयति (मैत्र सं 424)

28. सुमना: सुवीर्यान् देवान् यक्षि (मैत्र सं 427)

29. नमस्विन: स्वराजं उपासते (मैत्र सं 436)

30. पृश्निमातर: मर्तास: स्तोता अमृत: स्यात् (मैत्र सं 460)

31. यो वाधते सूनरं वसु ददाति स: अक्षिति श्रव: धत्ते (मैत्र सं 485)

32. ऋतं यते पन्था: सुग: अनृक्षर: च (मैत्र सं 493)

33. देवयन्तं घ्नन्तं शपन्तं मा प्रति वोचे (मैत्र सं 497)

34. सुम्नै: इत् व: आ विवासे (मैत्र सं 497)

35. दुरुक्ताय न स्पृहयेत् (मैत्र सं 498)

36. चतुर: ददमानात् आ निधाता: बिभीयात् (मैत्र सं 498)

37. देव! अंह:वि न: पुर: प्र सक्ष्व (मैत्र सं 499)

38. य: अघ: वृक: दु:शेव: न: आदिदेशति, तं पथ: अप जहि (मैत्र सं 500)

39. त्रातारं अहं स्तविष्यामि (मैत्र सं 522)

40. दैव्यं जनं नमस्य (मैत्र सं 523)

41. उषर्बुध: स्वर्दृश: देवान् (मैत्र सं 526)

42. पारं एतवे ऋतस्य पन्थां: साधुया (मँत्र सं 552)

43. उषा: सूनरी योषा इव प्रभुंजती (मँत्र सं 571)

44. सूर्य अद्य उद्यन् मम हृद्रोगं हरिमाणं च नाशय (मँत्र सं 597)

45. यस्य मानुषा: वि चरन्ति, त्यं इन्द्रं गीर्भि: मदत (मँत्र सं 600)

46. इन्द्र: अनुव्रताय अपव्रताय रन्धयत् (मँत्र सं 608)

47. आभूधि: अनाभुव: श्नथयन् (मँत्र सं 608)

48. त्वं पृथिव्या: भुव: प्रतिमानं (मँत्र सं 627)

49. यस्य व्यच: द्यावापृथिवी न अनु (मँत्र सं 628)

50. रजस: सिन्धव: अन्तं न आनशु: (मँत्र सं 628)

51. एक: अन्यत् विश्वं चकृषे (मँत्र सं 628)

52. जनेषु इन्द्रियं प्रब्रुवाण: (मँत्र सं 655)

53. महान् द्यौ: वीर्य अनु ममे (मँत्र सं 670)

54. अस्य त्वेषसा सिन्धव: रन्त: अयच्छत् (मँत्र सं 703)

55. येन न: पूर्वे पितर: गा: अविन्दन्, पद्ज्ञा: (मँत्र सं 710)

56. कुत्साय शुष्णं अहन् (मँत्र सं 724)

57. शतं हिमा पुष्येम् (मँत्र सं 744)

58. देवा: ऋतस्य व्रता अनु गु: द्यौ: न भूम (मँत्र सं 748)

59. योनो जाया इव सर्वस्मै अरं (मँत्र सं 760)

60. य: शिक्षात् रयिं दयस्व (मँत्र सं 781)

61. अग्नि: विश्वानि देवत्वा अश्या: (मँत्र सं 791)

62. अर्य: दिधिष्व: विभित्रा: अतृप्यन्ती: प्रयसा देवान् जन्म वर्धयन्ती: (मँत्र सं 809)

63. अग्ने! कवि: सन् अभिविदु:, पित्र्याणि सख्या मा प्र मर्षिष्ठा: (मँत्र सं 816)

64. रूपं जरिमा मिनाति, अभिशस्ते: तस्या: पुरा अधि इति (मँत्र सं 816)

65. पद्व्य: अग्ने: परमे पदे तस्थु: (मँत्र सं 818)

66. ऋतज्ञा: राय: दुर: विदन् (मँत्र सं 824)

67. य: सत्यमन्मा कृत्वा विश्वा विज्ञनानि नि पाति (मँत्र सं 828)

68. हित: मित्र: पृथिवीं उपेक्षति (मंत्र सं 829)

69. अनवद्या पतिजुष्टा नारी विश्वधाया: (मंत्र सं 829)

70. सूरय: ददत: विश्वमायु: वि (मंत्र सं 831)

71. ऋण्वते मंत्रं वोचेम (मंत्र सं 837)

72. महे सौमनसाय देवान् यज (मंत्र सं 852)

73. कवि: सन् कविकभि: यजस्व (मंत्र सं 855)

74. अद्भुतस्य रथी: (मंत्र सं 858)

75. कश्चन् त्वावान् न, न जात:, न जनिष्यते (मंत्र सं 898)

76. सुन्वते यजमानाय भद्रा शक्ति: (मंत्र सं 911)

77. य: एषां भृत्यां ऋणधत्, स: जीवात् (मंत्र सं 930)

78. श्रिये कं व:तनूषु अधि वाशी: (मंत्र सं 965)

79. भद्रा: अदब्धास: अपरीतास: उद्भिद: क्रतव: विश्वत: न: आ यन्तु (मंत्र सं 969)

80. ऋजूयतां सुमति: भद्रा: (मंत्र सं 970)

81. देवानां सख्यं उपसेदिम (मंत्र सं 970)

82. जीवसे न: आयु: प्र तिरन्तु (मंत्र सं 970)

83. जगत: तस्थुष: पतिं धियं जिन्वं तं ईशानं वयं अवसे हूमहे (मंत्र सं 973)

84. वृद्धश्रवा: इन्द्र:, विश्वे वेदा: पूषा, अरिष्टनेमि तार्क्ष्य:, बृहस्पति न: स्वस्ति दधातु (मंत्र सं 974)

85. कर्णेभि भद्रं शृणुयाम (मंत्र सं 976)

86. अक्षभि: भद्रं पश्येम (मंत्र सं 976)

87. स्थिरै: अंगै: तनूभि: तष्टुवांस: यत् आयु: देवहितं वि अशेम (मंत्र सं 976)

88. शरदं शतं अन्ति इत् नु (मंत्र सं 977)

89. न: आयु: गन्तो: मध्या मा रीरिषत (मंत्र सं 977)

90. विद्वान् मित्र: वरुण: अर्यमा न: ऋजुनीती नयतु (मंत्र सं 979)

91. ऋतायते वाता मधु, सिन्धव: मधु क्षरन्ति (मंत्र सं 984)

92. न जीवातुं प्रियस्तोत्र: वनस्पति: (मंत्र सं 993)

93. त्वं च वश: न मरामहे (मंत्र सं 993)

94. ज्योति: एकं बहुभ्य: (मंत्र सं 1032)

95. जीवातवे धिय: प्रतरं साधय (मंत्र सं 1044)

96. विश्वा सनानि जठरषु धत्ते (मंत्र सं 1066)

97. अग्नि: दुरिता अति (मंत्र सं 1088)

98. स: एक: विश्वस्य करुणस्य ईशे (मंत्र सं 1095)

99. अस्य व्रते द्यावापृथिवी, वरुण:,सूर्य: सिन्धव: सश्चति (मंत्र सं 1110)

100. य: वशी: कर्मणि कर्मणि स्थिर: (मंत्र सं 1111)

101. श्रद्धे सूर्याचन्द्रमसा कं चरत: (मंत्र सं 1120)

102. जनुशा अशत्रु असि (मंत्र सं 1126)

103. यत् ते मनु: हितं तत् शं या: ईमहे (मंत्र सं 1170)

104. पितृणां शक्ती: अनुयच्छमाना (मंत्र सं 1191)

105. मर्तास: सन्त: अमृतत्वं आनशु: (मंत्र सं 1197)

106. स्वध्रा: अध्वा समान: अनन्त: (मंत्र सं 1238)

107. ग्रामे विश्वं पुष्टं अनातुरं असत् द्विपदे चतुष्पदे शं (मंत्र सं 1256)

108. देवानां अनीकं चित्रं चक्षु: (मंत्र सं 1267)

109. सुर्य जगत: तस्थुष: आत्मा (मंत्र सं 1267)

110. योषा ऋतस्य धाम न मिनाति , अह: अह: निष्कृतं आचरन्ती (मंत्र सं 1394)

111. संचक्षे अस्यै भुजे (मंत्र सं 1436)

112. विश्वं शत्रुं स्तृणोषि शत्रु: त्वा नहि स्तरते (मंत्र सं 1448)

113. मनवे अव्रतान् शासत् (मंत्र सं 1463)

114. (इन्द्र:) ऋतस्य क्षयं वा असि (मंत्र सं 1475)

115. उषास: भद्रा वस्त्रा तन्वते (मंत्र सं 1499)

116. सर्वदुधा धेनु: विश्वा वसूनि दोहते (मंत्र सं 1499)

117. विपन्यव: कृत्वा वुभुज्रिरे (मंत्र सं 1513)

118. साम्राज्याय प्रतर दधान: अस्तावि (मंत्र सं 1551)

119. सु प्रतीकस्य भानव: अजरा: (मंत्र सं 1567)

120. धीर: स्वेन मनसा यत् अग्रभीत्, प्रथमं न अपरं, वच: न मृष्यते (मंत्र सं 1582)

121. बृहत् ऋते आ घोषथ: (मैंत्र सं 1611)

122. यस्य विक्रमणेषु विश्वा भुवनानि अधिक्षियन्ति, तत् विष्णु: वीर्येण स्तवते (मैंत्र सं 1629)

123. उरुक्रमस्य बन्धु: (मैंत्र सं 1632)

124. विष्णो: परमे पदे मध्व: उत्स (मैंत्र सं 1632)

125. अद्रुह: पितु: मातु: मन हविमभि: मन्ये (मैंत्र सं 1658)

126. ऋभु:विभ्वा वाज: देवान् आगच्छत् (मैंत्र सं 1672)

127. यत्, तत् शुभनै: वोचे: (मैंत्र सं 1770)

128. यत् वशाम, कृत्वा (मैंत्र सं 1774)

129. स्वेन भामेन तविष: बभूवान् (मैंत्र सं 1775)

130. न मृषा श्रान्तं देवा: अवन्ति (मैंत्र सं 1888)

131. विश्वानि व्युनानि विद्वान् (मैंत्र सं 1975)

132. अस्मात् जुहुराणं एन: एधि (मैंत्र सं 1975)

133. भूयिष्ठां नम: उक्तिं विधेम (मैंत्र सं 1975)

134. स्वस्तिभि: अस्मान् विश्वा दुर्गाणि पारय (मैंत्र सं 1976)

135. पृथिवी पू: च उर्वी भव (मैंत्र सं 1976)

136. अन्-अग्नित्रा कृष्टी: अभि अमन्त (मैंत्र सं 1977)

Mandala Two

The Second *Mandala* contains 43 hymns and 429 stanzas. From the point of view of its content, seer *Gritsmada* is the composer of this Book. The maximum stanzas of it are dedicated to *Indra*. The names of the seer along with the number of stanzas composed by them are given below-

Seer	Hymns	Stanzas
1. Gritsmada	36	363
2. Somâhuti Bhârgava	4	31
3. Gârtsmada Kûrma	3	35
Total	43	429

As regards the number of *Mantras* pertaining to various gods, the position is as follows-

1.	Indra	136
2.	Agni	78
3.	Brâhmanaspati	28
4.	Vishwedeva	17
5.	Âditya	17
6.	Brahaspati	16
7.	Maruta	16
8.	Rudra	15
9.	Apanipata	15
10.	Ritu	12
11.	Savita	11
12.	Ashwini Kumâr	11
13.	Apri Sûkta	11
14.	Varuna	11
15.	Soma Pûshana	6

16.	Shakunta	6
17.	Saraswatî	4
18.	Dyâvâ Prithivî	4
19.	Sinivali	3
20.	Mitrâ Varuna	3
21.	Indra Twasta	2
22.	Raka	2
23.	Vâyu	2
24.	Indra Vâyu	1
25.	Indra Brâhamanaspati	1
26.	Indra Soma	1
	Total	429

Rigveda chooses an impressive style of conviction in it. In sheer contrast of maximum religious faiths of the world, it does not come out to preach the final truth pronouncing it from the highest seat of power. The theme is also different from the story telling art of later *Puranas* and scriptures. It tells in general the glories and heroic characters of those gods who while helpful to human beings can well become the models of an ideal world. The meanings of the *Mantras* simultaneously operate on all three levels, i.e.- the material, metaphysical and the spiritual. All the deities like *Indra* or *Agni* for instance, while manifesting outer divine and material forces, have also a definite place identifiable in our social hierarchy as well as in our spiritual being. Therefore, the appeal and the application of the text are manifold.

Agni

Agni, as usual again occupies an important place in the Second *Mandala*. Whereas the first *Mandala* begins with the prayer of Agni[1] so does the second.[2] As a matter of fact, barring 8 and

---

1 अग्निमीले पुरोहितं
2 त्वमग्ने द्युभिस्त्वमाशुशुक्षणि:

9 *Mandala*; all other Books begin with the invocation of this power. The very first *Mantra* of the second Book indicates how perfect the knowledge of the physical science of the ancient seers was. It points out 'Agni, you take birth in waters, stones and forests.'[3] They very well knew that smashing two particular stones or woods could create the fire. They were in fact producing fire (this continues till date) after rubbing two pieces of wood, which they called the churning of *'arani'*. The fire so created is the right fire for the performance of the rite of the sacrifice. As regards producing fire from water, it may have an indication for the power generation under hydro electro system, which is supposed to be only a modern invention. Further more Vedic seers far from considering fire just to be a physical force, in the third stanza of the first hymn of this Book it is stated, '*Agni,* you are brave *Indra* among the virtuous, you are all pervading *Vishnu* praised by many, you being full with glory of wisdom, are *Brahma* and because of the master of many arts you are *Medhâvi.*'[4] *Rigveda* invokes and prays and goes at length to appreciate certain qualities of the deity *Agni* in order to bring home the idea that they ought to be nurtured by human beings as well. It is very much in contrast with the systems, which openly not only advocate, but also admonish those who do not take such advice. Some of such traits specifically brought out are as follows-

Purity: Agni is absolutely pure. Everything whether waters, food or air- they get polluted but fire is always unadulterated. Even the objects, which are put in fire, get purified. A person need not always remain pure, but he should purify everyone coming in his contact.

Administrator: Fire is a good administrator. It is present everywhere. Its position is always commanding. It coverts and transforms every object as per its order.

Purifier: Fire has been addressed as' *Shuchi Kritu'*, the performer of righteous deeds. It is the principal agent of sacrifice. It also keeps the environment pure when putting medicinal herbs and purified butter one performs sacrifices by way of oblation in it.

---

3 त्वमद्भयस्तमनस्परि, त्वं वनेभ्यस्तवमोषधीभ्य

4 त्वमग्न इन्द्रो वृषभः सतामसि त्वं विष्णुरुरुगायो नमस्य
  त्वं ब्रह्मा रयिविद् ब्रह्मणस्पते त्वं विधर्ता सचसे पुरन्ध्या ।

Sublimity: Its flame always tends to be elevating and get sublime. The *Sanskrit* term for this characteristic is *'Oordhwa shochih'.* A human being should also be aspiring to reach higher.

All Encompassing: Fire is not only aspiring to go higher and higher, but it also tends to be spreading all around. It has been therefore called *'Sarvatah Shochi.'* It is that quality which is responsible for the removal of darkness.

Common Friend: It is everybody's friend.[5] It is never discriminating among people. It can be made use of by any one who chooses for it.

Alertness: Fire is never lazy or inactive. It is incessantly alert and prepared to carry out its duty. It is very much law abiding and does never break the rule

Ruler of Masses: Fire is the ruler of masses.[6] *Agni* is present in all living beings in the form of vital force, *prana*. The matter becomes a living animal because of the presence of this force. A ruler should represent this trait of fire, as he must transform his people into an organic whole.

Effulgence: Fire is born out of effulgence.[7] It continues to be effulgent. A man should remain equally unblemished in his life.

Indra, Varuna and all other gods similarly have many such exemplary traits that a human being should nurture in his life for attaining success here and after. It has been advised that proper knowledge elevates human being as compared to one who is ignorant.[8] Only the superiority of the knowledge is the right distinction because it is through this quality alone that a man not only makes himself sublime but also is instrumental in the transformation of the whole society.

---

5 मित्र इव जन्या

6 नृणां नृपति:

7 द्युभि: जायसे

8 ब्रह्मणा वा चिंतयेमा जनां अति
अस्माकं द्युम्नंमधि पंचं कृष्टिशुंचा स्व:र्ण शुशुचीत दुष्टरम् ।

Concern for Community

The concern of Vedic seers for an ideal human society is evident all over. Elements responsible for disrupting the harmony of it are criticized and a willing preparedness is accepted to fight against such evil forces. It is desired time and again that evil forces inimical to human beings and gods may never come to possess power and rule.[9] The ruler in such society should also be particularly cautious and help protect his subjects by punishing such forces.[10]

Human beings living in an ideal society like this will also be magnificent, rich and glorious. A society consisting of poor, ignorant and defeated people can never be an ideal human society. *Indra* is the ideal of all human aspirations because he is capable of achieving his goals.[11] It has been repeatedly stressed that gods are not supporting the tired and idle people.[12] It is in all fitness of logic and reasoning therefore, that the valour and courage of *Indra* is appreciated. He is capable of dismissing his enemy from his seat even when he is dismissed himself. His adventures remain undeterred whether there is a mountain or an Ocean falling in his way.[13] It does not make him arrogant or a supporter of arrogant either. *Indra* is never extending help to such person.[14] He is always rewarding those people who are forsaking and willing to give things for others. *Indra* makes the bounty full in case of such people.[15] *Indra* is thus the giver of superior knowledge, riches, fortune, freedom from disease and sweet voices. Virtually, *Indra* accomplishes all such and many other unparalleled feats, therefore all the appreciation for him.[16]

---

9 देवस्य मर्त्स्य च आरातिः नः मा ईशत (67)

10 पशुपते अस्मत् द्वेषांसि युयोधि (61) मानुषं अमानुषं नि जूर्वात् (99)

11 यः लक्षं जिगीवान् सः इन्द्रः (114)

12 न ऋते श्रान्तस्य सख्याय देवाः

13 यः अच्युतच्युत् सः इन्द्रः (119)
   ते रथः समुद्र।ः पर्वतैः न (163)

14 यः शर्धते न अनु ददाति (120)

15 यजतःदित्सतं भूयः चिकेत (148)
   दाशुषे पुरूणि अप्रतीनि दाशत् (191)

16 ता प्रथमं अकृणोः स उक्थ्यः (127)

Stress on Action

The performance of proper action has been stressed and it is the indicator of real greatness in a man's life. *Indra* was born with a superior spirit of action. It holds true in respect of every human being since his progress in life depends on his virtuous and valiant deeds. (214) An action is the right protector and works like an armour of an intelligent person. All wise men therefore perform superior actions for their well being and protection. [17]

The Vedic seer knew that the life and its longevity is important for the performance of uninterrupted action. He therefore prays that till his objectives of life are achieved, the threads of his cloth should not break and his senses may also remain potent and active. [18] Each human being must do his job. He should not be living on others' earning. He desires that he should not be depending for enjoying riches accumulated and earned by others. [19] Seer *Gritsmada* is all for social harmony. He expects that one who speaks nicely and means welfare of others, should be closer, just next on the right side and one who speaks ill should never exercise control on us. [20]

Superiority of Knowledge

Virtuous knowledge is the sole recommendation of the seer. *Brah*aspati, the divine teacher of gods has been invoked to lead on such paths. Persons following it do not commit sins. The divine teacher punishes those who are envious of the right knowledge and finally destroys them. [21] one who is under the protection of this master of superior knowledge, remains unharmed by all violent force. All evil forces, sins, enemies, cheats etc. are incapable of harming him (220). Even when a shrewd person tries to harm such person of pure intellect, he only ruins himself in consequence. It was their firm conviction that their pure intellect can redeem them from all ills. They were sure that one who is a hypocrite and deceitful shall never succeed in his life. [22]

---

17 अवस्यव: वयुनानि तक्षु: (195)

18 मा तन्तुश्छेदि वयतो धियं मे मा मात्रा शार्यपस: पुर ऋतो: (281)

19 अहं अन्यकृतेन मा भोजम् (285)

20 सुमंगलो भद्रवादी शकन्ते ।

   मा न: स्तेन ईशत माघाशंसो (425)

21 ब्रह्मद्विषा तपन: मन्यु मी: असि (219)

22 अरण: नकि (241)

The great epic *Mahabharata* speaks in this line alone when it declares that even though an unholy man may make progress and defeat his enemies in the beginning, but he is sure to get ruined along his whole clan in the end. It has been reminded in this book that gods with innumerable eyes are constantly keeping watch on all our actions and they very well understand where a man is honest or dishonest in his deeds.[23] No place is far for these shining gods however distantly it is placed.[24] Seer *Gritsmada* in this Book is constantly praying gods (*Varuna* for instance, in stanza 281-82) to strengthen and energize people to always move on the path of righteousness, make them fearless and remove all sins from them the way delicate calf is kept free from the rope.[25]

Gritsmada, the Seer and His Visions

As compared to *Mandala* 1, *Mandala* 2 is a better compact piece of hymns as the seer of it is only *Gritsmada* with two others of his own school of thought. It will appear that the gods who have been invoked in it are nearly common as the realisation of truth can be just one in the deep state of *Smâdhi*. But the characteristic distinction is also a marked one. Interestingly for instance, *Acharya Vinoba Bhave* believes this seer to be a great devotee of *Ganesh* (reference drawn to the stanza 216 or the first *Mantra* of the hymn 23.) Two syllables of his names *Gritsa* and *Mada* respectively stand for *Prana*, inhalation and *Apâna*, exhalation respectively involving the exercise of *Prânâyâma* attributed to *Shri Ganesh*, the god marked with a long nose (elephant's trunk). He was further a great mathematician, an agricultural scientist as well as an efficient weaver. According to him[26] the seer lived in the village *Kalamba* of present *Yavatmal* of the *Mahârashtra* State about twenty thousand years back. This thickly forestland falling between river *Narmada* and *Godavari* demonstrated a marked progress in the cotton cultivation as well as the use of cotton in cloth weaving. There are quite a number of

---

23 भूर्यक्षः अन्तः वृजिना उत साधु पश्यन्ति (262)
24 सर्व राजाभ्यः परमा चिदन्ति (262)
25 दामेव वत्साद् (281)
   गणानां त्वा गणपतिं हवामहे (282)
26 From the book 'Veda chintana'

internal references available in this Book to prove that the men and women were involved in cloth weaving and the life span of a man is well comparable with this process. When the Sun withdraws its rays in the evening, the weaving woman also winds up her half-woven day's cloth.[27] *Gritsmada* has a special request to make to *Varuna* so that he does not allow the weaver's thread break in between and lets the course of full life finish honourably in the performance of the noble deeds.[28] He was a staunch believer of the life of action and therefore wished that living and enjoying on others' earning is not fair on his part.[29]

The contribution of this seer in the field of Mathematics is particularly memorable. There is lot much talked and spoken about the Vedic Mathematics these days propounded by late *Shri Bhârti Krishna Teertha*. Seer *Gritsmada* in Book two here has simple memorable multiplication for the beginners while fairly demonstrating the decimal, which marks the epic progress in human understanding. He prays *Indra* to come in the chariot of two horses first and in case he has a preference there is firstly the table of two and later the table of ten for him to opt as far as the selection of the number of horses is concerned. '*Indra,* you come soon to me boarding in the chariot of two horses, four horses, six horses, eight horses and ten horses. If this table does not suit you any further, then come in the chariot of ten horses, twenty horses, thirty horses, forty horses ... hundred horses.'[30]

Gritsmada was the son of *Shunhotra*, a seer of the *Angirâ* dynasty. He was a great friend of *Indra*. He even once allowed demons catch hold of him while saving *Indra* from their captivity. *Indra* very much pleased after his accomplishment gave him the other name *Shaunaka*. According to *Mahabhârataa (Anushâshana*

---

27 पुन: समव्यद् विततं वयन्ती (381)

28 मा तंतुश्छेदि वयतो धियं मे (281)

29 माहं अन्यकृतेन भोजम् (285)

30 आ द्वाभ्यां हरीभ्यामिन्द्र या ह्या चतुर्भिरा षड्भिर्हयमान:
आष्टाभिर्दशभि: सोमपेयं अयं सुत:सुमुख मा मृधस्क:
आ विशत्या त्रिंशता याह्यर्वाङ्ग आ चत्वारिषता हरिभिर्युजान:
आ पंचाशता सुरथेभिरिंद्र आ षष्ट्या सप्तया सोमपेयम्
आशीत्या नवत्या याह्यर्वाङ् आ शतेन हरिभिरुह्यमान:
अयं हि ते शुनहोत्रेषु सोम: इन्द्र त्वाया परिषिक्तो मदाय (182-184)

Parva) Gritsmada was the son of king *Veethavya*. This king once hides himself in the place of seer *Bhrigu* because of the fear of the king of *Kâshi* named *Pratardana*. When *Pratardana* reached there, the seer declared that there lived no warrior in his centre and the king *Veethavya* thus got transformed into a seer's clan with his son *Gritsmada* as his descendent. He came in this manner to be known as *Bhargava*. He is therefore also stated to be *Ângirâs Bhargava*.

In stanza eight of the hymn nineteen of this Book, there is a direct mention of the seer *Gritsmada* invoking *Indra* in highly pleasing terms. Scholars having no pride (literally the name *Gritsmada* also suggests this meaning) always pray *Indra* for their assistance and they are sure to attain all kinds of riches and glories.[31] Again in the hymn 39 stanza 8, the seer while addressing *Ashwini Kumârs* refers back to himself as the composer and requests them to shower their grace for attaining fame and prosperity.[32]

This direct touch and appeal of the invocations of the present seer is the special feature of this part. There are scholars believing that the homogeneous texture of this *Mandala* characterizes it to be the first one since the first *Mandala* appears to be a compilation of many later compositions quite evident by the varied contents of the various seers. The outlook and the vision of *Gritsmada* are very broad. He does not just typify gods in a particular fashion. *Agni* for instance, is not a mere physical fire or god of sacrifice for him. He is *Indra* in valour, *Vishnu* for being all pervading and *Brahma* as he is all knowing. The rite of sacrifice is also not an act performed solely for the individual benefit as the 'food put in fire during sacrifice reaches immediately in all parts of earth and heaven.'[33] Similarly seer *Gritsmada's Indra* represents all finer virtues of a good ruler as well as an ideal person of a good society. He is a queer combination of all divine and worldly accomplishments for human beings to follow and worship for attaining highest good on earth.

---

31 एवा ते गृत्समदा: शूर मन्म अवस्यव: (195)
32 एतानि वामश्विना वर्धनानि ब्रह्म स्तोम गृत्समदासो अक्रन् (396)
33 यत् पृक्ष: ते अत्र विभुवत् द्यावापृथिव्यौ अनु (15)

All other gods such as *Brahaspati, Varuna, Âditya, Saraswatî* etc. are also important because of their special relationship with men on earth. *Brahaspati,* for instance is the proper guide on a righteous path (221), *Varuna* is prayed to be prolonging the thread of life while performing worldly obligations (281), *Âditya* for inspiring human beings to perform action (378) and *Shakunta* for permitting a person to speak when he is speaking nice words for the welfare of others. (425)

Important Key-notes from Mandala Two

1   Wise men place the performer of good deeds on a high altitude.

2   May we become supreme acquiring high knowledge.

3   May the enemy of gods and mankind not reign over us.

4   Wise men perform good actions for their well being.

5   May virtues never forsake us.

6   Man makes progress by valour and courage.

7   May he never rule over us who wants to keep us suppressed.

8   Let us get rid of all sufferings by superior knowledge.

9   A hypocrite can never be successful in life.

10   Words should be filled with love and grace.

11   Let me give up all sins treading on the path of virtues.

12   Gods are great because of their truthfulness.

13   One should have longer life for experiencing world well.

14   A donor always transcends all other virtuous deeds.

15   May I live in broad and fearless lights.

16   May enduring darkness never overcome us .

17   Brave persons winning enemies enjoy this and the world beyond.

18   I should never have pride after attaining large wealth.

19   I want to perform good deeds for my advancement.

20   People perform good deeds for attaining fame.

21   May you allow us *Rudra!* to live for hundred years with the help of your medicines.

22   That very god is aflame in the water without any firewood.

23   Sun rises regularly everyday for inspiring human beings to work incessantly.

24   Let only a person uttering good and well wishing words address the audience.

1   सुदंससं देवा: बुध्ने एरिरे (19)

2   ब्रह्मण सुवीर्य जनान् अति चितयेम (26)

3   देवस्य मर्त्स्य च आराति: न मा ईद्धात (67)

4   अवस्यव: वयुनानि तक्षु: (195)

5   भग: न: मा अति धक् (205)

6   वीर्यै: साकं जात: (214)

7   दुशस: अभि-दिप्सु: न: मा ईशत (225)

8   मतिभि: प्र तारिषीमहि (225)

9   स: अरण: नकि (241)

10 इमा: गिर:: धृतस्नू (260)

11 प्रणीतौ दुरितानि परि वृज्यां (264)

12 व: मत्विं ऋतेन महि (267)

13 विचक्षे सुधितानि आयूंषि अश्याम (269)

14 वसुदावा विदथेषु प्रथम: याति

15 उरु अभयं ज्योति: अश्याम् (273)

16 दीर्घा: तमिस्त्रा: न: मा अभिनष्न् (273)

17 पृत्सु आजयन् उभा क्षयौ याति (274)

18 सुयमात् राय: मा अवस्थाम् (276)

19 एता उत् यता वशिम (312)

20 आयव: नव्यसे सं अतक्षन् (312)

21 त्वा दत्तेभि: शंतमेभि: भेषजेभि: शतं हिमा: अशीय (322)

22 स: अप्सु अनिध्म: दीदाय (354)

23 स्य: देवा सविता सवाय शश्वत्तमं अस्थात् (378)

24 सुमंगल: भद्रवादी इह वद (425)

Mandala Three

The number of hymns and stanzas composed by various seers in this Book is as follows-

Seer	Hymns	Stanzas
Gâthin Vishwâmitra	46	466
Gâthi Kaushika	4	20
Prajapati Vaishwâmitra	4	62
Rishabha Vaishwâmitra	2	14
Katya Utkila	2	13
Kato Vaishwâmitra	2	10
Devâshrva Devavrata	1	5
Kushik Yeshirathi	1	22
Nadi	1	4
Ghor Angirâsa	62	617

As regards the number of stanzas invoking various gods, the position is following-

1.Indra 229, 2. Agni 186, 3.Vishwedeva 34, 4.Vaishwânar Agni 29, 5. Âpri Sûkta 11, 6. Ashwini Kumâr 9, 7. Indra Agni 9, 8. Mitra 9, 9.Yupa 9, 10. Nadi 8, 11. Ushâ 7, 12. Abhishapa 4, 13 Ribhu 4, 14. Rathanga 4, 15. Indra Ribhu 3, 16. Indra-Varuna 3, 17. Pushâ 3, 18. Brahaspati 3, 19.Maruta 3, 20. Mitra-Varuna 3, 21. Vishwâmitra 3, 22. Savita 3, 23. Soma 3, 24. Âtma 2, 25. Vâk 2, 26. Agni-Indra 1, 27. Indra-Parvata 1, 28. Ritu 1, 29. Ritwija 1, 30 Prishya Agni 1, 31. Vishwamitropâdhyâya 1, 32. Brischana 1.

Vishwâmitra

Vishwâmitra is the principal *Rishi* (seer) of Book three of the *Rigveda*. All other *Rishis* generally belong to his family. Mythological references about this seer are many. He was by birth a *Kshatria*, born in a royal family but achieved the status of a Brâhmin seer by his firm resolution and penance. Characteristically he is depicted in *Purânas* as fiery and strong. He introduces himself in the *Mantra* 219 of this *Mandala* as 'born out of fire, light is my eye and nectar rests in my mouth.'[1] He confesses that his relationship with fire is not that of one life. He has worshipped this god performing sacrifices in past many lives, which entitles him to be described as that.[2]

Vishwâmitra is the seer of one of the representative *Veda Mantras*, composed in the *Gâyatrî* metre. It has later come to be known and remembered as *Gâyatrî Mantra*. It is the tenth stanza of the sixty- second hymn of this Book (609 *Mantra* of the third *Mandala*). The god invoked here is *Savita*, the Sun 'whose brilliant effulgence is worth meditating upon so that he directs our intellect in the righteous path'.[3] Lord *Krishna* also makes a reference to this as a metre only in the tenth chapter of *Gîta* while describing his glories and attributes. 'Out of various metres, I am the metre *Gâyatri*[4], He declares. Strangely enough this *Gâyatri Chhanda*, the metre, has now come to be identified with the goddess *Gâyatri* as her *Mantra* with its further elevation as *Veda Mâta*, the mother of *Vedas*. The reason behind this generalization and sublimation of the word *Gâyatri* may be attributed to the immense purifying effect of this sacred *Mantra* now used in every rite or *Samskara* of *Hindu* tradition. As the elevation of an individual in the society and the sublimation of his character for the common good are the central theme of *Vedas*, this aspiration manifested in this metre duly entitles it for such recognition. It is said that out of twenty-four letters of this *Mantra*, each contributed to the composition of the 24 thousand verses of the *Vâlmiki Râmâyana*.

The story of *Vishwâmitra* is narrated with many elaborated colourings in *Puranas*. His rivalry with another *Rishi Vashishtha*, the seer of the seventh *Mandala*, is of particular mention as he did all sort of penance for attaining *Brahma Gyâna*, the absolute knowledge which made *Vashishtha* invincible for him. In hymn 53 of the Book under context, there is an indirect reference to this effect, which seems to have, been further extended in later *Puranic*

---

1   अग्निरस्मि जन्मना जातवेदा घृतं मे चक्षुरमृतं म आसन्

2   जन्मन्जन्मन् निहितो जातवेदा विश्वामित्रेभिरिध्यते अजस्र: (3.21)

3   तत् सवितुर्वरेण्यं भर्गोदेवस्य धीमहि धियो योन: प्रचोदयात् ।

4   गायत्री छनदसामहम् (गीता 10.35)

literature. Following the interpretation of *Sayana*, it means: 'These sons of *Bharata*, *Indra*, understand severance (from *Vashishtha*), not association (with them); they urge their steeds (against them) as against a constant foe; they bear a stout bow (for their destruction) in battle.'[5] As regards mention of the origin of the seer, stanza 2-3 of the hymn 26 inform that he was a *Kaushika*, born in the dynasty of *Kushik* who were so learned that they knew the secret of the origin of this world.[6] *Vishwâmitra* directly refers himself to be the 'son of *Kushik*' (3.33.5) as he submits his requests before the rivers *Vyasa* and *Satlaj* allowing him to cross them without drowning. According to some interpreters, *Vishwâmitra* was working as a priest of King *Sudasa* and it was with the intention of finding a way for the forces of his mentor to attack King *Samvarana* of *Punjab* that he prayed these rivers. According to *Sâyana*, however, it was the problem of carrying great wealth achieved from *Sudâsa* that inspired him to invoke these rivers to provide him a passage.

There are some further hints available about the rivalry of *Vishwâmitra* with the son of *Vashishtha*, *Shakti*. While interpreting the fifth stanza of the fifty-third hymn of the third Book, therefore, commentator *Sayana* interprets '*Sasarpari*' as the name of Voice or Speech as the daughter of the Sun. At a sacrifice of king *Sudasa*, the power of speech of *Vishwâmitra* was completely vanquished by *Shakti*, son of *Vashishtha*. Having been so overcome *Vishwâmitra* became very much dejected. *Jamdagni* then drew from the domain of Sun a voice called '*Sasarpari*' and gave her to him. Being gladdened by receiving the Voice, he paid homage to the *Jamdagnis* praising them with the two verses. Western commentator Ludwig and Roth are of the view that '*sasarpari*' may mean a war trumpet, which inspires the combatants and dispels their fear of the enemy.

Salient Features of the Book

Some important contents of *Mandala* three can be well illustrated under following headings-

---

5   इम इन्द्र भरतस्य पुत्रा अपपित्वं चिंकितुर्न प्रपित्वम् (3-53-24)
6   प्रथमजा ब्रह्मणो विश्वमिद् विदु:(3-29-15)

Nationalism and National Integration of Bharata

Bhârata, the then India is very dear to the Vedic seers. They ardently desired that the people of this land should speak in a manner, which is satisfying to others.[7] The ancient people in it were very brave and they 'only knew to vanquish their foes rather than nurturing them'.[8] When river *Vyasa* and *Satlaj* provide passage to *Vishwâmitra*, the sage further requests they to offer safe passage to other '*Bhârtah*' and only then they should start overflowing.[9] *Vishwâmitra* thus made a difficult path quite easy for '*Bhâratas*' to pass.[10] They also believed that the knowledge superior is a great protecting force of *Bhârata*.[11]

Superiority of Knowledge

Knowledge is an all-superior talent in human beings. It is through knowledge alone that a man becomes happy.[12] Only a man of knowledge can be a rightful ruler.[13] It is a fact universally acknowledged that the learned ones will prefer living in the company of learned people. The Vedic seer thus says that 'a learned man will be followed by other learned people.'[14] Knowledge is important both as an individual and a member in the society. As an individual it helps cross the darkness and attains light[15]. This knowledge alone is the representative characteristic of India and it is an important factor protecting Indians from all odds.[16]

Importance of Action

Action forms an important part of the Vedic life. 'Happiness rests in action',[17] Learning and practising the proper art of action is equally important in human life. Only wise people know the

---

7   भारती भारतीभि: सजोषा: (57)

8   भरतस्य पुत्रा: अपपित्वं चिकित: न प्रपित्वं (509)

9   यदह्न त्वा भरता: संतरेयु र्गव्यन् ग्राम इषित (330)

10 अतारिषुर्भरता गव्यव: स मभाक्त विप्र: सुमतिं नदीनाम् (331)

11 इदं ब्रह्म भारतं जनं रक्षति (497)

12 शूषं प्रविदा (88)

13 विप्र: एषं यन्ता (143)

14 विद्वान् विदुष: आ वक्षि (149)

15 विजानन् तमस: ज्योति: वृणीत (393)

16 इदं ब्रह्म भारतं जनं रक्षति (497)

17 यस्मिन् अपांसि, तस्मिन् सुमनननि (41)

correct technique of it. Naturally such people always act more efficiently and earn appreciation from others. *Richâ* 230 of this Book states that 'persons performing acts wisely get selections (in high places.)'[18] As a matter of fact, noble deeds bestow status and reputation to a man.[19] *Rishi Vishwâmitra* does not just stop here but goes on to stress that the action in life is not an end but a means to make him immortal.[20]

Significance of the Holy Order

Everyone must follow *Rit,* the law divine. This is the cardinal principle of the Vedic discipline. This is the first definition to be remembered and followed.[21] People should get up early in the morning and follow the footprints of the wise people. Intelligent people always adhere to this rule (61). A person speaking truth soon earns fame. And it is also a fact that those who follow the righteous path are capable of speaking always truth.[22] People have in general a feeling that riches earned by whatever means are ultimately gains only and they are important in human life. This Book, however, gives a warning that only such money lasts long which has been earned without committing any sin.[23] Following the divine dictate of living in holy order is itself a bliss. Seer *Vishwâmitra* prays *Indra* to 'set our voices in order by *Rit,* the holy-order so that we get rid of all evils.'[24]

Respect for Woman

The Vedic seers firmly believed that man and woman should live in peace and harmony in house. Particularly, it is the responsibility of a man that he gives proper treatment to his wife. It is not only a case of trust or treatment but also that of the conviction. Sage *Vishwâmitra* therefore, declares 'woman is the home'.[25]

---

18 धिया चक्रे वरेण्य:

19 महद्भि: कर्मभि: सुश्रुत: (355)

20 सुकृत्या अमृतत्वं एरिरे (588)

21 ऋतं अनुव्रतं इति आहु(56)

22 व्रतं दीध्याना: ऋतं आहु: (90)

23 अद्रोघेण वचसा रयि: सत्यं (153)

24 प्र सूनृता दिशमान ऋतेन दुरश्च विश्वा अवृणोदप स्वा: (301)

25 जाया इत अस्तं (487), जाया इत् योनि: (489)

Another source of happiness in household is that of having good and obedient offspring. They always desired that they have an issue who is' brave, performing virtuous deeds, intelligent and aspiring to attain divinity.'[26] They were also praying gods to particularly bless them for this purpose. *Vishwâmitra* advises to worship *Agni* in particular for the fulfilment of the desire of having 'a long living son.'[27]

---

26 वीर: कर्मण्य: सुदक्ष: देवकाम: जायते (58)
27 आयुनि सु-अपत्ये जरस्व (45)

Important Key-notes from Mandala Three

1. Only riches earned without shame are worth appreciation.
2. Where there are deeds, happiness rests.
3. To follow the path of truth is the right resoluion.
4. Each one's knowledge should conform to the other.
5. May there is a son born who is brave, intelligent and aspiring to attain divinity.
6. One who gets up early attains knowledge like all early risers.
7. Happiness comes through knowledge.
8. A man in high spirits is always happy.
9. Learned man can only rule others.
10. A true leader is like a friend, a father and the mother.
11. May your pure intellect act for the welfare of others.
12. A man attains fame by his noble deeds.
13. Always look fresh and energetic.
14. Man should strive to attain new means of protection.
15. Knowledge is the best purifier of your head.
16. Woman is the right abode.
17. A strong man should not torture the weak.
18. A farsighted plan yields high results.

19. Let us not follow the paths, which are unbecoming for our children.

20. May all food and herbs be tasteful and sweet.

21. May everyday for us be bright and joyful.

1   अन्हयं वाजं ऋग्मियं (27)

2   यस्मिनि् अपांसि, तस्मिन् सुम्नानि (41)

3   ऋतं अनु व्रतं इति आहु: (56)

4   सरस्वती सारस्वतेभि:(57)

5   वीर: कर्मण्य:, सुदक्ष:, देवकाम: जायते (58)

6   उषस: चेकितान: कवीनां पदवी: अवोधि (61)

7   शूषं प्रविदा (88)

8   तृष्टं ववक्षति सुमना अस्ति (107)

9   विप्र: एषां यन्ता (143)

10   सखा इव पितरा इव साधु: भव (173)

11   ते सुमति: भद्रा (265)

12   महद्भि: कर्मभि: सुश्रुत: (355)

13   सद्य: जात: वृषभ: कनीन: (451)

14   नूतनस्य अवस: बोधि (471)

15   ब्रह्मणा शिर: (477)

16   जाया इव अस्तं (489)

17   वाजिना अवाजिनं न हासयन्ति (508)

18   कवय: नाम महत् चारु (526)

19   न: गन्तो: अनपत्यानि युयोत (527)

20   ओषधी: मध्वा सं पिपृक्त (530)

21   विश्वा अहा न: दिदीहि (531)

Mandala Four

Rishi Vâmadeva Gautama is the principal seer of Book four. He is the composer of 55 hymns of it out of 58 in all. The other two seers are Trasdasyu Pourukutsua and Purumilhalmijhau Sohotra who have been credited with one and two hymns respectively. As regards the number of Mantras composed by various seers, the position is as follows-

Vâmadeva Gautama	562
Trasdasyu Pourukutsya	10
Purumil Hajmilhau Sohotra	14
Indra	2
Aditi	1

Various deities of this Mandala along with the Mantras allocation to them are following-

1.	Indra	193
2.	Agni	126
3.	Ribhu	48
4.	Ashwini Kumâr	23
5.	Dadhikra	19
6.	Ushâ	18
7.	Indra-Varuna	15
8.	Rakshoh-Agni	15
9.	Vaishwanar-Agni	15
10.	Savita	13
11.	Agni-Sûrya-Apa	11
12.	Vishwedeva	10
13.	Indra-Vâyu	9
14.	Brahaspati	9

15. Indra-Brahaspati	8
16. Dyâva-Prithivî	8
17. Shyena	8
18. Vâyu	7
19. Trasdasyu	6
20. Vâmadeva	5
21. Agni-Varuna	4
22. Indra-Ushâ	3
23. Rita	3
24. Ksetrapati	3
25. Indrashwa	2
26. Shunasira	2
27. Sita	2
28. Somaka Sahdevatâ	2
29. Shunah	1
30. Sûrya	1

Visions and Compositions of Seer Vâmadeva

Vâmadeva Gautama (*Vâmadeva* being the son of *Gautama* is referred as *Vâmadeva Gautama* in 4.16.18) introduces himself in stanza 1 of the verse 26 of this Book in the following words- 'I was born as *Manu*, as *Sûrya*. I am the wise seer *Kakshiwân*. I have made *Kutsa*, the son of *Arjuni* competent. I am the far seeing poet *Ushanâ*.'[1]

Evidently there is some mysticism in the statement of this seer when he claims that he had come to understand the secret of the origin of gods when he was just in the womb of his mother.[2]

---

1 अहं मनुरभं सूर्यश्च अहं कक्षीवां ऋषिरस्मि विप्र:
  अहं कुत्समार्जनेयं न्यृंजे अहं कविरुशना पश्यता मा (294)
2 गर्भे नु सन्नन्वेषमवेदं अहं देवानां जनिमानि विश्वा (301)

This seer was a great perceiver of the ultimate truth and he was at the same time a *Jâtismar* (knowing all the details of his past lives). He was aware of his past lives as *Manu* and *Sûrya*. He talks about triple birth of living beings. The first according to him is at the time of conception; the second at the time he comes out from the mother's womb and the third is the rebirth after death. This extraordinary talent in him made him aware of the truth that his life and birth may be a fact of the body and not the soul. He therefore thinks that he is redeeming himself from the iron cage of the body like a falcon flying forcefully at the strength of his knowledge. He in this way thought it fit not to take birth from the womb of his mother but 'from the side obliquely will I issue'[3]

Vâmadeva is one of the profoundest seekers of truth through a very high mysticism. There are definite seeds of Non-dualistic philosophy of later Indian thought quite deep rooted in him. In his deep state of consciousness of being one with the Almighty, he can easily declare that ' I had created land for *Âryans* to live, I am the donor of rains for those who have right sense of sacrifice, I have shown the path for rivers to flow; all gods follow my path of knowledge'[4]

Vâmadeva was the chief priest of king *Dasharatha*. *Vâlmiki* in his *Râmâyana* and *Tulsidâsa* in his *Ramcharit Mânasa* make repeated mention of this seer. Although *Rigveda* does not make any mention of king *Dashratha*, but there is the reference of a priestly king *Kutsa* in the stanzas of verse 16 of this Book. *Kutsa* was the son of a priestly king called *Ruru*. Once upon a time when his enemies defeated *Kutsa*, his father made special prayers for *Indra*, who after appearing on such call, defeated the enemies. *Indra* and *Kutsa* thus became very good friends. *Indra* even took his friend to his high abode and made him share his royal seat and attain his divine form. This sight bewildered the wife of *Indra*, *Shachi* who found it difficult to recognize her husband. Seer *Vâmadeva* naturally has all praises for *Indra* for his high touch of human divine and qualities.

---

3 नाहमतो निरया दुर्हैतत्तिश्चता पाश्वर्चान्निर्गमाणि (208)

4 अहं भूमिमददामार्याय अहं वृष्टिं दाशुषे मर्त्याय
   अहमपो अनयं वावशाना: मम देवासो अनु केतमायन् (295)

The last 57th hymn of this *Mandala* is the most mystical of all Vedic hymns. Outwardly looking, the hymn is in the praise of *Ghrita,* the clarified butter used in sacrifices but a choice of deities is offered in the index of gods- *Agni, Sûrya, Waters* and Cows. Owing to its deep mystical note, Wilson goes on to comment like this-'a good specimen of Vedic vagueness, and mystification, and of the straits to which commentators are put to extract an intelligible meaning from the text.'

Vâmadeva talks about two oceans in it. In the beginning he says that a honeyed wave climbs up from the ocean and by means of this mounting wave the *Soma* attains immortality; that wave or *Soma* is the secret name of clarity (*ghrita*); it is the tongue of the gods; it is the nodus (*nâbhi*) of immortality. Shri Aurobindo in his famous work on *Veda* has following comments to make-

'Certainly *Vâmadeva* does not mean that a wave or flood of wine came mounting up out of the salt water of the Indian Ocean or of the Way of Bengal or even from the fresh water of the river Indus or the Ganges and this wine is a secret name for clarified butter. What he means to say is clearly that out of subconscient depths in us arises a honeyed wave of Ânanda or pure delight of existence, that it is by this Ânanda that we can arrive at immortality; this Ananada is the secret being, the secret reality behind the action of mind in its shining clarities.'

The seer further speaks about the Creator who has four horns, three feet, two heads and seven hands etc. They have been interpreted in the context of fire, Sun and linguistics   by various commentators. The four horns are also identified as four *Vedas,* the three feet. As three daily sacrifices of morning, noon and evening, two heads as day and night and seven hands as the seven metres of *Veda* or the seven rays of the Sun.

Important Contents of the Mandala

Significance of Yajna

Vâmadeva is the master of the rite and all sacrificial rituals. Naturally this trait in him enabled him to be the chief priest of king *Dasharatha*. He was a firm believer of the theory that the supporter of the sacrifice deserves a Haining best the pure knowledge.[5] According to him the performer of the sacrifice is always held high and lives the life of grace. It is because the wise becomes wiser because of it.[6]

The sacrificial rite had traditionally three ingredients; god-worship, virtuous company and donations. The worship of god was important from the point of view of attaining divine grace for the achievements of worldly as well as other worldly objects. The virtuous company helped increase knowledge and donations served the cause of the needy class of the society.

Glorious *Indra*

As mentioned above, *Vâmadeva* as an intimate friend of *Indra* has special praises for him to offer. 'Indra, you are great!'[7] He declares. He is so great that while himself alone he is capable of defeating a number of enemies.[8] Whole world, whether animate or inanimate, tremble whenever *Indra* is furious.[9] *Indra's* might is just not an acquired one as he is invincible right from his birth. According to the seer, 'there has been no one capable of vanquishing him ever since he took his birth.'[10]

It is also not the just prowess of this mighty god that impresses the seer. 'A man performing good deeds, having righteous thoughts and protecting needy ones', he declares, 'is very dear to *Indra*.'[11]

---

5   यज्ञबन्धु: मनुष्य: चेतयत् (9)
6   ऊर्ध्व ऊ षु णो अध्वरस्य होर्तेंप्र वेधस्चित तिरसि मनीषाम् (87)
7   त्वं महान् (186)
8   एक: भूम च्यावयति (190)
9   विश्वं दृळहं भयत एजदस्मात् (195)
10 जनुषा अस्य वर्ता न अस्ति (237)
11 इन्द्रे सुकृत, मपायु:, सुप्रावी: प्रिय: (290)

Important Key-notes from Mandala four

1.   Make us full of charity and protect from miserness.

2.   All days of the worshipper of fire are fine.

3.   Superior knowledge of the seers should be propogated.

4.   You are the lord of the wealth existing in earth and heaven.

5.   A man passing through the right paths gains prosperity.

6.   Spicy meals make a man charming.

7.   A man pleasing god and performing right duty attains heaven.

8.   Agni is the origin of poetry, intellect and hymns.

9.   One controlling the world power commands supreme respect all over.

10.   Go to the learned one if you wish to do good to others.

11.   Let people having common views stay together.

12.   Rising Sun must be seen for long.

13.   Gods do not make them friends who are not taking pains.

14.   Good deeds make man a god.

15.   Man enjoys fruit of his good deeds.

16.   The One God, who created the space and the earth, pervades them.

1 दितिं रास्व अदितिं उरुष्य (31)

2 विश्वानि दिनानि सु (62)

3 मनीषां महि साम प्र वोचत् (74)

4 दिवि पृथिव्यां यत् द्रविणं अस्य त्वं क्षयसि (82)

5 अध्वन: परमं (83)

6 अरूक्षितं अंनं रूप: (133)

7 वेपसा गृणते खं (134)

8 काव्या मनीषा: राध्यानि उक्था त्वत् जायन्ते (135)

9 य: विश्वा भुवना अभि बभूव अमितं ववक्ष (५69)

10 नृमण: कविं अच्छ गा (173)

11 सरूपा स्वे योनौ निषीदतम् (174)

12 उच्चरन्तं सूर्य ज्योक् पश्यात् (289)

13 न ऋते श्रान्तस्य सख्याय देवा (389)

14 सुकृत्या देवास: अभवत् (408)

15 धीभि: सनिता (424)

16 य इमे द्यावापृथिवी जजपन स: इत् सुअपा: भुवनेषु आस (566)

Mandala Five

Rishi Atri is the principal seer of this Book. The total number of the seers of all 87 hymns and 727 stanzas of this *Mandala* is 43 but they basically belong to the family of this seer only. As regards the number of hymns dedicated to various gods, the position pertaining to few important ones is as follows-

Gods	Number of stanzas
1. Agni	184
2. Vishwedeva	120
3. Maruta	118
4. Indra	102
5. Mitra Varuna	59
6. Ashwini Kumâr	48
7. Ushâ	16
8. Savita	14
9. Âpri Sûkta	11
10. Parjanya	10
11. Varuna	8
12. Indragni	7
13. Atri	4
14. Prithivî	3
15. Sûrya	1
16. Rudra	1
17. Vâyu	1

Seer Atri and his Vision

Mandala four is termed as *'Âtreya'* as the seers of the family of *Atri* are the composers of it. He is one among the seven principal *Rishis* mentioned in *Vedas* and figuring prominently in *Purânas*. *Bhâgwata Purâna* mentions about *Atri* taking birth from the eye of *Brahma*, the Creator. *Ansûyâ* is the wife of *Atri* who is very famous for her devotion to her husband. Literally *Atri* stands for one who transcends *'tri'* (three) *gunas*, elements, namely; *Satwa, Rajas* and *Tamas*. *Ansûyâ* means one who is above all fault finding. This couple has been held so high in the *Puranic* literature that *Brahma*, *Vishnu* and *Shiva* became little babies when they wanted to test her chastity.

In *Mandala* one of the *Rigveda* (hymn 51 and 112) *Atri* is described to be under a gracious cover of *Ashwini Kumârs*. Once when the seer was in deep *Samâdhi* the demons took him away and put him in a fiery pond. The twin gods saved him from that ordeal. (1.118.7, 1.119.6) In the tenth *Mandala* again, it is mentioned that when he became very fragile and weak after long penance, these gods restored his young age. (10.141.1)

In *Mandala* five it has come to be mentioned that *Atri* had to face imprisonment because he was always siding public for its rights. (5.66) He had naturally some confrontations with the rulers on this accord. This book also mentions the names of some of his sons such as *Vasuyu* and *Saptavadhri* who are in the category of some other seers of the Book. (5.25-26, 5.78)

Hymn 51 of this Book whose seer is *Swasti Atreya* deserves our special attention. Especially *Mantra* 11 to 15 of it are the verses written and sung for the welfare of entire human race. These hymns are therefore called, '*kalyana Sûkta /Mangala Sûkta* or *Shreya Sûkta*'. Whenever there is a good work or welfare activity to be started, the *Vedic Pandits* start chanting these *Mantras* so that the result of that action is an overall good for all mankind. In this particular hymn *Ashwini, Bhaga, Pushâ, Dyava-Prithivî, Brahaspati, Âditya, Vaishwânar, Savitâ, Mitrâvaruna*, Sun and the Moon have been invoked to shower their grace for the common good. This is one of the representative poetry and prayer of the Vedic lore.[1]

---

1 स्वस्ति नो मिमीतामश्विना भग: स्वस्ति देव्यर्दितिरनर्वण:
स्वस्ति पूषा असुरो दधातु न: स्वस्ति द्यावापृथिवी सुचेतना (432)
स्वस्तये वायुमुप ब्रवामहै सोमं स्वस्ति भुवनस्य यस्पतिं
बृहस्पतिं सर्वगणं स्वस्तयेस्वस्तय आदित्यासो भवन्तु न: (433)
विश्वे देवा नो अद्या स्वस्तये वैश्चानरो वसुरग्नि: स्वस्तये
देवा अवन्त्वृभव: स्वस्तये स्वस्ति नो रुद्र: पात्वहंस: (434)
स्वस्ति मित्रावरुणा स्वस्ति पथ्ये रेवति
स्वस्ति न इन्द्रश्चाग्निश्च स्वस्ति नो अदिति कृधि (435)
स्वस्ति पन्थमनु चरेम सुर्याचन्द्रमसाविव
पुनर्ददताघ्नता जानता सं गमेमहि (435)

Towards the end, in the 82nd hymn of this Mandala the seer again prays god Savita that he should 'remove all our obstacles, pains and sufferings and help us achieve that which is good and in our interest.'[2]

While forwarding the hymns of *Atri Shri Aurobindo* distinctly states that there 'literal and external translation gives either a bizarre, unconnected sequence of sentences or a form of thought and speech strange and remote to the uninitiated intelligence. It is only when the figures and symbols are made to suggest their concealed equivalents that there emerges out of the obscurity a transparent and well linked though close and subtle sequence of spiritual, psychological and religious ideas.' Referring to the hymn to *Agni* where the seer cries 'O *Agni*, O Priest of the offering, loose from us the cord' the mystic scholar goes to interpret, ' He (the seer) is thinking of the triple cord of mind, nerves and body by which the soul is bound as a victim in the great world-sacrifice, the sacrifice of the *Purush*.'[3]

Seer *Atri* is highly poetic and has an impressive description for record when he invokes the god of thunderstorms and rains as the creator and one who nourishes plants and living creatures. It is much like Shelley in his famous 'Ode to West Wind' when the seer sings-

'Like a car-driver whipping on his horses, he makes the messengers of rain

Spring forward

Far off resounds the roaring of the lion, what time Parjanya fills the sky

With rain-cloud.

Forth burst the winds; down come the lightning-flashes: the plants shoot up,

The realm of light is streaming

---

2 विश्वानि देव सवितर्दुरितानि परा सुव
   यद् भद्रं तन्न आ सुव (687)

3 From '*On the Veda*' by Sri Aurobindo

Food springs abundant for all living creatures, what time Parjanya quickens

Earth with moisture.'

And yet again much alike 'Lift me like a wave, a leaf, a cloud', the Vedic seer has following –

'Lift up the mighty vessel, pour down water, and let the liberated stream rush forward

Saturate both the earth and heaven with fatness, and for the cows let there be

Drink abundant.'[4]

Astronomy occupies important place in the Vedic school of thought and experience. This is more so because astronomy was put to the service of rituals making it an indispensable part of the priestly craft. This called for careful observation of the heavens marking the approach of the seasons. It would thus appear how Vedic calendar and Vedic astronomy was born.

Atri is one such seer whose heavenly observation is distinct and marked when he talks about the eclipse of the Sun. In stanza five of hymn 40 of the Book five, when *Asura's* descendent *Swarbhânu* 'pierced' sun 'through and through darkness, all creatures looked like one who is bewildered, who knows not the place where he is standing.' Like a good scientist seer *Atri* at this occasion does not only dispel darkness 'by his fourth sacred prayer' but also 'discovers *Sûrya* concealed in gloom' (shadow).[5]

Themes and Techniques

Agni Glorified

Like all other seers, *Atri* glorifies *Agni* in his own style. He states that *Agni* has been worshipped from the beginning and shall continue to be worshipped forever. No force can ever replace it in future. 'There was no one for being worshipped before fire

---

4   *Rigveda* Mandala 5, hymn 83 (stanzas 3,4 and 8)
5   स्वर्भपोरध यदिप्द्र माया अवो दिवो वर्तमापा अवाहन्
     गूळहं सूर्य तमसापव्रतेन तुरीसेण ब्रह्मणापिन्दुदत्रि: (307)

and nor shall there any one be in future.'[6] This statement is also firmly in line with the first hymn of *Rigveda* where seer *Madhuchhandâ* talks about the 'ancient' and 'new' seers praising *Agni* likewise. The seer of this Book is of the opinion that if human beings welcome *Agni* at their houses, they are sure to be blessed with progenies.[7]

The Warring God, *Indra*

Indra is basically that aspect of creation that represents motion, change and volatility. He possesses the power of dynamism in abundance. *Indra* is the solar *Prâna* ruling over all the objects while keeping them alive and glowing. Seer *Atri* thus declares that '*Indra* is the creator of this universe by his might.'[8]

Another function of *Indra* is to be known as *Satya*. Water always flows downwards, the fire rises, air always flows horizontally, and no horns grow on human beings while cattle always have horns. These laws are the inherent attribute of *Rit; Satya* represented by *Indra*, which can never be violated. *Indra* in the form of supraphysical energy is always regulating every object in the universe- earth, water, sun, air, space, planets, stars, speech, eyes and so forth. He actually performs various roles and while manifesting in different organs and different forms, he is the listener, the seer, the knower and the thinker. *Atri* may well be al right when he speaks in stanza 217 of this Book about the *Indra* who alone controls all his foes and in 230 who transgresses every one in his supremacy.[9]

Yajna the Act of Acculturation

According to Vedic theme of creation, *Prajâpati* while himself being the Creator also bears the structure of *Veda*. He as a matter of fact endures through this process of *Yajna* only. Much like the process of *Prana,* inhalation and exhalation in human beings, the *Yajna* at the subtle level (and well represented by the physical act of sacrificial rite), this process goes on forever. The Vedic seer is

---

6 त्वत् पूर्व: यजीयान न, पर: काव्यै: न (29)
7 यस्या अतिथि: भवासि, स: मर्तान् वनवत् (29)
8 जनुषा वीर्येण एता भूरि विश्वा चकृवान् (212)
9 युधये एक: चित् भूयस: वेषीत् (217) त्वत् वस्य: अन्यत् नहि अस्ति (230)

therefore advocating it always, as it is an integral part of the cosmic existence. According to seer *Atri,* therefore, a person performing such duty acts in tune with the forces of nature and consequently attains glories bestowed by it. [10]

Acting in Tune with the Laws of Nature

It cannot be disputed that the universe has an origin. To say that it originated without a cause is simply over-stretching the imagination. As a matter of fact there cannot be any order in creation if a thing can originate or appear without a cause. This would mean that the principle of cause and effect has no value. As a matter of fact, the logical sequence of cause and effect has a great significance in the practical life and the very assurance of their interdependence makes human beings meaningfully act in a logical manner.

Even when the cause is not obvious, it has got to be inferred from the effect. Each occurrence must have a cause. That is the rule. This rule of the cosmic creation is called *Rit,* the divine order that should not be violated. Seer *Atri* therefore advises intelligent people to patiently follow these rules. It is indeed after abiding by these laws alone that a human being attains glory. [11] Cosmic laws are insurmountable even by gods and the seer has therefore to assert that *Mitrâvaruna* is a strict disciplinarian in this regard. [12]

---

10 येषु चित्रा दीधिति: (142)

11 धर्मणा मित्रावरुणा विपद्धिचता व्रता रक्षथे असुरस्य मायया

   ऋतेन विद्धवं भुवनं वि राजथ: सूर्यमा धत्थो दिवि चित्र्यं रथम् (570)

12 न व देवा अमृता आ मिनन्ति व्रतानि मित्रावरुणा ध्रुवाणि (603)

Important Key-notes from Mandala five

1.   A man of pure consciousness should be held high.

2.   Such man attaining divinity transcends dark ignorance.

3.   Persons using foul language in their behaviour with good people ultimately ruin-themselves.

4.   Hymns are to be remembered by heart after constant repetitions.

5.   A man should shine in his glory like the undiminished light of the Sun.

6.   A man of high learning can reach *Indra*.

7.   *Indra* exercised control over his mind immediately after his birth.

8.   In whose kingdom *Indra* has *Soma* to drink, the king rests in peace.

9.   Such a person is capable of achieving unachieved as well as protecting that which rests in his possession.

10.   He becomes dearer to Fire and the Sun.

11.   *Rudra* is the abode of all medicines.

12.   May mother earth never allow ill will among people.

13.   Those who are not hypocrites attain heaven.

14.   One who toils, attains goals.

15.   The best of all hymns becomes famous even beyond the shores of sea.

16.   *Yajna* comprising of hymns is free from all kind of violence.

17.   One who respects society and its order, attains success here and after both.

18.   The *Yajna* is the source of all actions.

19.   One who keeps awake is chosen by *Richâ*, the *mantra*.

20.   One who keeps awake, *Sama* (musical notes of *Sama Veda*) reach him.

21.   To the one who is awake, this *Soma* (divine drink) says 'I am yours'.

22.   A woman treading the path of virtues deserves all praises.

23.   Guests, wise men, and their wives deserve best service in *Yajna*.

24.   Let us move on the path of common good like sun and moon.

25.   *Marut*-brothers live all united forgetting who is old or young.

26.   The woman, who understands human sufferings, is worth appreciation.

27.   Wise people patiently follow the path of virtues.

28.   Human beings attain glory following the path of truth.

29.   *Ashwini Kumârs* never torture wise and virtuous men.

30.   A man earns good company by being virtuous.

31.   *Savita*, you one alone is the king and the lord of every one born and living.

32.   Oh god *Savita*, you take away all demerits from us.

33.   That which is for the general well-being may reach us.

34.   May we never commit a sin towards our motherland and remain obedient to the Sun.

35.   A person who works honestly whether day or night is the forerunner.

36.   A leader should behave like a brother, a friend, and a wellwisher.

1 सुमना: ऊर्ध्व: अस्थात् (2)

2 महान् देव: तमस: निरमोचि (2)

3 ऋजूयते वृजनानि ब्रुवन्त: स्वयं अधूर्षत (110)

4 आसन् उक्था पान्ति (142)

5 जप अजरं सूर्य इव क्षत्रं सुवीर्य (192)

6 बुबुधाना: नर: इन्द्रं अशेम (215)

7 जात: मन: स्थिरं चकृषे (217)

8 यस्मिन् इन्द्र: सोमं पिबति स राजा न व्यथते (290)

9 योगे क्षेमे अभि भवाति (291)

10 सूर्ये अग्नौ प्रिय: भवाति (291)

11 विश्वस्य भेषजस्य क्षयति (341)

12 माता पृथिवी न: दुर्मतौ मा धात् (346)

13 मायाभि: पर: नाम ऋते आस (367)

14 य: स्वयं वहते स अरं करत् (373)

15 आसां अग्निमा समुद्रं अवतस्थे (374)

16 यस्मिन् आयता सवनं न रिष्यति (374)

17 य: ई गणं भजतेअ स: वरा उभा प्रति एति (377)

18 विश्वासं धियां ऊध: (378)

19 य: जागार, तं ऋच: कामयन्ते (379)

20 य: जागार, तं सामानि यान्ति (379)

21 य: जागार, तं अयं सोम: आह, तव अस्मि सख्ये नि ओक: (379)

22 सरमा ऋतस्य पथा गा: विदद् (388)

23 अत: अतिथीन् नृन् पत्नी: दशस्यत (419)

24 सूर्याचन्द्रमसौ इव स्वस्ति पन्था अनुचरेम (436)

25 अज्येष्ठास: अकनिष्ठास: एते भ्रातर: (532)

26 या जसुरि तृष्यन्तं कामिनं वि जानाति , वृणते (542)

27 विपश्चिता धर्मणा व्रता रक्षेथे (570)

28 ऋतेन विश्वं भुवनं वि राजते (570)

29 संस्कृतं न प्र मिमीत: (644)

30 धर्मभि: मित्र: भवति (681)

31 एक: इत् प्रसवस्य ईशिषे (682)

32 देव सवित: ! विश्वानि दुरितानि परा सुव (687)

33 यत् भद्रं तत् न: आ सुव (687)

34 सवितु सवे अदितये अनागस: (688)

35 उभे अहनी अ-प्रयुच्छन् सु-आधी:, पुर: एति (690)

36 अर्यस्य: मित्र: सखाय: सदं भ्रातर: अरण: (711)

Mandala Six

Seer *Bhâradwâja* and his family descendents are the composers of this Book. The names of various seers and the number of hymns as well as stanzas composed by them are indicated below-

Seer	Hymns	Stanzas
Bârhaspatya Bhâradwaja	59	529
Suhotra Bhâradwâja	2	10
Shunhotra Bhâradwâja	2	10
Nara Bhâradwâja	2	10
Bârhaspatya Shanyu	4	93
Garga Bhâradwâja	1	31
Rijishwa Bhâradwâja	4	63
Payu Bhâradwâja	1	19

As regards the stanzas dedicated to various gods, the position is as follows-

Gods	Number of Stanzas
Indra	279
Agni	162
Vishve Deva	65
Pushâ	40
Indrâgni	25
Ashwni Kumâr	22
Vaishwânar Agni	21
Maruta	18
Saraswatî	14
Ushâ	12
Indra Varuna	11

MitraVaruna	11
Indra Vishnu	8
Go	8
Indra Pûshana	6
Dyâva Prithivî	6
Savitâ	6
Indra Soma	5
Soma	5
Ishada	4
Ratha	4
Soma Rudra	4
Sarjaya Prastoka	4
Brabustaksha	3
Brahaspati	3
Dundubhi	2

Other gods who have been invoked by just one *mantra* are namely; *Dundabhi Indra, Ashwa, Jartni, Ishudhi, Jya, Devabrahmnani, Devbhumi Brahaspat Indra, Dyâva Bhumi Prashni, Dhanu, Pratoda, Brâhman Pitrisoma Dyâva Prithivî Pûshana, Yusdhabhumi Kavach Brâhmanaspati, Rathgopa, Varma, Varmasoma Varuna, Sârathi Rashmi, Hastaghna.*

Seer Bhâradwâja and His Visions

Bhâradwaja, is the seer of the son of *Brahaspati* mentioned as *Bârhaspatya Bhâradwâja*. 59 hymns comprising 529 stanzas, which form the maximum part of this Book. All other ten seers of the Book are his sons along with one daughter called *Ratri*. The names of his sons appearing in it are- *Rijiswa, Garga, Nara, Payu, Vasu, Shasa, Shirambitha, Shunahotra, Sapratha* and *Suhotra*. There is a mention of one *Rishika* called *Kashipa* in the *Sarvanukramni* (indexing) of *Rigveda* as a daughter of *Bhâradwâja* also. There are thus twelve descendent seers of *Bhâradwâja*.

According to *Mahâbhârataa*, *Brahaspati* was the father and *Mamta* the mother of *Bhâradwâja*. There was a dispute among his parents about his custodianship. Later on the king of *Vaishali* took up the responsibility of his upbringing. He became the priest of *Divodâs*, the son of *Sudeva*, the king of *Kâshi*, well known as the founder of *Vârânsi*. When a king Veethavya once defeated this king, the seer provided him shelter and also performed a sacrificial rite for him. This enabled him to be blessed with a son called *Pratardana*. He was a great warrior and ultimately defeated his father's enemy winning back the throne of *Kâshi.*

There is a story mentioned in *Taittariya Brâhman* about the ardent interest of *Bhâradwâja* in the study of *Vedas.* Since he could not complete the study of the vast storehouse of knowledge, he prayed *Indra* who offered him hundred years to complete his task. When he appeared second and third times again on request, the life span was extended for three hundred years and the saint was still in demand for time. *Indra* thereafter materialized three big mountains before him and taking out a handful dust said, 'All your accumulated knowledge like it is comparable with these mountains (symbolizing three older *Vedas, Rik, Yaju, Sama*). Can you think of completing the job in just one life? That is just impossible. You can at present understand this much that *Agni* is the embodiment of all knowledge.' He also revealed to him the secret of *Savitryâgni* (fire leading to sun) mystic knowledge, which ultimately united him with the Sun.

Bhâradwâja was highly skilled in the use of medicinal science. This was also a reason of his comparatively very long life. According to *Charak Samhitâ,* a book on Indian medicine, he also wrote a book called '*Ayur-Veda Samhitâ.*' In *Yetreya Âranyaka* he has been called '*Deerghajivitama*' living. He had learnt grammar from *Indra* and taught it afterwards to his disciples. *Maharishi Bhrigu* was his teacher for philosophy of religions that later enabled him to write '*Bhâradwâja Smiriti.*' According to *Mahâbhârataa* (*Shântiparva 210-21*), he was also a teacher of *Dhanur-Veda* (the science of archery) as well as *Râja Shastra*, Political Science, (58-3) to have subsequently come to be mentioned by *Kautilya* in his famous *Arthashâstra.*

Lastly this seer wrote a comprehensive book called *'Yantra Sarvaswa'*, all encompassing machine. Some part of it has been published by *Brahma Muni* as *'Vimâna Shâstra'*, the science of spacecraft. It mentions about various metals used in the low and high- flying airplanes.

It is thus to be concluded that *Rishi Bhâradwâja* was a great seer- scientist as well as a philosopher, a thinker on humanities and also a great writer on various disciplines like Grammar, Religion, Education, Political Science, Economics, Archery, Medicine and Physics. Book ten of the *Rigveda* further mentions that *'Bhâradwâja* learnt music (*Brahatsâma*) from *Dhâtâ, Savitâ, Vishnu* and *Agni'* (Rik 10-181-2). He is one of the four most prominent Vedic musicians of whom other three being *Gotama, Vâmadeva* and *Kashyapa*. This Vedic vocal music form has the strength of immediate and direct physical results when applied in sacrificial rites in the prescribed manner.

The world vision of seer *Bhâradwâja* is progressive and broad. He does not consider it to be a bondage or a place meant for sufferings. It is neither an illusion nor an unreality, which would render it meaningless. It has a definite and positive strength and status, and it should be properly made use of. The world exists as per divine plan for human beings to attain ultimate good. This superior most design of the Supreme Being operates in consonance with human nature and tendencies. All human quests tend to seek happiness. There cannot be a better place than this world for the fulfilment of this most original and fundamental urge in man. There is water here for quenching thirst, fire for removing cold, air to breathe and food to eat. There are stars and planets and clouds putting gravitation, atmosphere and climate of earth in order. All this happens without any contribution from our side and the abundance of the availability of all that we require could never be disputed. The glorious rising sun, the greenery around us, big snowy mountains, vast oceans and shining starry heaven all could nothing be except the manifestation of One Supreme Soul deeply concerned with us and our happiness. This exquisitely beautiful and bounteous world, according to this great seer, is suggestive of living and enjoying in its fullness. In stanza four of the first hymn of this Book, he rightly advises to' take pleasure in the enjoyable form of the Almighty who is all set to do welfare alone.'[1]

The seer becomes naturally poetic when he starts singing in the praise of the great Lord whose glory is much greater than the earth and heaven.[2] One Who is actually responsible for dispelling darkness around the world,[3] Whose protections extend like branches of a giant tree,[4] Who can take any form he desires,[5] and Who actually is every object and the subject of all creation.[6]

It may be questioned how this Creator who is often likened with human beings never tires, does not become old and keeps tolerating all ills of nature and beings. *Bhâradwâja* has all convincing answers for these queries. According to the great seer, the Supreme is involved in action incessantly which is evident by the full course of nature working under his supreme command. It is also not a dull prosaic activity like a machine either. The seer says that the Creator has 'one action today and the other tomorrow.'[7] Because his own course is so much integrated in an eternal activity of constant change, he is never becoming old under the influence of 'days, months and years.'[8] Lastly the seer has the ultimate assurance to offer which is well available to humanity and all beings. This is also the keynote of all religions and a ground to indicate why he does not inflict miseries immediately to the wrong doers. 'He is father as well as the mother of mankind,'[9] is the declaration.

Divine worship Hailed

The intimate relationship between gods and human beings is the central note of all Vedic lore. As compared to human beings,

---

1 ते भद्रायां सन्द्रष्टौ रणवन्त (4)
2 पुरुमायस्य महित्वं दिव: पृथिव्या: मह्ना अति रिरिचे (231)
3 तम: सूर्येण वयुनवत् चकार (232)
4 वृक्षस्य वया: ऊतय: वि रुरुहृ: (265)
5 मायाभि: पुरुरूप: ईयते (468)
6 रूपं रूपं प्रतिरूप: बभूव (468)
7 अद्य अन्यत् कर्वरं अन्यत् उ श्व: (267)
8 शरद: न जरन्ति, मासा: द्याव: न अवकर्षयन्ति (269)
9 मनुष्याणां सदं इत् मातापिता (5)

gods have power to exercise on forces of nature and have a larger control on the space and time faculties of creation. Human beings on the other hand are gifted with the power of action, *Karma,* devotion, *Bhakti* and knowledge, *Jnân.* These faculties are very important since they bring a man closer to the divine existence and make him blessed with their added capacity of energy and intelligence. Seer *Bhâradwâja* therefore, while invoking fire, states, '*Agni!* If some offers prayers in your praises intelligently, he is protected from all ills and makes progress steadly.'[10] Such an intellect which leads human kind towards attaining divinity is appreciated everywhere. In stanza 85 of this Book, the seer also congratulates such a mind.[11] The other side of this truth lies in the fact that the people of this high intellect are also dearer to god.[12]

Agni, for instance, is worthy of our prayers because he represents vital life force, immortality and is a regular guest of us all. The effulgent Sun, likewise, should inspire a human being to spread light of knowledge like its rays.[13]

Pure and Proper knowledge Advocated

The Vedic seer ardently believes that knowledge is the source of all prosperity. It definitely brings worldly as well as other worldly bliss. It has been therefore advised to acquire good knowledge. According to the seer of this Book, a man of knowledge should be skilled in science (*Pracheta*), should work for the welfare of others, (*Sukratu, Kavih*), must be free from all envies, (*Adhruk*) and should be showing path to others through his light of knowledge.[14] In order to establish the superiority of knowledge, persons having envy with the man of knowledge have been severely criticized and exemplary punishments prescribed for them.[15]

---

10 धिया मर्त: शशमते
ऊती ष बृहतो दिवो द्विषो अहो न तरति (17)
11 त्वे वष्टि धिष्णा धन्या (85)
12 धीवत: सखा (598)
13 विश्वायु: अमृत: अतिथि: जातवेदा: (34), भनुमद्भि: अर्कैं: सूर्य: न (38)
14 ज्योतिषा तम: अन्तर्वावित् अकृणोत् (64)
15 मानुषे जने विश्वेषां यज्ञानां होता हित: (126), होता मनुर्हित: (134)

Yajna Glorified

Like all other seers, *Bhâradwâja* is also a great advocate of sacrificial rite. This act brings glory to a human being (120). Such a person is the true servant of humanity.

This act on the part of human being is also contributory to the divine cause of cosmic development and growth. In stanza 232 of this Book, the performer of this right helps the lord of heaven, *Indra,* live and rule from the state of immortality as 'Yajna increases the longevity of *Indra.*[16] *Agni* being the principal deity of this important rite, it becomes the most celebrated god of the Vedic hymns. Quite evidently, therefore, according to seer *Bhâradwâja* 'Agni* is highly intelligent, efficient and farsighted divinity.'[17]

Behavioural Morality Advocated

Various stanzas of the hymns composed by seer *Bhâradwâja* are suggestive of ideal human behaviour in an elegant society like ours. The ruler, for instance, according to him should be leading the life of a holy person.[18] Human speech should always be sublime and dignified because such people are sure to reach their goals fast.[19] Contempt and criticism of others is a great evil of human society. It does not only increase enmity among people, but also hampers progress of both. The seer therefore has a message to spread in stanza 563 of this Book 'May I never utter ill words for others.'[20]

Health Care

Human body is believed to be the temple of god. Definitely it requires a worthy treatment for it. It is wrong to believe that Indian stress on the life of austerity tend to neglect body. Seer *Bhâradwâja* distinctly advises to worship the body.[21] Likewise in

---

16 यज्ञः इन्द्रं वर्धात् (355)

17 अग्निः प्रचेताः वेधस्तमः ऋषिः (102)

18 राजानः शुचिव्रताः (149)

19 विश्वाभिः गीर्भिः पूर्ति अभि अश्याम् (100)

20 परिचक्ष्याणि वचांसि मा वोचं

21 तव स्वां तन्वं यजस्व (84)

stanza 430, it has been desired that a man should make himself healthy taking proper food grains. It has also been pointed out that the water while benefiting human beings by its purifying effect is also a great medicinal agent for his health. Finally, the seer has a cautioning- 'Keep awake, only persons with awakened intellect earn reputation.' [22]

Holy Cow

In all Vedic literature in general and in this 6th Book of seer *Bhâradwâja* in particular, cows are treated very respectfully. They virtually symbolize prosperity on the material plain and divine height on the spiritual. In stanza 302, the seer says that the 'cows are the real glory' and that 'these cows are virtually *Indra*' [23]. In the next stanza the seer again states that the milk of the cows makes a weak and frail person strong. They turn our home to be a good living home. The milk of a cow, then, is the best food known. [24] This nectar like food keeps death away. (493) Naturally, the seer advises us to keep the cow healthy after taking its due medical care. [25] Even the words used for calling a cow should be sweet and spoken soft. [26] In fact, a cow is the embodiment of a vibrant joy in a house. [27]

---

22 जागृवांस: रयिं अनु ग्मन् (3)

23 गावो भगो गाव इन्द्रो मे अच्छान् गाव: सोमस्य भक्ष:
   इमा या गाव: स जनास इन्द्र   (302)

24 गो अग्रा: इषां: (357)

25 गो-इष्टौ प्र चिकित्स (470)

26 नव्यसा वच: सबर्दुघा धेनुं आ (492)

27 सुम्नै एव यावरी (493)

Important Key-notes from Mandala Six

1.   Man should first harbour to possess divine qualities.

2.   Human looks should be as sacred and sin free as the sun.

3.   A man should get up early at dawn.

4.   The food that has not fallen be consumed.

5.   One should salute and serve by raising hands.

6.   Great deeds are imperishable.

7.   Knowledge helps *Indra* grow up.

8.   Forces controlled by God are many.

9.   His forces of protections never diminish.

10. God manifests in different forms through various objects.

11. Plants should not be uprooted.

12. Friendship should be free from hidden secrets.

13. Man is the issue of Immortal God.

14. Gods lead us on the path of truth.

15. We look for a house around which roam cows.

16. We look towards a home where people behave straightwardly.

17. I am looking for a house that can spare a young man for the battlefield.

1 नर: प्रथमं देवयन्त: (2)

2 सूर: न अस्य दृशति: अ-रेपा: (27)

3 मर्त्येषु उषर्भत् (34)

4 यत् अच्युतं, तत् अत्ति (107)

5 उत्तनहस्त: नमसा आ विवासेत् (171)

6 यानि दाधार, न कि: आ मिमाति (313)

7 ब्रह्म इन्द्रं वर्धात् (355)

8 अस्य प्रणीतय: मही:: (406)

9 अस्य ऊतय: नक्षीयन्ते (406)

10 रूपं रूपं प्रति रूप बभूव (468)

11 वनस्पतिं मा उद् वृह: (498)

12 सख्यं अवृकं अस्तु (499)

13 अमृतस्य सूनव: (558)

14 ऋतावृध: देव: (559)

15 यत् गाव: अनुस्फुरान् छर्दिष: अभिष्टि: (703)

16 ऋजिप्यं धृष्णुं (703)

17 यत् रणे वृषणं युनजन् (703)

Mandala Seven

Seventh Book of *Rigveda* belongs to seer *Vashistha* and his family seers. The names of these seers along with the number of hymns and stanzas attributed to them are given below.

Seer	Hymns	Stanzas
Maitrâ Varuni Vashistha	102	834
Shakti	1	2
Vashistha Putra	1	5

Important gods and goddesses in the order of higher number of stanzas attributed to them are also mentioned below-

1. Indra — 172
2. Agni — 118
3. Vishwedeva — 82
4. Ashwini Kumâr — 56
5. Maruta — 50
6. Ushâ — 41
7. Mitra Varuna — 38
8. Indra Varuna — 30
9. Varuna — 27
10. Indrâgni — 20
11. Vaishwânarâgni — 19
12. Âditya — 16
13. Sûrya — 11
14. Vishnu — 11
15. Savitâ — 10
16. Indra Vâyu — 10
17. Mândûka — 10

18. Parjanya   9

19. Saraswati   8

Some other important gods invoked by a couple of stanzas worth naming are, *Vâyu, Âpah, Brahaspati, Rudra, Bhaga, Vasishtha, Soma, Ilâ, Twashtâ, Ahi* etc.

The central note of this Book is the desire of the general welfare of all living beings. The word *Swasti* standing for general well-being appears in it again and again. The seer prays *Indra, Agni, Varuna, Bhaga, Aryamâ, Dhâtâ, Ashwini, Dyâvâ Prithivî, Vasu, Rudra, Soma, Sûrya, Aditi, Marut, Vishnu, Parjanya, Vishwedevâ, Saraswatî, Gau, Ribhu, Pitar* etc. in the thirty five hymn for a lasting peace.

The famous *Mahâmrityunjaya Mantra* has its origin in this Book only. Three-eyed Lord *Shiva* has been invoked in it for removing the shackles of death for us to live eternally. The mantra reads like this-

त्र्यंबकं यजामहे सुगन्धिं पुष्टि वर्धनम्

उर्वारुकमिव बन्धनान्मृत्योर्मुक्षीय मामृतात् । 7-59-12

The life for the Vedic seer is very precious and the body being a vehicle of it must be protected for long. The following mantra from this Book is the regular prescription for a Hindu in his daily routine prayer-

पष्येम शरद: शतं जीवेम शरद: शतम् (7-66-16)

In stanza 947 again the seer gives expression to the common desire to live hundred years of happiness and strength-

सुवीरा: शतहिमा: मदेम्

Seer Vashishtha and the world of his Visions

There are a number of stories narrated about the origin of *Vashishtha*. He is at times reffered to as the mental creation of *Brahma* but also informed as the son of *Mitravaruna, Agneya* and a manifestation of the Vital Force (*Prana Tattva*). He is one among the seven luminous seers. His wife is *Arundhati*, an ardently devoted wife who occupies a permanent seat along with his husband in the sky near seven stars.

Seer *Vashishtha* comes out to be acknowledged in later mythology as a strong and determined character that not only gives tough fight to his rival seer *Vishwâmitra* but also serves the long dynasty of *Sûryas* right from *Ikshwâku* to *Râma*. He is the glorious master of *Râma*, an accomplished character of Indian mythology in bravery, intelligence and all brilliant human traits.

The most important side of his character is his high tolerance arising out of his pure intelligence of *Brahmnical* order. Although *Vishwâmitra* had an inimical behaviour with him, but he never took revenge and even forgave that seer when he killed his (*Vashishthas*) hundred sons. The Book seven also mentions that *Vashishtha* was in possession of thousand cows and was a great master of knowledge and action.[1] *Indra* used to participate in his *Yajna* even when he was occupied otherwise. The sons of *Vashishtha* crossed river *Sindhu* quite easily by the blessings of *Indra* only. There were a number of demon enemies of *Vashishtha* and *Pârashar* but they could not do any harm to him because of his special protection (7.18.21). *Indra* was able to protect king *Sudâsa* in great *Dâshrâj* war because of *Vashishtha's* powerful *mantras*, as he happened to be the priest of this king as opposed to *Vishwâmitra*, the priest of the ten opponent kings. The account of this war finds place in three hymns (18, 33 and 83) of this Book.

There are names of twelve sons of *Vashishtha* mentioned in *Rigveda*. These seers are—*Manyu, Upmanyu, Vyaghrapat, Mrilika, Vrishagana, Pratha, Indra-Pramati, Dyumnika, Chitramaha, Karnashrut, Vasukra* and *Shakti*. Four seer grandsons, further, are *Vasukrida Vasukra, Vasukarna Vasukra, Pârashar Shâktya* and *Gaurviti Shâktya.*

His sons had visualized the origin of his father in the state of deep *samâdhi*, which finds mention in the 33 hymn of the Book. In the tenth stanza of this hymn, the seer states that *Mitra Varuna* first noticed him in form of a flame prepared to take human body. That was his first state of origin. In the next stanza he is described as born out of the determination of *Urvashî*, the mother.[2]

---

1 इदं वच: शतसा: संसहस्रमुदग्नये जनिषीष्ट द्विबर्हा: (7-8-6)

2 विद्युतो ज्योति: परि संजिहानं मित्रावरुणा यदपश्यतां त्वा
तत् ते जन्मोतैकं (7-33-10)
द्युतो ज्योति: परि संजिहानं मित्रावरुणा यदपश्यतां त्वा
उतासि मैत्रावरुणो वसिष्ठोर्वष्या ब्रह्मन् मनसोऽधि जात: (7-33-11)

Vashistha's Poetry of Nature

Seer *Vashistha* has tremendous love for nature. His 41 stanzas written in praise of *Ushâ*, the dawn, and 50 for *Maruts*, the winds, 9 for *Parjanya*, the clouds and 10 for *Mânduka*, the frogs are some specimen of it. During rainy season when the seer sees clouds roaming in the sky, pouring rains, the flashing of lightening and the blowing of cyclic wind, and hears the rhythmical chantings of frogs, his fanciful imagination becomes active. Although according to Max Muller, *Vashishtha's* hymn on frog (103) is 'clearly a satire on the priests'; the poetry of the text no way gets undermined. Following passage from the text is an ample evidence of its superb poetry of nature-

'When at the coming of the Rains the water has poured upon them as they yearned and thirsted,

One seeks another as he talks and greets him with cries of pleasure as a son of his father.' (103-3)

The seer has composed four songs (vii. 38, 45, 62, 63) in honour of the Sun. The first one begins with the description of the rising Sun. The poet rightly asserts that his songs are sweet. The Sun is beautifully jewelled. He is the brilliant glory of the mid-region. He is brought fourth by his speedy steeds. His golden hands extend unto the bounds of heaven. They are sublime, lovely and easy in their motion. Even the tongue of the Sun is pleasant.[3] The mounting Sun rolls up the darkness as if it were leather. Sun's well- harnessed steed carries the well-rounded wheel onward. The poet thereafter compares him with a falcon that flies through the region. It is all very picturesque. The direct touch of a blissful joy is exquisitely present in the following stanza-

'Refulgent from the bosom of the mornings, he, in whom singers take delight, ascends. This god Savitar is my chief joy and pleasure that does not break the universal statute.'[4]

3　आ देवो यातु सविता सुरत्लोऽन्तरिक्षप्रा वहमानो अश्वै:
हस्ते दधानो नर्या पुरूणि निवेशयंच प्रसुवंच भूम (409)

4　विभ्रजमान उषसाममुपस्थाद्रेभैरुदेव्यनुमद्यमान:
एष मे देव: सविता चच्छन्द य; समानं न प्रमिनाति धाम (530)

The Sun and the Dawn are often most fertile footing for the poetry of the Vedic seers. The most ancient love poetry owes its origin to the Sun and Dawn. Sun following dawn and dawn waiting for sun incessantly is a variously fond imagery here. The sun is the lover and the dawn a beloved. They are following this routine but never getting united like the lovers in 'Ode to the Grecian Urn' of Keats. Seer *Vashishth* naturally is full of appreciation of Dawn, as she is still waiting from the beginning like a most beloved woman not married.[5]

Dawn in fact plays a still greater role in making many myths of the mysterious Vedic concepts. According to Max Muller this beautiful sight to the early gazer and thinker was the 'problem of all problems' According to him "What we simply call the sunrise, brought before their eyes everyday the riddle of all the riddles, the riddle of existence...The whole theory and philosophy of the ancient world centered in the Dawn, the mother of the bright gods, of the sun in his various aspects, of the morn, the day, the spring: herself the brilliant image and visage of immortality."[6]

---

5 तानीदहानि बहुलान्यासन् या प्राचीनमुदिता सूर्यस्य
यतः परि जार इवाचरन्त्युषो ददृक्षे न पुनर्यतीव (7-76-3)

6 Max Muller's Lectures on the Science of Language Vol. II

Important Key-notes from Mandala Seven

1.   People brought up well live unitedly in a society.

2.   Let us not dwell in a house that does not contain sons and grandsons.

3.   The son should be seeking hiqher knowledge.

4.   Let us be free from the misfortune of bearing bad cloths.

5.   Let us never live in ignorance.

6.   Learned people show path to humanity at large.

7.   Learned people should honour the goddess of learning.

8.   A truthful person knows about the origin of gods.

9.   Guests must be served during day as well as night.

10.   Old person, joy seeker, learned and virtuous men- all get up before dawn.

11.   A learned person must be gifted with ample money.

12.   A wise man is the virtual leader of earth.

13.   Wise men are naturally dear to all.

14.   We long for a spacious house, which is comfortable and brings us good repute.

15.   Brave peonle earn reputation by their strength.

16.   People engaged in sensuous pleasures are unaware of divine glories.

17.   The people do not know the extent of the glories of God.

18. May your grace bring us happiness to us.

19. There is one god (*Indra*) all benevolent to human kinds.

20. May we be blessed by your pleasure!

21. May we live in blissful well being!

22. Learned people spread divine knowledge.

23. Wise men do not interfere with the divine doings.

24. I will not use money for committing sin.

25. Like a father to his son, O God, you teach us and make powerful.

26. Sun is the witness of everything in whole universe.

27. The dawn is the daughter of space who nourishes all worlds.

28. We should control our words by our intellect.

29. May cruel ones never rule over us!

30. The goddess of knowledge opens paths of riches and glory.

31. Gracious goddess of learning does all good.

32. No one understands the glories of God.

33. One who is born or is to be borne can never understand your glories.

34. The creator has provided the spacious earth for human beings to live.

1 सुजाता नर: समासते (4)

2 शुने मा निषदाम (11)

3 तनय: अक्षरा समेति (14)

4 दुर्वाससे न: मा दा: (19)

5 सचा दुर्मतये मा प्रवोच: (22)

6 विप्रा जातवेदसा मानुषेषु कारू (32)

7 सारस्वतेभि: सरस्वती सजोषा (33)

8 सत्यतर: देवानां जनिमानि वेद (35)

9 अतिथिं दोषा उषसि मर्जयन्त: (41)

10 जार: मन्द्र: कवितम: पावक: उषसां उपस्थात् अबोधि (87)

11 पुरंधिं राये यक्षि (92)

12 जातवेदा वैश्वानर: (107)

13 सूरय: प्रियास: सन्तु (133)

14 दीर्घश्रुत शर्म यच्छ (134)

15 महित्वा तविषीभि: आ पप्राथ (185)

16 ते महिमानं रजांसि न विव्यंग (197)

17 ते राधा: वीर्य न उदश्नुवन्ति (209)

18 ते सख्यानि अस्मे शिवानि सन्तु (210)

19 देवत्रा एक: मर्तान् दयते (215)

20 ते मही सुमतिं प्रवेविदाम (222)

21 अस्मे प्रियाणि भद्राणि सश्वत (234)

22 विप्र: ब्रह्म जनयन्त (118)

23 तस्य व्रतानि धीरा: न मिनन्ति (119)

24 पापत्वाय न रासीय (131)

25 पुत्रेभ्य: पिता त्वं न: कतुं शिक्ष आभर (138)

26 सूर्य: विश्वा भुवना अभिचष्टे (203)

27 दिव: दुहिता भुवनस्य पत्नी (237)

28 धिया धेना: ऐरयाम: (266)

29 दु:शंस: न: मा ईशत (267)

30 भुवनस्य भूरे: राय: चेतंती (270)

31 भद्रा सरस्वती भद्रं इत् कृणवत् (273)

32 ते महित्वं न अंश्रुवन्ति (276)

33 ते महिम्न: परं अंतं न जायमान: न जात: आप (278)

34 एष विष्णु: एतां पृथिवीं मनुषे क्षेत्राय दशस्यन् (282)

Mandala Eight

This Book contains 103 verses of 1716 stanzas. The principal seer of it is *Kanva* and his traditional disciples who are 66 in number. The principal deity again is *Indra* who has been invoked in as many as 867 stanzas. The next is *Agni* (371) and the other important gods are *Ashwini Kumâr* (198). *Marut, Vishwedeva, Âditya, Soma, Varuna* and *Vâyu* also, prominently figure in it.

Seer Kanva and his family tradition

Seer *Ghora* had two sons, *Kanva* and *Pragatha. Kanva* literally stands for a word dearer to the ear. He should have been probably the family priest of *Yadu* dynasty as one seer *Devâtithi* prays *Indra* to make *Yadu* and *Turvashu* happy (8.4.7). This seer received 60 thousand cows as gift from a lucky king *Kuranga. Kanva* is the seer of *Angirâsa* dynasty. There is a story narrated about *Kanva* in *Rigveda* (1.119.8.). The demons locked up *Kanva* in a dark chamber for him to disclose when there was dawn in order to test his intuition. *Ashwini Kumârs* helped him by playing on *Vina* at the arrival of dawn at that occasion. The descendents of this seer are reported to us to have been greatly equipped in the performance of the rite of *Yajna* (8.1.8)

Mythologically, *Kanva* is the famous godfather of *Shakuntalâ* who has been memorably characterized in the famous drama *Abhigyân Shâkuntalam* by the poet *Kâlidâsa*. This illustrates the theory that the characterization of *Vedic* seers gets developed in later mythological literature. Another great mythological saint *Nârada* is said to be the descendent of the *Kanva* dynasty (8.13).

Seer *Nabhaka* of this family tradition is a great worshipper of *Indra* and *Agni*. 'The great grand earth gets happily settled in the lap of *Indra* and *Agni*' (8.40.4), he declares.

Indra, the Central Figure

Indra is the central figure of *Mandala* eight. He has innumerable attributes. His valour and strength has no match. 'There is no heroism that *Indra* has not performed. Where is a heroic deed which is not attributed to *Indra* only? He the vanquisher of *Vrittra* is famous for his super power since very inception.'[1]

Indra has a strong physique with every limb full of strength. His neck is thick and arms well muscled. His stomach is full of fats. He holds *Vajra* in his mighty hand to hit his enemy hard. This weapon is made of steal. *Indra* is also capable of defeating his enemy by his fists. He is also competent to wage a pseudo war with a clever enemy. He does not envy others, but if his enemy starts envying with him, his destruction is imminent. His army consists of *Maruts*, the wind gods. They help him in every war. Whatever number of the enemy's force, and whatever their strategy of surrounding him from all sides, *Indra* destroys the enemies force completely.

Indra's greatest of all traits is his capacity to annihilate enemies. He is a great protector that way. He is therefore the most adored divinity in a *Yajna*. *Indra* himself is *Shatkritu* (86), the performer of hundred sacrificial rites. He performs actions with full concentration- *Vishwagurta* (108). His deeds aim at the overall good of mankind. He is very rich and keeps on distributing all sorts of riches among his worshippers, particularly those who perform *Yajna*.

The horses and the chariot of *Indra* also find a special mention in this Book. The horses of his chariot are as bright as sun. The two horses are white in colour. His chariot is golden- *Hiranyamaya* (110) driven by two the horses.

Indra is wise- *Vipra* (151), learned-*Surah* (267), seer- *rishi* (283) and righteous- *Satwa* (151).

---

1. कत् नु पौर्स्य अस्ति अस्य इन्द्रस्य अकृतं,
   केन श्रोतमेन न श्रुतम् । वृत्रहा जनुषा परि (616)

Important Key-notes from Mandala Eight

1. Be the devotee of one Supreme Lord and suffer never .

2. My Lord, you are certainly superior to my father but only equal to my mother.

3. May our speech be fulfilling our desires bearing good fruits, positive and ornamented!

4. Who is not demanding from his Lord!

5. Untiring gods forsake lazy persons.

6. One should keep awake for his upliftment.

7. *Indra* keeps earth and heaven wrapped under his might like leather.

8. All our prayers reach One God.

9. Friends must be helped always.

10. Gods have set all worlds in cosmic order.

11. They are always winning whom *Indra* favours.

12. The persons following the righteous path attain reputation.

13. A learned man is at the top of wise ones.

14. One Lord alone governs all creatures.

15. *Indra* is the friend of the performers of *Yajna*.

16. *Indra* also speaks that it is impossible to command a woman's mind.

17. One who performs good deeds with happiness is worshipped among gods.

18. Wise *Varuna* nourishes all forms in heavenly grandeur.

19. The position and place of *Varuna* is unalterable.

20.   He is the right ruler who treats his subjects equally living in different parts of his state.

21.   I am never demanding from my son and my friend.

22.   Supreme are the glories of the Absolute One.

23.   Fire in one form burns out in many ways.

24.   One God alone manifests Himself in many forms.

25.   This fire lives as an immortal among mortals.

26.   A man attains fame by his labour and deeds.

1   अन्यत् चित् मा शंसत मा रिषण्यत

2   मे पितु वस्यां असि- मे माता च समा

3   सर्व दुधां सुदुघा अस्या अलंकृत:

4   ईशानं क: न याचिषत्

5   अतन्द्रा: प्रमादं यन्ति

6   वृधे बोधि

7   इन्द्र: रोदसी चर्म इव सं अवर्तयत्

8   मति: इन्द्रं वनन्वती

9   मित्रस्य सनि:

10 ते विश्वा भुवनानि येमिरे

11 येषां इन्द्र: ते जयन्ति

12 ऋतावान: नमस: पदे

13 जातवेदसं यज्ञेषु पूर्व्य

14 एक: इत् विश्वा: कृष्टी: अभि अस्ति

15 सुन्वत: सखा

16 इन्द्र: चित् तत् अब्रवीत स्त्रिय: मन: अशास्यं

17 मुदा परुकाव्या पुष्यति देवेषु यज्ञिया

18 कवि: स: काव्या पुरुरूपं द्यौ: इव पुष्यति

19 वरुणस्य सदा ध्रुवं

20 परुत्रा: विश्वा: विश: अनु सदृङ प्रभु:

21 सख्यु: पुत्रस्य शूनं मा आ विदे

22 अ-नूनस्य श्रव: महि

23 एक: एव अग्नि: बहुधा समिद्ध:

24 एकं वा इदं सर्व वि बभूव

25 मर्त्येषु अमृत:

26 कृत्वा यशश्वत:

Mandala Nine

Book nine has a special feature as far as the contents of it are concerned. Although it is not entirely the composition of one predominant seer and his family who in the present case is *Angirâ* but unlike all the other Books almost all the hymns of this Book are addressed to *Soma*. He can be appreciated as a nectar juice, Moon, *Brahaspati* or an herb containing the celestial drink which is exhilarating in its effect. *Soma* is much less anthropomorphic deity than *Indra* or *Varuna*. Hence very little is said about his human form or action. Symbolically, *Soma* is the Lord of delight and Immortality. As the Moon-God pours down his ambrosial rain through the sieve of heaven, he is also addressed and worshipped as *Pavamâna* (Self-Purifying), represented by the *Soma* juice as it undergoes purification by flowing through the wool which is used as a filter or strainer. The *Soma* plant is said to have come from heaven to be brought by an eagle.

As the theme of the Book progresses, it comes to be understood that *Soma* is the real Lord of delight as it symbolizes the wine of immortality. Like fire, he is present in the plants, the growths of earth, and in the waters. It is abundantly used and prescribed in the sacrificial rite. It is extracted with ten fingers, which are figuratively called the ten maidens. The *Soma* juice after being extracted is kept in a jar. It is then mixed with milk or water. This admixture is figuratively described as garment or shining robe. Admixture of ghee is also repeatedly mentioned. The pressing stone, *adri*, which is suggestive of the thunderbolt, presses it out. (Indra's weapon is called by this name as well.)

Soma is also addressed as *Brâhmanaspati*, a word applied to other gods, but normally standing for *Brahaspati*, the godly priest. He has a creative power of his own and thus *Soma* comes to represent a creative power by way of *Ananda* or bliss.

It has been stressed and reiterated time and again that the preparation and the sustenance for this divine drink are also necessary for which there are cautioning given in a mystified language. It has necessarily got to be purified after squeezing it so that it no longer disturbs the mind or hurts the body and is also not spilled or lost.

Vedic seers further develop this concept from divine manifestation to the divine person and the *Soma* becomes *Gandharva*, the god of music guarding the world of bliss. The rite of sacrifice involving this process of manifestation is well explained by Shri Aurobindo in his famous work 'On *Veda*' in following words-

"*Soma* manifests here as the offering, the divine food, the wine of delight and immortality, *havih,* and as the *deva,* lord of that divine offering, *havismah,* above as the vast and divine seat, the superconscient bliss and truth, *brahat,* from which the wine descends to us. As the wine of delight he flows about and enters into this great march of the sacrifice which is the progress of man from the physical to the superconscient."[1]

Soma has been called *Amrita,* meaning imperishable. *Soma* is thus that essence of human existence, which is never destroyed. In other words it is that substance of supraphysical from which all objects in the world are made. It is the basic material cause of all objects in nature. It permeates the entire atmosphere and has no form, smell or taste. However all objects which do possess a form, taste, smell or tactile quality come into existence on the basis of contact with *Soma.* According to Shri Rishi Kumâr Mishra, 'When the *Soma* clashes with another and the latter retaliates so that they crush or rub up against each other, a *Bala* is generated known as *Saha. Agni* arises spontaneously from *Saha,* and *Yajna* is the process by which *Agni* is born from the friction and attrition of one *Saha* with another.

'*Havana* is the act of offering a substance to *Agni* for its consumption. When *Soma* is offered in *Havana* to *Agni,* it is transformed into *Agni. Agni* then converts itself into flame and radiates outwards until there is light. When it travels that point, *Agni* loses its fieriness and is transformed back into *Soma.* The continuously recurring *Soma-Agni* cycle is called *Yajna.*'[2]

Agni and *Soma,* according to the Vedic philosophy are two such basic elements, which constitute the cosmic order of creation.

---

1   From 'On the Veda' page 373
2   From 'Before the Beginning and after the End' by Shri R. K. Mishra published by Rupa & Co.

The relationship of these two may outwardly appear to be that of consumer and the consumable respectably, but they are very close allies of each other. The existence and the continuation of *Agni* solely depend on the oblation, the fuel of *Soma* to be poured into it. Lord *Krishna* while describing the constituents of his cosmic form mentions that he is both this fire as well as *Soma*-'I nourish all herbs taking the form of *Soma*, the essence'

पुष्णामि चौषधी: सर्वा: सोमो भूत्वा रसात्मक: (15-13)

See Angirâ and his visions

The name *Angirâ* or *Angirâs* has been generally applied to *Brahaspati*. In Book five seers *Atri* attributes the discovery of fire to this seer (VII-6). It is also to be noted that *Angirâ* is used at places as an epithet in connection with the image of the dawn and the cows. It occurs as a name of *Agni* as well while *Indra* is said to have become *Angirâs*. Even the *Ashwins* are addressed collectively as *Angirâs*. It has therefore been concluded by some interpreters that it is just not merely the name of a family of seers, but is important for the distinct meaning of the word itself. The word is derived from the root *Ang,* a nasalised form of *ag,* the root of *Agni.* In Book X and hymn 62 attributed to *Angirâs* it is said that these seers are sons of *Agni* born in different forms in heaven.

Mythologically this seer is said to be doing such hard penance at one point of time that *Agni* had to keep himself protected in waters. He then went to the seer and admitted 'you are the virtual *Agni*.'

Angirâ finds mention along with *Manu* and *Yayati* in *Rigveda Mandala* 1(31.17) and with *Bhrigu* in *Mandala* 8(43.13). Again in *Mandala* 1(39.9) he figures with *Kanva* and *Atri. Indra* sends *Saramâ* in a class of *Angirâ* (1.62.3). According to a reference of *Mandala* 10.67 *Brahaspati* was the son of *Angirâ. Angirâs* once requested a cow from gods after satisfying them. Gods granted him a cow but he did not know how to be milking it. He therefore took the assistance of *Aryaman* for this purpose (1.139.7). *Angirâs* was also responsible for removing darkness from the world after forwarding his prayer to *Indra* (1.62.5).

Angirâs was initially a human being but got transformed into godhead and attained knowledge (4.4.13). They first mastered the sound principle then they understood metre (4.2.16).

As a matter of fact seer *Angirâ* and his descendents find maximum mention in the entire *Rigveda*. The hymns composed by this school of seers are like the beautiful pillars standing still at the gates of knowledge (1.51.14). He was believed to be the sun of *Brahma* born out of mental determination. His wife is sometimes mentioned to be *Shraddhâ* and at other times as *Smriti*.

Angirâs were responsible for the release of cows under captivity of *Panis*. They had taken the assistance of spy *Saramâ* in this adventure. They destroyed *Panis* by the powers of *Mantras* (1.71.1). *Kutsa*, the son of *Angirâ* narrates the story of the cows stolen away by *Panis* in detail (1.101.5). He was consequently thrown into a well from where he got released by *Indra* (1.106.6). The cows were kept hidden in mountain caves where *Panis* were having their fort. *Angirâs* were capable of knowing the strategy of these dacoits. They used fire as their most effective weapon (2.24.7).

Angirâs were the great exponents of *Yajnas*. They were fond of performing *Yajnas* continuously for ten months. They were the chief priests of king *Sudâsa* of the solar dynasty (3.53.7). They were thus making the two, this and the other world, happy places for the people (10611.60). They destroyed *Balasura* by the strength of *Yajna*.

Hiranyastoop, the son of *Angirâ* is the composer of 1.31 to 35.9.4 and 9.69 hymns of *Rigveda*. Another son *Nrimedha* composed 27 and 29 hymns of the Book 9. Some other important names of these seers are *Hiranyastoop, Saptagu, Sankputa, Priyamedha, Sindhusit, Veethavya, Abhivarta, Samvarta* and *Havirdhana* etc.

The Book 9th containing 114 hymns in all is also known as 'Pavamâna Mandala' because of the purifying effect of these hymns. They are just not the potential prayers of *Soma* but also a deep chemistry in process for pleasing Almighty *Indra* and making human life happier here as well as in the world beyond. Some Vedic scholars believe that all hymns to *Soma Pavamâna* appearing in

Book 1 to 8 were removed and a single collection of thematic unity was compiled in this Book. It may have been the requirement of the chanting priests performing sacrifices. The diction and recondite allusions in the hymns of this Book suggest that they are later part than those of the proceeding Books; but some of them may be early also accompanying the *Soma* ritual. The hymns of the first part of this Book (1-60) are arranged according to the decreasing number of their stanzas beginning with ten and ending with four. In the second part (61-114), which contains some very long hymns (one of forty-eight and another of fifty-eight stanzas); this arrangement is not followed. The two parts also differ in metre: the hymns of the first are, excepting four stanzas, composed in *Gâyatrî*, while the second consists mainly of groups in other metres; thus 68-84 form *Jagati* and 87-97 a *Trishtup* group.

Important Key-notes from Mandala Nine

1.   Fill our houses with food grains.

2.   Let knowledge, speech and language adore our *Yajna*.

3.   Like the very soul of *Yajna*, Soma keeps sharpened the intellect of the priest.

4.   When *Soma* is invoked in a *Yajna* with high poetry, *Indra* prepares himself for attending it.

5.   May earth produce food grain!

6.   Grant us cows, horses, intellect and all type of riches.

7.   You are the highest source of joy.

8.   Bring our friends close who are living away from us.

9.   Bring larger fame for us.

10.   *Soma* is sweet, sacred and purifying.

11.   May you grant food grain at the time of war.

12.   Make uncultured cultured.

13.   Provide us variety of such food which not causing any disease.

14.   *Soma*! Purifier, you remove all obstacles and be seated as a scholar on the seat.

15.   May all our prayers reach you!

16.   Perform your right job becoming strong.

17.   According to all scriptures, friend expects appreciation from friend.

18.   *Soma,* take away the fear which is close, that which is far and that which has just arrived before me.

19.   We wish to live in this earth near heaven without hatred.

20.   May all living beings whether two footed or four, live here in peace!

21.   May earth and heaven protect us by their divinity!

22.   Our description divides the earth and heaven.

23.   The shines of the immortal *Soma* rays never get dim by any force.

24.   Move us away from the sin inflicting torture ahead us.

25.   *Soma* juice gets purified in *Yajna* after squeezing it by hands and grinding on stone.

26.   Priests invoke *soma* with love through prayers.

27.   *Soma,* the purifier, receives well the prayers worded nicely.

28.   Evildoers never tread the righteous path of Yajna.

29.   That wise one watches everything all over in his subtle form.

30.   Incapable performers of actions fall from their positions.

31.   Like the tongue of *Yajna, Soma,* is sweet and lovely.

32.   *Soma* makes the priest happy in the manner a wife does her husband.

33.   You are the Supreme Lord of this world and the worlds beyond.

34.   *Soma,* you are our first abode.

35.   You are the shelter of earth and heaven.

36.   All these worlds have love for you.

37.   You perceive the doings of all human beings on earth.

38.   May we lead a long life in this world!

39.   You are good to me like a very dear friend.

40.   You are very smart in protecting the worthy one.

41.   You protect us always by your noble deed.

42.   This human preparation (*Soma*) is just nectar.

43.   You take joy in different kind of speech.

44.   A friendly ruler does not torture his subjects.

45.   *Soma*! You be seated in the *Kalash* (jar) meant for you.

46.   *Soma* is invoked by intuitive prayers of *Vipra* (learned people).

47.   You are the antiviral of the roots of all diseases.

1   न: वस्यस: कृधि (31)

2   भारती पवमानस्य सरस्वतीला मही इमं नो यज्ञमा गमन् (48)

3   आत्मा यज्ञस्य रंह्या प्रत्नं नि माति काव्यम् (59)

4   परि यत् काव्या कवि (64)

5   पृथिव्या अधि द्युम्नं (77)

6   गां अश्व मेधं स्व: सन (87)

7   मदेषु सर्वधा असि (156)

8   अपस्तस्थुष: उप शिक्ष (168)

9   बृहद् यश: अभ्यर्ष (173)

10   सोम: मध्व: शुचि: पावक: उच्यते (204)

11   भवा वाजस्य संगथे (244)

12   अनिष्कृतं परिष्कुर्वन् (290)

13   अयक्ष्मा बृहतीरिष: (347)

14   त्वं सोम पवमानो विश्वानि दुरिता तर कवि: सीद नि बर्हिषि (393)

15   अभि विश्वानि काव्या (453)

16   वृषा धर्माणि दधिषे (489)

17   अभि विश्वानि काव्या सखा सखिभ्य ईड्य: (549)

18   यदन्ति यच्च दूरके भयं विन्दति मामिह पवमान वि तज्जहि (599)

19   अद्वेषे द्यावापृथिवी हुवेम (620)

20 न: निवेशे द्विपदे चतुष्पदे शं (627)

21 द्यावा पृथिवी न: देवै: प्रावतं (630)

22 उभे द्यावा पृथिवी काव्येन विशश्रये (632)

23 अस्य अमृत्यव: अदाभ्य: केतव: अनुयन्तु (635)

24 पुरा न: बाधात् दुरिता अति पवस्व (639)

25 अद्रिभि: गभस्त्यो: सुत: पवते (643)

26 ई प्रियं गिरा आ रिणन्ति (646)

27 पवित्रवन्त: वाचं परि आसते (661)

28 ऋतस्य पन्थां दुष्कृत: न तरन्ति (664)

29 विश्वा भुवनानि विद्वान् स: अभिपश्यति (667)

30 अप्रभु: कर्त अब पदाति (666)

31 ऋतस्य जिह्वा प्रियं मधु पवते (678)

32 जाया पत्यै इव शेव अधि मंहसे (715)

33 विश्वस्य भुवनस्य पति: राजासि (743)

34 सोम त्वं प्रथम: धामध: असि (766)

35 त्वं द्यां च पृथिवीं च जभ्रिषे (767)

36 तुभ्यं इमानि विश्वानि भुवनानि येमिरे (769)

37 त्वं विश्वत: नृचक्षा: असि (776)

38 वयं भुवनेषु जीवसे स्याम (776)

39 प्रिय: मित्र: न त्वं शुचि: असि (803)

40 अर्य एव दक्षाय्य: असि (803)

41 यूयं स्वस्तिभि: सदा न: पात (816)

42 य: अमृत: मर्त्येभि: नृभि: मृजान: (818)

43 विश्वेषु काव्येषु रन्ता भुवत् (825)

44 मित्रं न धीर: राजा न प्र मिनाति (879)

45 इन्दो! सोमधनं कलशं आ विश (900)

46 विप्रा: मतिभि: सोमं पृच्छमाना: (902)

47 अमीवां अप बाधमान: (910)

Mandala Ten

Much like Book One Book Ten comprises of 171 hymns and the seers composing it are quite large in number. For quite a few commentators of *Vedas*, it seems to be the final addition of Vedic compilation. Its language and subject matters also suggest that it is later in origin as compared to other Books. Its composition is also indicative of the fact that its character is supplementary to the first Book. In spite of its generally more modern character, it contains some hymns quite old and poetic. The important gods of it as usual, are *Indra, Agni,* and *Vishwedeva* invoked in 48, 35 and 30 hymns in number respectively. Other gods worth mentioning are *Ashwini Kumârs, Yama, Brahaspati, Soma, Vâyu, and Sûrya* etc. This Book is most important in the sense that it contains maximum hymns conveying the basic philosophical themes of the Indian mind. It thus has the *Purush Sûkta* (Supreme Being- 90), *Hiranyagarbha* (Golden Womb-121), *Nâsadiya* (Beginning less One-129), *Vishwakarmâ* (The Architect of the Universe-81-82) and *Gyâna* (Knowledge-71). It is famous for its dramatic depictions of *Saramâ Pani* (108) and *Urvashî Pururava* (95) stories and a graphic presentation of the marriage of the daughter of Sun- *Sûrya Vivâha* (85).

Seers

Saptarshi, seven seers in India are traditionally believed to be the forefathers of the whole human race. How were they born? According to stanza 15 of hymn 27 of Book Ten 'Seven seers were born out of the womb of the Creator symbolized as *Indra.* They became the fathers of eight *Bâlkhilya.* Later on nine *Bhrigu etc.* and afterwards ten *Angirâ* seers were born. The seven seers had first invoked *Sûrya* (10.64.5). *Vishwakarmâ,* the divine architect is later stated to be witnessing the places of these seven seers.

Angirâ, Atharva and *Bhrigu* are important fore fathers (10.14.6). *Angirâs* were the chief exponents of *Yajna* by which they assured happiness here and the world beyond (10.61.10). They destroyed *Balâsura* by this technique. They advocated truthfulness in life, were straightforward, behaved like intelligent persons and were good singers of the hymns of *Sâmaveda* (10.78.5).

Evidently the seer of 10/174 is *Angirâs Abhivarta, of 10/113 Angirâsa Dhruva, of 10/172 Angirâsa Samvarta, of 10/164 Angirâsa Pracheta, of 10/128 Angirâsa Vihavya, of 10/117 Angirâsa Bhikshhu, of 10/107 Angirâsa Divya, of 10/96 Angirâsa Varu, of 10/47 Sngirasa Saptagu* and of 10/12-12 *Havirdhan*, another son of *Angirâ*.

The son of *Vâmadeva* called *Brahaduktha* is the seer of hymns 54 to 56 of this Book. The seven stanzas of the hymn 56 are very important for their philosophical approach to the question 'where does soul go after death?' The seer points out in the seventh stanza-'The way people cross the river by boat, the way they move in different directions of earth and the way obstacles are removed following righteous path, I have helped my dead son (*Baji*) get merged into the secret elements of fire, sun and the space.'[1]

Women Seers

An important aspect of the seers of this Book worth notice is this that quite a few among them are females; *Ghosa, Suryâ* and *Vâgambhrani* are some such names.

Ghosa

Ghosha was the daughter of seer *Kakshivân*. She was suffering from leprosy since her childhood. She was not getting married because of this illness. Later on she having been treated by *Ashwini Kumâr* became all right and got married. *Ashwini Kumârs* taught her *Madhu Vidyâ*, the science of secret learning. She thus became a great scholar that is evident by her invocations in hymns 39 to 41 of this Book.

'Great *Ashwini Kumârs!* Your grace has made me fortunate. May your grace shower good rains for my husband to grow good grains from his field! Your kind looks also save my future husband from the violence. Let me find a young and handsome husband to live with him for long.

'The way father offers education to his son, you teach us good lesions. I am ignorant. May your grace save us from the impending misfortune! May you bless me with sons, grand sons and great grand sons to lead a life of success! May I live happily in the abode of my husband!'[2]

---

1 नावा न क्षोद: प्रदिश: पृथिव्या: स्वस्तिभिरति दुर्गाणि विश्वा
 स्वां प्रजा बृहदुक्थो महित्वा ऽऽवरेष्वदधादा परेषु   (567)

2 इयं वामह्वे शृण्पुतं मे अश्विना पुत्रायेव पितरा मह्यम् शिक्षितम्
 अनापिरज्ञा असजात्यामति: पुरा तस्या अभिशस्तेरव स्पृतम् (403)

Suryâ

Suryâ is the composer of 47 stanzas of the hymn 85 of the tenth Book. It is highly poetic and picturesque to see *Suryâ* departing from her father's abode after her marriage with *Ashwini Kumârs*. She was at that time flying in the chariot of her mind whose two wheels were made of the Sun and the Moon. The cloth of high heaven was covering her from above and the winds were leading her long path to her husband's house.

Sûryâ first propounds in the initial five stanzas the significance of *Soma*. It starts with a profound philosophical note of the Vedic order in which the most fundamental principles of cosmic character are illustrated. According to her-

'Truth is the basis on which earth exists and heavens get sustenance from *Sûryâ*, the Sun. *Âdityas* stand secure by the cosmic law and *Soma* holds his place in heaven. Because of *Soma*, the *Âdityas* strong and the earth is mighty. Thus *Soma* occupies an important place in the midst of all these constellations.'[3]

Sûryâ talks about that ideal state of family relationship, which should serve as the best model for any society in any situation. The love and affection for a bride is generally not long lasting as human relationship in a joint family becomes so complex that the house starts dividing as soon as the young persons start getting married off. This is most important because there is a sense of superiority prevailing in the family of the bridegroom where the bride finds totally a foreign atmosphere. Whereas her senses of security needs to be strengthened, she should receive the most humble attention and feel as if she is in the absolute commanding position in the house of husband. It is with this assurance that *Sûryâ* blesses the bride in following words-

'Over your husband's father and your husband's mother you bear full sway

---

3   सत्येनोत्तभिता भूमि: सूर्येणोत्तभिता द्यौ:
    ऋतेनादित्यास्तिष्ठन्ति दिवि सोमो अधि श्रित:
    सोमेनादित्या बलिन: सोमेन पृथ्विी मही
    अधो नक्षत्राणामेषा मुपस्थे सोम अर्हित: (869-870)

Over the sister of your husband and over his brothers as well, your rule be supreme.'[4]

Vâgambhrani

The female seer *Vâgambhrani* was the daughter of seer *Ambhrana*. She was a great scholar of high repute and realization. She had reached that state of realization that she is now identified as the Goddess of Knowledge Herself. 8 stanzas of hymn 125 of this Book she composed are known as 'Vâk Sûkta'. *Vâk* is the speech personified. The word, the first creation and representative of Spirit, she is the means of communication between men and gods. Her identity with the Almighty Cosmic Force is so complete that she is able to claim it in following words-

'Through me alone all eat the food that feeds them-

Each one who sees, breaths, hears, the word outspoken

They know it not, but yet they dwell beside me. Hear, one and all, the truth as I declare It.'[5]

Themes and Techniques of the Mandala

Mandala ten is abundantly rich in the employment of eternal themes of perennial philosophy, cultural evolution and mythological narratives in superb poetry and drama. A few instances from the Book are given below for illustrations.

Concept of Creation

The theory of evolution is supposed to be the greatest revolution of the modern scientific research. Hymn 90 of this Book is perhaps the first recorded document vividly presenting how this evolution took place. The hymn known as 'Purush Sûkta' begins with the description of the Supreme Being Who is ' thousand- headed, thousand-eyed, thousand-footed pervading the universe in all sides, all directions and extending far beyond them. He while transcending all material existence is the Lord of

---

4 सम्राज्ञी श्वशुरे भव सम्राग्री श्वश्वां भव
   ननान्दरि सम्राज्ञी भव सम्राज्ञी अधि देवृषु (85-46)

5 मया सो अन्नमत्ति यो विपश्यति य: प्राणिति य ई शृणोत्युक्तम्
   अमन्तवो मां त उप क्षियन्ति श्रधि श्रुत श्रद्धिवं ते वदामि (125-11)

Immortality. All beings are just a quarter of Him whereas the rest of three-quarters make up immortal supreme regions, which continue to remain abstract. The first one-quarter consisting of animate and inanimate beings comes into existence through the divine energy of the Supreme Being. The dynamic universe (*Virâta*) first came into existence and thereafter in the course of evolution of the universe; the earth and the other habitable planets took birth. Simultaneously, souls also manifested themselves in the form of living beings and thus the life came into existence.

'With the adaptation of the primordial matter into the primeval activities, the changes in the atomic composition of matter also came about. The Vedic seer calls it a cosmic sacrifice,which produced substances to sustain life like vegetation, grains, fruit, flowers etc. that increased both energy and life span and made it possible for animals to thrive.

'Three kinds of animals came into being in this process of creation. Domestic animals like- horses, donkeys, etc, which possessed two sets of teeth, upper and lower; cows, goats, sheep possessing only the lower set of teeth and the most advanced specie human being possessing superior intellect and displaying divine qualities. There were ascetics, hermits and sages well versed in the knowledge of *Vedas* born who contemplated intensely on how to integrate and organize society.'[6]

Hymn 121 called *Hiranyagarbha* (Golden Womb) *Sûkta* depicts the most characteristic exposition of Indian mind, which epitomizes the basic human philosophy of the world. According

---

6 सहस्रशीर्षा पुरुष: सहस्राक्ष: सहस्रपात्
   स भूमिं विश्वतो वृ5त्वा ऽत्यतिष्ठद्द्दशांगुलं
   पुरुष एवेदं सर्व यद्भूतं यच्च भव्यम्
   उतामृतत्वस्येशानो यदन्नेनातिरोहति
   एतावानस्य महिमा ऽतो ज्यायांश्च पूरुष:
   पादोऽस्य विश्वा भूतानि त्रिपादस्यामृतं दिवि
   त्रिपादूर्ध्व उदैत पुरुष: पादोऽस्येहाभवत् पुन:
   ततो विष्वङ् व्यक्रामत् साशनाशने अभि
   तस्मात्विराळजायत विराजो अधि पूरुष:
   स जातो अत्यरिच्यत पश्चाछ् भूमि मथो पुर: (90, 1-5)
   तस्मादश्वा अजायन्त ये के चोभयादत:
   गावो ह जज्ञिरे तस्मात् तस्माज्जाता अजावय: (90,10)

to it, 'In the beginning was *Hiranyagarbha* the seed of all elemental existence. That He was the only Lord of all that was born. He upheld the heaven and earth together. To what God other than Him, could we dedicate our life?'[7]

The Vedic seer here does not represent a school of teacher who goes on issuing commandment or dictates. He has time to pause, think and move along with all other seekers of truth. He is all honest and sincere in his search and can thus express his doubt about the All Knowing Creator-

'Where this Creation has come;

Who holds or does not hold;

He who is its surveyor in the highest heaven

He alone knoweth,

And yet doeth He knows?'[8]

The Hound of Heaven – Hymn 108 called *Saramâ-Pani Sûkta* is a vivid description of the emissary of *Indra Saramâ*, a hound from heaven talking to *Panis* for the return of the cows of *Angirâs*. The *Panis* address *Saramâ* who has found her way to the rocky stronghold in which the stolen cows are imprisoned. Characteristically *Panis* speak in uneven stanzas with the exception of stanza 11 and *Saramâ* in the even. It is necessary symbolically to fix up the identity of *Saramâ* and the exact function of the *Panis*. According to the great Vedic scholar *Shri Aurobindo*, *Saramâ* stands for a power of light and *Panis* the darkness or envious demons, who, have carried off the cows or the rays of light which *Indra* wishes to recover. *Saramâ* leads in the search for the radiant herds and thus becomes the forerunner of the dawn of truth in the human mind. She represents that character of human kind who is a traveller and seeker on the great path and although not possessing her self helps find that which is lost.[9] Her final warning

---

7 हिरण्यगर्भः समवर्तताग्रे भूतस्य जातः पतिरेक आसीत
स दाधार पृथिवीं द्यामुतेमां कस्मै देवाय हविषा विधेम

8 इयं विसृष्टिर्यत आबभूव यदि वा दधे यदि वा न
यो अस्याध्यक्षः परमे व्योमन् त्सो अङ्ग वेद यदि वा न वेद (129,7)

9 From 'On the Veda'

to the evading yet challenging *Panis* is more of a word of caution as the light of truth is just decreed for the true seekers of it-

Hence far away you go *Panis*

Let the cattle come out as the holy law commanded

Kine which *Brahaspati,* and *Soma, Risis.* Sages and pressing stones have found when hidden.'[10]

---

10 दुरमित पणयो वरीय उद्गावो यन्तु मिनतीऋतेन
   बृहस्मतिर्या अविन्दन्निळहा: सोमो ग्रावाण ऋषयश्च विप्रा: (118-11)

Important Key-notes from Mandala Ten

1.   The fire of *Yajna* accepts oblation that is without violence.

2.   We shall move on the path set by gods.

3.   The earth is always rewarding those who move on the righteous path.

4.   Wise men filter out their speech the way flour is filtered out for meals.

5.   Knowledge pours down on the deserving the way a wife unrobes herself for her husband.

6.   Long before gods were born, non-being gave birth to being.

7.   The Creator is all seeing, all facing, all embracing and all moving.

8.   Celestial thoughts were her cover and the earth and heaven her treasuries.

9.   She was moving in the chariot of her fancy with the parasol of high heaven above her head.

10.   I take your hand, my beloved, for your fortune; you live with me in happiness till old age.

11.   You (wife and husband) live here together and never get separated.

12.   O dear one (bride) you live as the mistress of your in laws and rule like a queen in the new house.

13.   The Moon originated from His (Creator's) mind, The Sun from His eyes, *Indra* and *Agni* were born from His mouth and His breath gave birth to winds.

14.   A woman's friendship is never enduring.

15.   I cannot think of him dying as he (Creator) is the destroyer of all.

16.   He is not a friend who cannot spare for his friendship.

17.   He is the One Lord of every one that is born.

18.   I am the Supreme Force of this world and the store house of all riches.

19.   It was neither non-being nor being in the beginning.

20.   It was neither death nor life in the beginning.

21.   Who knows how this world came into being and who can in future claim how this world was born?

22.   Cosmic order and Existence were the first products of His great penance.

23.   Assemble, speak together: let your minds be all of one accord.

24.   The place is common, common the assembly, common the mind, so be their thought united.

1   अध्वरस्य होतारं अग्नि (5)

2   देवानां पन्था अपि आगन्म (10)

3   स्वस्तिरिद्धि प्रपथे श्रेष्ठा (661)

4   सक्तुमिव तितउना पुनन्तों (758)

5   जायेव पत्य उशती सुवासा: (760)

6   देवानां युगे प्रथमे ऽसत: सदजायत (770)

7   विश्वतश्चक्षुरुत विश्वतोमुखो विश्वतोबाहुरुत विश्वतस्पात् (843)

8   चितिरा उपबर्हणं... द्यौ भूमि: कोश आसीद्

9   मनो अस्या अन आसीद् द्यौरासीदुच्छदि: (878)

10 गृभ्णामि ते सौभगत्वाय हस्तं मया पत्या जरदिष्टिर्यथास: (904)

11 इहैव स्तं मा वि यौष्टं (910)

12 सम्राज्ञी श्वशुरे भव सम्राज्ञी श्वश्र्वां भव

ननान्दरि सम्राज्ञी भव सम्राज्ञी अधि देवृषु (914)

13 चन्द्रमा मनसो जातश्चक्षो: सूर्यो अजायत

मुखादिन्द्रश्चाग्निश्च प्राणाद्वायुरजायत (1013)

14 न वै स्त्रियाणि सख्यानि सन्ति (1090)

15 नाहं तं वेद दभ्यं दभत् स (1250)

16 न स सखा यो न ददाति सख्ये (1337)

17 भूतस्य जात: पतिरेक आसीत (1374)

18 अहं राष्ट्री संगमनी वसूनां

19 नासदासीन्नो सदासीत तदानीं (1442)

20 न मृत्युरासीदमृतं न तर्हि (1443)

21 को अद्धा वेद क इह प्र वोचत् कुत आजाता कुत इयं विसृष्टि: (1447)

22 ऋतं च सत्यं चाभीद्धात् तपसोऽध्यजायत (1748)

23 सं गच्छध्वं सं वदध्वं सं वो मनांसि जानताम् (1752)

24 समानो मंत्र: समिति: समानी समानं मन: सह चित्तमेषाम् (1753)

Khil Sûktas of Rigveda

According to the commentator of *Neelkantha*, '*Khil*' stands for the contents belonging to other school of interpretation necessary for grasping the meaning by a different branch.'[1]

Different texts have different sets of *Khil Sûktas* with many common hymns. These *Khil Sûktas* belong to the four nearly extinct *Rigvedic Shâkhâs* namely *Bâskala, Ashwalâyana, Shânkhâyana,* (or *Sânkhyâyana)* and *Mandukayâna,* as evidenced by the fact that many ancient texts like the *Brahmanas* and *Brahaddevtâ* refer to the *Mantras* in these *Khil* hymns. Thus these *Khil* hymns are part of Rigveda in a strict sense and are not merely popular hymns, which were appended to Rigveda by their admirers.

There are a number of appendices of Rigveda available now. The most important among all is -*anukramanian*, the contents which are important from the point of view of understanding the true form of Rigveda. They are virtually testifying the age-old intact form of Rigveda till date.

Two seers- *Kâtyâyana* and *Shaunaka* have contributed immensely in keeping Vedic literature intact in its original form. *Kâtyâyana* wrote *'Rigveda Sarvanukramni'* and *Shaunak* wrote as many as ten analytical books including *'Shaunaka Smriti'.*

As pointed out earlier in the book, Vedic indexing is of two types, Mandalas (Books) and *Ashtakas*. The number of *Sûktas* and *Mantras* based on the *mandal* classification is as follows-

---

1   खिल लक्षण- परशाखीयं स्वशाखायामपेक्षावशात्पठ्यते तत्खिलमुच्यते । म.भा. धां. 323.10 नीलकंठ टीका

Mandala	Number of Sûktas	Number of *Mantras*
First	191	2006
Second	43	429
Third	62	617
Fourth	58	589
Fifth	87	727
Sixth	75	765
Seventh	104	841
Eighth	92	1636
Ninth	114	1108
Tenth	191	1754
Total	1017	10472
Vâlyakhilya Sûktas	11	80
Grand Total	1028	10552

The classification based on *Ashtakas* is also provided as below-

Ashtaka	Sûktas	Mantras	Akshras
First	121	1370	48931
Second	119	1147	51718
Third	122	1209	47636
Fourth	140	1249	49762
Fifth	129	1263	48022
Sixth	124	1650	48212
Seventh	116	1263	47562
Eighth	146	1281	52178
Total	1017	10472	394221
Valkhilya	11	80	3044
Grand Total	1028	10552	397265

Parishishtani Khil Sûktani (the appendix verses) are 36 in numbers consisting of 292 *Mantras*. Some of the well known *Khil Sûktas* commonly chanted are the *Shri Sûkta, Medhâ Sûkta, Sauparna, Shiva Sankalpm,* and *Hridya.* The *Khil* hymns in *adhyâyas 5 through 7* namely the *Nivids, Puroruchas* and the *Prashas* belong to the oldest Rigvedic period. All the 11 *Vâlahkilya* hymns in the Rigveda 8.49 through 8.59 are also part of *adhyâyas* 3 of the *Khil.* The accent marks for the same *Khil Sûkta* found in different books are substantially different. The texture and the language of this part is however discernible from the main in the sense that there are different forms and substitutes available suggesting interpolations added in course of time. *Sûkta* 2 of *khil,* for instance, is supposed to be appended after the last *Sûkta* of *Mandala* 1. This verse deals at length with the poison of insects, scorpion and many other animals. The *Khil Sûkta* invokes *Garuda* and reminds the snake about the promise it gave to *Astika.* It also talks about the seer *Jaratkâru* and remembers the river *Narmadâ* as a protector of the venom of a serpent. There are thus quite numerous references and characters to be tallied with as recent works as *Mahâbhârata.*

Sûkta 11 called *Shri Sûkta* is a very famous verse of the appendix. It is the prayer of the goddess of wealth who while removing poverty and sorrow brings prosperity and fame. The seers of this verse are *Ânand-Kardam-Shrid-Chikleeta* and *Shri Putra.* The gods invoked in it are *Shri* and *Agni.* In the second verse of the hymn, the seer has following prayer to make-

'O *Jâtaveda* (fire), make me feel the presence of *Lakshmi* who will stay here for ever, Who will bestow on me enough gold, cow and horses.'

Laksmi is not merely the goddess of wealth; she is the mistress of all types of wealth, all virtues, goodness, beauty, and psychological and physical perfections in our body. According to the Aurobindonian interpretations and symbols, *gam,* cow symbolizes knowledge, *Ashwa;* horse is the symbol of *prânic* energy needed for executing our tasks. *Purush* means the courage needed to solve all problems in life. It can also mean the soul; i.e. the prayer is for *Lakshmi* to activate our soul forces, which are covered by a veil of ignorance.[2]

---

2 There have been a number of researches of many kinds conducted on this hymn by researchers and scholars. They include from the chemistry of making gold to the reformation of this composition with a view of providing it the original Rigvedic character, as there appeared to be many interpolations in it for them. I was narrated an interesting anecdote by one Vedic scholar Acharya Durgacharan Shukla in this context. Late king Devendra Bahadur Singh of the erstwhile Orchha state once came to him with the information that he had come to hold that only the 9th stanza of the hymn was purely Vedic in character and he would be bringing out the text accordingly. But he wanted his (Shri Shukla's) confirmation for it. Shri Shukla admitted his incompetence for the purpose but advised the ex ruler to contact Shri Karpatriji who happened to be in the town at that time. Shri Singh came back after about an hour and was virtually under tears (he was that way as simple as that!) as Karpatri was just furious on this attempt and warned the king that he was surely doomed to dwell in hell for this act of violating the *Shastra* in an arbitrary manner. This time the king had come to seek Shri Shukla's advice for his redemption. Shri Shukla sent him back to the Swami again, who, he assured, would definitely show him the way. Shri Singh was full of repentance and as usual, Karpatriji told him that the Vedic text including the appendices, is absolutely pure and it has been kept intact historically for the past twenty five thousand years. It is not because such ideas did not come across other scholars but because they had full trust in the tradition of ancient Vedic scholars and their talents.

Brâhmana, Aranyaka and Upanishads of Rigveda

Vedas classify actions and applications into two categories of material and the supraphysical kind. The former one aims at worldly attainments with the application of some techniques to be employed. *Brâhmanas* are those books of injunctions that reveal these techniques and their applications. They describe at great length those actions, which are to be performed with necessary material input to yield the desired results.

There can be hardly any doubt that the oldest hymns that we possess, are purely sacrificial, and made basically for sacrificial purposes. Strictly speaking, the rule regarding the performance of a rite of sacrifice went by the name *Brâhmana* but afterwards the term, which is applied to a single dictum, was applied to the whole collection. Each Veda has a *Brâhmana,* or collection of the dicta of *Brahmana* priests, of its own. It may have taken many centuries before endless number of rites could form themselves into such a regular system of sacrificial rules as we find exhibited in the *Brâhmana*. Thus through the long course of history they came to serve as manuals or the text books to the sacrificial priests. The *Yajna* to these authors was like the latent power of electricity in an electrifying machine, requiring only the operation of a suitable apparatus in order to be elicited. It is supposed to extend when unrolled from the sacrificial fire into which all oblations are thrown, to heaven, forming thus a bridge or ladder, by means of which the sacrificer can communicate with the world of gods and spirits and even ascend to their abodes.

The questions on the age of these treatises is determined beyond all doubt by an astronomical observation provided by the *Brâhmanas* as early as the 12th Century before Christ by the date to be elicited from the observation itself. It is also an historical proof that these texts were definitely complete before the origin of *Buddhism* as the criticism of these rites became an important subject for this cult to evolve.

As regard the subject matter of *Brahmanas*, they basically contain following -

1. *Karmavidhâna* or *Vidhi*, i.e. rules about the performance of particular rites.

2. *Arthavada*. This term comprises the numerous explanatory remarks on the meaning of *Mantras* and particular rites, the reasons why a certain rite must be performed in a certain way.

3. *Nirvâchana*, etymology. Various names of gods and important terms employed in rites have been explained on the basis of their origin, root and grammatical principles.

From a practical point of view these texts were to guide to the chanters of *Mantras* of the *Rigveda* in some of their most important performances; but as regards the theoretical one, the author seems to be intending to instruct them on their profession as well, viz. to make the performer believe that he attains everything he wishes.

Aitareya and *Kaushitaki* are two *Brâhmanas* belonging to the *Rigveda*. The former consists of forty whereas the later of thirty *adhyâyas* (chapters). In the third chapter of the former again, the famous story of *Shunahshepa* is narrated at length, who got transformed into a great seer in the tradition of *Vishwâmitra*.

Aranyaka and *Upanishads* are distinct in the sense that they do not lay stress on the material input and output of such actions. In brief, the way *Brahmanas* form the *Parshishta*, appendix, later part of *Samhitâs,* so do the *Âranyakas* and *Upanishads* also. They form very important links in between. The seers of *Samhitâs* were naturally becoming introverts by this time and they were pondering upon the complicated philosophical issues of their concern. The credit for the development of *Prâna Vidya*, the knowledge of the vital force goes to the *Aitareya Âranyaka*, one of the two *Âranyakas* (the other one being *Shankhâyan Âranyaka*) belonging to the branch of the *Rigveda*. According to this text (2.1.6), whatever *mantras*, whatever, *Vedas* and whatever sounds, all are the various forms of *Prâna*. At least there is one *'Brahadârânyakopnishad* that speaks of both the later category of books. *Âranyaka* literally coming out from the root *'Aranya'* stands for something emanating in or from the forest. They prescribe methods and modes of life for saints and mendicants living in forests. *'Upanishad'* has its root in *'Upâsnâ'* which means to 'sit near.' It is generally translated as 'worship', 'homage', and 'service' or 'offering.' It necessarily involves knowledge, devotion reasoning and thought processing.

The first main category pertains to human behaviour in relation to the world and universe whereas the second one takes human quest for attaining and understanding God. *Upanishads* come at the close of *Âranyakas*. To put it ornamentally, it may be stated that if the *Mantra* or *Samhitâ* part of the *Veda* is the tree, the *Brahmana* is the flower, the *Âranyaka* the fruit (in its unripe stage), and the *Upanishads* are the mellow or fully ripened fruits.

Upanishads are also known as *Vedânta*, which suggests that they form the final part of the *Vedic* literature. As a matter of course, beginning with *Samhitâ*, and then the *Brâhmanas* followed by *Âranyakas* and *Upanishads* should make a complete study of *Vedas*.

Upanishads contain the teachings imparted by a *Guru* to his disciple sitting close by. This long drawn company between the two always proved to be fruitful as it unraveled the mysteries of life and secrets of the other world before the seeker.

As regards the names of these so called commentaries of *Rigveda*, *Brâhmanas* namely are *Yetreya* and *Kaushitaki*, *Aranayaka* also *Yetreya* and *Kaushitaki* and the *Upanishads Yetreyopnishad* and the *Kaushitaki Upanishad*. The *Samhitâ* of the *Sânkhayâna Shâkhâ* of Rigveda is almost lost to us. Only the *Kaushitaki* is available now. The *Bâskal Mantropnishad* from *Rigveda* is also available at present. (A palm-leaf manuscript of the same is reported to be available in a library in Chennai, the capital of the State of Tamilnadu, India)

Yetreyopnishad

Chapter 4,5 and 6 of the second *Yetreyâranyaka* constitute *Yetreyopnishad*. This classic is predominantly dealing with the knowledge of the Supreme Creator. The book consists of three chapters. The first chapter is divided into three and the rest two in one part each. The first chapter explains that in the beginning of creation there was one Being and nothing else. He desired to create formed *Ambha, Marichi* and *Mara* three worlds by sheer determination. He then thought of creating the Governors, *Lokpala* of these worlds and consequently gave form to a person from water. This cosmic individual was bestowed with senses, their objects and the respective ruling deities. When these deities came in the great waters for performing their duties, they felt hungry. They therefore prayed for providing some object that they could occupy and eat with. The God then offered a cow, which they argued that it was inadequate for the purpose. The horse was the second offer, which was declined also. The God thereafter created human being that was unanimously accepted and the deities occupied various places such as speech, eyes, ears and breath. Food grain was also created accordingly but it started running away. The gods tried to hold it through the medium of speech, eyes, ears, breath but they did not succeed. They thus tried to hold it through *Apâna*. Thus when the whole world came to exist, the Almighty One also decided to occupy it Himself. He thus entered into human body through the center of his head. He in this manner forms an integral whole with man but since He is realized as '*Idam*' (this or that) indirectly, He is often called '*Indra*'.

The second chapter talks about three births of mankind – 1 Conceptual, 2 coming out of the womb and 3 Rebirth after father's demise. It is described in it that the heart, mind, knowledge, science, intellect, vision, patience, memory, determination, action, desire etc. are all the names of *Pragyâna* (knowledge). It also consists of the creator, *Indra, Prajapati,* all deities, five basic elements all other kind of species. Thus the Knowledge is at the root, the process and the end of all being.

6

Yajurveda

As suggested by the word 'Yaju' standing for worship, Yajurveda is the compilation of Mantras meant for the performance of the sacrificial rite. Again the mantras of Yajurveda are mainly in prose as against poetic form of the Rigveda or the Sâmaveda. It is also said to be the book of *'Adhwaryu'*, the chief supervisor of the sacrifice as against *hota*, the performer of the Rigveda. In *Vajsaneyi Samhita,* one of its main codes, for instance, the *mantras* have been compiled in order of specified *Yajnas* suggesting the fact that this Veda was to take the form of a textbook for the performer of sacrifices.

According to *Manusmiriti* Rigveda owes its origin to *Agni*, *Yajurveda* to *Vayu* and the *Sâmaveda* to the *Sûrya* . Obviously, the Sun represents knowledge and *Vayu*, the speed. The speed is indicative of action, which in the case of Yajurveda is definitely Yajna, the sacrifice. This Veda, in this manner, is a scripture of a life in action. The action in it is also not confined to its physical part alone. It encompasses the mental, intellectual and the imaginative faculties of human beings also.

Branches

The ancient interpreter of Vedas *Maharṣhi Patanjali* mentions about hundred branches of the Yajurveda.[1] There are, however, only six branches known and available at present. Yajurveda has basically two classifications, *Shukla* and *Krishna Yajurveda*. The *Shukla Yajurveda* has two namely, *Madhyandin* and *Kanwa* whereas the *Krishna, Taittireyi, Maitrayani, Kathaka* and the *Kapishthalkath* branches.

---

1   एकशतमध्वर्युशाखा

Shukla and Krishna Yajurveda

According to the *Shatapatha Brahmana*[2] there are two schools called *Âditya* and *Brahma* representing *Shukla* and Krishna *Yajurveda* respectively. *Shukla* literally means something that is pure. *Shukla Yajurveda* thus is a compilation of the text and *Mantras* only whereas, *Krishna Yajurveda* comprises of illustrations as well as interpretations also. There is a story narrated about the creation of the *Krishna Yajurveda*. *Vedvyâsa* first taught this scripture to his disciple *Vaishampâyana* who in turn preached this to his disciple *Yâgyavalkya*. One day, however, annoyed with *Yâgyavalkya, Vishampâyan* demanded back the knowledge he had imparted. *Yâgyavalkya* vomited out all that he had stored but the knowledge being so precious was picked up by his fellow disciples taking the form of partridges. *Shri Bhâgwat Purâna* (12.6) further goes on to say that after getting so emptied, *Yâgyavalkya* invoked god Sun who, having pleased, preached him *Shukla,* pure *mantras* of this Veda after taking the form of a horse.

One major point in this context worth mentioning is the fact that the *Shukla Yajurveda* became the textbook of the northern India whereas the *Krishna Yajurveda* predominantly influenced south. The later Vedic literature also consequently influenced *Krishna Yajurveda* considerably as compared to the former one.

Subject Matter of Krishna Yajurveda

Out of four branches namely, *Taittariya, Maitrayani, Kathak* and *Kapisthal –Kathav* available of this *Yajurveda* now, *Taittariya Samhita* is well known and important. There are seven divisions of this book, which are divided in 44 chapters. These chapters are further divided into 631 heads. The subject matter of this text is exclusively the rituals and their detailed procedure.

The first division deals with the '*Darsh Purna Mâsa Yajna'.* It also discusses the *mantras* of *Agnishtom Vajpeya* and *Râjsuya Yajna* along with the procedural rituals necessary for it. The second division begins with the animal rites. It prescribes *Yajnas* for the

---

2 आदित्य नीमानि शुक्लानि यजूंषि
वाजसनेयेन याज्ञवल्क्येनाख्यायन्ते (श.14.9.5.33)

purposes like progenies victory, glory etc. It has been discussed at length what procedure and which mantras are appropriate for targets like glory, realization, victory over enemy, enlistment and securing place in heaven. The third division deals with the supplementary acts necessary in *Somyâg*. There is the detailing of *mantras* of the construction of altar and the selection of fire. The fifth division elaborately tells about the procedure of *Ashwamedh*. The sixth contains a variety of information such as the initiation of an aspirant, the selection of site and containers for the sacrifice and the donations to be given afterwards. The seventh is associated with the sacrifice called *Jyotishtom*.

Subject matter of Shukla Yajurveda

Another name for *Shukla Yajurveda* is *Vâjseneyi Samhita* because *Vâjseneyi Yâgyavalkya* was its first preacher. It has two branches known as *Kanva* and *Madhyandin*. Ordinarily all references made to *Yajurveda* pertain to it only. It has forty chapters. The first three chapters deal with the *mantras* regarding *darsh*, *paurnamasa*, *agnihotra* and *chaturmâs*. From fourth to tenth chapter there is the compilation of *mantras* pertaining to *Somayâga*, *Vâjpeya, and Râjsûya* etc. In chapters beginning from eleven unto eighteen, exhaustive details of the construction of altar for sacrifice are given. The procedure has been called *Agni chayan*, the selection of fire. The altar is to be made by 10800 bricks, which are collected from the specified places specially prepared in form prescribed. Its shape conforms to a bird expanding its wings. There are spiritual meanings ascribed to the number and the forms of these bricks interestingly.

The sixteenth chapter is dedicated to Lord *Shiva* who initially being *Rudra* in *Rigveda* attains attributes of an all potential powerful Lord working for the general well being. In 19-21 chapters, there is the procedure laid down for *Sautramani Yajna*. It has been said that *Indra* became ill because he drank too much *Soma*. *Ashwini Kumars* cured him from this illness. This sacrifice is for the persons who have been usurped from the throne. Chapters 22 to 25 throw light on the *mantras* related to *Ashwamedha* sacrifice. This sacrifice is prescribed for becoming the monarch of the whole world and has been dealt in detail in *Shatpath Brahman* and

Kâtyâyan Shrotsutra. Chapters 26 to 29 are the compilation of supplementary *mantras* prescribed for the completion of various sacrifices. The oblations here have symbolical meanings. The sacrifice thus is not any physical rite but an inner action of spiritual imagination.

The 31st chapter comprises of the famous *Purush Sûkta,* which is known for its spiritual height all the world over. It is worth remembering that while *Rigveda* contains 16 *mantras* in this *Sûkta, Yajurveda* has those 22 in number and a different order. In the beginning of chapter 32, there are some *mantras* of *Hiranyagarbha Sûkta.* In the beginning of 34th chapter figures the famous *Shiva Samkalpa Sûkta.* This hymn analyses deeply with an obvious scientific accuracy how powerful the mind is. Human mind, the hymn says, travels fast while awake or asleep and is the light of all lights. It is present in past, present and future alike. Its power is well symbolized by *Rik, yaju* and *Sam* Vedas. The Vedic seer thus, aware of its immense potential, wishes the mind to have always desires of doing well. The thirty- fifth chapters are a compilation of *mantras* pertaining to *Pitrimedh,* the sacrifice for the welfare of departed forefathers. From 36 to 38 chapters is the description of *pravargya yâga* in which a cauldron is put on flames and when it becomes red due to fire, it is worshipped like sun. The milk is boiled thereafter and offered to *Ashwin.*

The last chapter of the *Shukla Yajurveda* is *Ishâvâsyopnishad* complete as such. It is the smallest and the first of all *Upanishads* and its text is directly borrowed one from the *Yajurveda.* The last *mantra* of this chapter states that the face of truth is hidden behind a golden jar.[3]

Chapters 1 to 25 of Yajurveda are supposed to be original by the scholars. Even by tradition, 10 chapters, chapter 26 to 35 are believed to be later interpolations. According to western scholars, only the first eighteen chapters are original as they represent a true prose and verse character of this Veda. Indian scholars, however, do not agree with this contention. According to to them entire *Yajurveda* is a queer combination of prose and verse.

---

3 हिरण्मयेन पात्रेण सत्यस्यापिहितं मुखम्

It is true that *Yajurveda's* central theme is the performance of the ritual of sacrifice. The famous *Purush Sûkta* declares *Yajna* to be the first and foremost *Dharma*, way of life. This very act is at the basis of all creation. *Atharvaveda* further points out that the sacrifice is naval point of Creation.[4] However, this does contain a lot about psychology, philosophy, spiritualism and environment. Thus *Yajurveda,* like other three *Vedas* represents a holistic approach of life and society aiming at achieving perfection in it.

Important Sûktas of Atharvaveda

Rudra Sûkta

Chapter sixteen of *Yajurveda* is wholly dedicated to *Rudra* whose form as a benefic god as compared to fierce one of *Rigveda* is quite developed in it. The composition of this hymn is emphatically woven in familiar Vedic meters in an exquisite rhythmic flow. *Rudra,* to whom there are salutations made from all sides is a queer combination of all attributes, good and at times evil as he is the virtual commander of all forces. He is a great protector of those who take refuge in him. Simultaneously, he exercises due control over, thieves, spies, smugglers, dacoits, exploiters and cruel rulers.[5] He is present in all beings, whether sleeping or awake, whether static or in move. He is the very form of an assembly, is the chair person, and is himself the army, the commander in chief of it, a charioteer, the pot maker, the sculptor, the black smith and a scholar at the same time. *Rudra's* form in this manner, is fairly matching with the cosmic form of *Nârayâna* of the *Purush Sûkta*. However, it is to be noted that *Rudra* well a personal and subjective god whose benefic role for an individual and the society is remarkably noted.

Purush Sûkta

The first statement of evolution of society and culture in the world has its origin in the 90th hymn of the tenth *Manadala*

---

4 प्रजापतिश्चरति गर्भे अन्तरजायमानो बहुधा वि जायते
तस्य योनिं परि पश्यन्ति धीरस्तस्मिन् ह तस्थुर्भुवनानि विश्वा 31-19
5 नमो वंचिते परिवंचते स्तायूनां पतये नमो नमो निषंगिणे इषुधिमते
तस्कराणां पतये नमो नमो निषंगिणे ककुभाय स्तेननां पतये नमो
नमो निचेरवे परिचरायां रण्यानां पतये नमः ।40.20

of *Rigveda*. It has sixteen stanzas in it. The thirty-first chapter of *Yajurveda* while reproducing all sixteen stanzas in a little different order further adds up six more stanzas to it. The hymn begins with the description of the Almighty Supreme Person who exists enveloping the whole manifest universe, cognizing through every mind (literally head), seeing through every eye and working though every limb (literally foot) while transcending the universe as well. Essentially, the whole universe is He Himself; whatever was, whatever is, and whatever will be- all are his manifestation. It is He who confers on all immortality by which alone they live.

The existence of this Supreme Being is far beyond the realm of the world as only a part (literally one fourth) has manifested in the form this universe out which have emanated the living and non-living beings. This world came to be evolved in stages. From the First and Foremost one emerged the Cosmos, called *Virâj* (technically all-pervading). The first- born Being gradually grew; he created first this earth and then the various bodies, both divine and demonic. *Devâs* then performed a sacrifice. This First and the foremost person himself became the sacrificial offering. The spring became the mustered butter, the summer the faggots and the autumn the rice offering. Out of this sacrifice appeared *Rik, Yajur* and *Sâma Mantras* and various Vedic meters. Again, from this sacrifice only sprang up the horse (having one row of teeth) and other animals having two rows of teeth, different varieties of cows, goats and ewes.

Coming down to the evolution of human society, the hymn exclaims ' One cannot imagine how much thought went before projection of human beings! Which of the limbs of the Supreme Person could represent which section of man, what could be his head, the two hands, the two thighs, and the two feet?' It came to be so determined, afterwards, that the *Brahmans* could represent the head of the social being whereas *Kshatriyas* the arms, *Vaishya* the thighs and the *Shudra* the feet. From Him alone were born luminous beings and bodies- the moon from mind, the sun from eyes, fire and *Indra* from mouth and the wind god from the breath. Likewise, the space emerged from His naval, the world of gods from his head, the earth from His feet and the various quarters from His ears. This knowledge of the Cosmic Form of the Creator fills Vedic seer with great joy and he declares this that after understanding the Supreme One in this manner 'a person verily attains immortality- there is no other way for spiritual perfection.'

In conformity of its sculpture and design, *Yajurveda* has its characteristic conclusions to draw in the additional stanzas of it. It points out that although the Creator is above all life and death, but He incarnates in various forms the secrets of which are known to only great seers like *Marichi*. Sun is one such visible god who when understood well, a man become capable to even control gods. *Laxmi,* the goddess of wealth is His wife, the day and night His arms, heavenly stars His forms and the earth, heaven and the space live in Him. Such Omnipotent and Omniscient God must redeem us here and now and bestow all happiness on us.[6]

Shiva Samkalpa Sûkta

First seven stanzas of chapter thirty-four of the *Yajurveda* are known as *Shiva Samkalpa Sûkta.* They speak about the power

---

6 सहस्रशीर्षा पुरुष: सहस्राक्ष: सहस्रपात्
   स भूमिं विश्वतो वृत्वात्यतिष्ठद्दशाङ्गुलम्। 1।
   पुरुष एवेदं सर्वं यद्भूतं यच्च भव्यम्
   उतामृतत्वस्येशानो यदन्नेनाति रोहति ।2।
   एतावानस्य महिमातो ज्यायाँश्च पुरुष:
   पादोऽस्य विश्वा भूतानि त्रिपादस्यामृतं दिवि।3।
   त्रिपादूर्ध्व उदैत्पुरुष: पादोऽस्येहाभवत् पुन:
   ततो विष्वङ् व्यक्रामत् साशनानशने अभि।4।
   तस्माद्विराळजायत विराजो अधि पूरुष:
   स जातो अत्यरिच्यत पश्चाद्भूमिमथो पुर:।5।
   तस्माद्यज्ञात् सर्वहुत: सम्भृतं पृषदाज्यम्
   पशून् तांश्चक्रे वायव्यानारण्यान् ग्राम्याश्च ये ।6।
   तस्माद्यज्ञात् सर्वहुत ऋच: सामानि जज्ञिरे
   छन्दांसि जज्ञिरे तस्माद्यजुस्तस्मादजायत ।7।
   तस्मादश्वा अजायन्त ये के चोभयादत:
   गावो ह जज्ञिरे तस्मात् तस्माज्जाता अजावय: ।8।
   तं यज्ञं बर्हिषि प्रौक्षन्पुरुषं जातमग्रत:
   तेन देवा अयजन्त साध्या ऋषयश्च ये ।9।
   यत्पुरुषं व्यदधु: कतिधा व्यकल्पयन्
   मुखं किमस्य कौ बाहू का ऊरू पादा उच्येते ।10।
   ब्राह्मणोऽस्य मुखमासीद्बाहू राजन्य: कृत:
   ऊरू तदस्य यद्वैश्य: पद्भ्यां शूद्रो अजायत ।11।
   चन्द्रमा मनसो जातश्चक्षो: सूर्यो अजायत

of mind in an extreme scientific order. Analyzing the individual mind in order of actual growth, the collective mind duly figures here as the proper cause of sequential creation. This hymn basically aims at developing the positive strength of mind for the general well being.

The mind which travels quite far when awake and also takes us much farther when one is asleep; one that is brighter than the affluent, may always make us full of determinations of general well being.

The mind that helps wise people engaged in noble deeds perform *Yajna,* one that dwells in the centre of all living beings' body and the soul, may always make us full of determinations of general well being.

The mind that is intelligent, conscious and patient and dwells among living beings in an ever lasting bright form and without the help of which any action can never be performed; may that mind make us full of determination for the general well

मुखादिन्द्रश्चाग्निश्च प्राणाद्वायुरजायत ।12।

नाभ्या आसीदन्तरिक्षं शीष्र्णो द्यौः समवर्तत

पद्भ्यां भूमिदिशः श्रोत्रात् तथा लोकां अकल्पयन् ।13।

यत्पुरुषेण हविषा देवा यज्ञमतन्वत

वसन्तो अस्यासीदाज्यं ग्रीष्म इध्मः शरद्धविः।14।

सप्तास्यासन् परिधयस्त्रिः सप्त समिधः कृताः

देवा यद्यज्ञं तन्वाना अबध्नन् पुरुषं पुरुषं पशुम् ।15।

यज्ञेन यज्ञमयजन्त देवा-

स्तानि धर्माणि प्रथमान्यासन्

ते ह नाकं महिमानः सचन्त

यत्र पूर्वे साध्याः सन्ति देवाः ।16।

अद्भयः सम्भृतः पृथिव्यै रसाच्च विश्वकर्मणः समवर्तताग्रे

तस्य त्वष्टा विदधद्रूपमेति तन्मर्त्यस्य देवत्वमाजानमग्र ।17।

वेदाहमेतं पुरुषं महान्तमादित्यवर्णं तमसः परस्तात्

तमेव विदित्वाति मृत्यमेति नान्यः पन्था विद्यतेऽनाय ।18।

प्रजापतिश्चरति गर्भे अन्तरजायमानो बहुधा वि जायते

तस्य योनिं परि पश्यन्ति धीरास्तस्मिन् ह तस्थुर्भुवनानि विश्वा ।19।

यो देवेभ्य आतपति यो देवानां पुरोहितः

पूर्वो यो देवेभ्यो जातो नमो रुचाय ब्रह्मये ।20।

रुचं ब्राह्मं जनयन्तो देवा अग्रे तदब्रुवन्

यस्त्वैवं ब्राह्मणो विद्यात्तस्य देवा असन् वशे ।21।

श्रीश्च ते लक्ष्मीश्च पत्न्यावहोरात्रे पार्श्वे नक्षत्राणि रूपमश्विनौ व्यात्तम्

ठष्णान्निषाणामुं म इषाण सर्वलोकं म इषाण ।22।

being.The mind which encompasses all elements of past, present and future and that which performs sacrifice (action) through seven agents (five senses, mind and intellect), may it make us full of determination for the general well being.The mind that keeps *Richas* (stanzas of *Rigveda*), that keeps *Sâma, Yajush* in it the way spokes dwell within a wheel of a chariot and that keeps interwoven all the conscious living beings- may that mind make us full of determination for the general well being.

The way a goodcharioteer takes speedy horses farther away, the mind carries human beings this or that way, the ageless potent mind that dwells in the heart may make us full of determination for the general well beings.

Ishopnishad

Adhyâya forty of *Yajurveda* is a complete philosophy and thus characteristically finds a place among the category of *Upanishads*. It has virtually come to be known as *Ishopnishad* separately. Its deep philosophy combines seemingly different and even opposite ideals of knowledge and action of the world. It is indeed the central note of the Indian philosophy. Further, the philosophy of this hymn suggests that the ideal of the Vedic seer was never one sided but one of a full and complete cycle of birth. Mahatma Gandhi drew lot of inspiration from this by reciting it in his every day prayers. Ravindra Nath Tagore, the noted poet and the nationalist humanitarian was also very fond of it. They naturally

---

7   यज्ज्ञाग्रतो दूरमुदैति दैवं तदु सुप्तस्य तथैवैति
दूरङ्गमं ज्योतिषां ज्योतिरेकं तन्मे मन: शिवसंकल्पमस्तु ।1।
यंन कर्माण्यपसे मनीषिणो यज्ञे कृण्वन्ति विदथेषु धीरा:
यद्पूर्वं . यक्षमन्त: प्रजानां तन्मे मन: शिवसंकल्पमस्तु ।2।
यत्प्रज्ञानमुत चेतो धृतिश्च यज्ज्योतिरन्तरमृतं प्रजासु
यस्मान्न ऋते किं चन कर्म क्रियते तन्मे मन: शिव संकल्पमस्तु ।3।
यंनेदं भूतं भुवनं भविष्यत् परिगृहीतममृतेन सर्वम्
येन यज्ञस्तायते सप्तहोता तन्मे मन: शिवसंकल्पमस्तु ।4।
यस्मिन्नृच: साम यजूषि यस्मिन् प्रतिष्ठिता रथनाभाविवारा:
यस्मिश्चित्तं सर्वमोतं प्रजानां तन्मे मन: शिवसंकल्पमस्तु।5।
सुषारथिरश्वानिव यन्मनुष्यान्नेनीयते भीशुभिर्वाजिने इव
हृतप्रतिष्ठं यदजिरं जविष्ठं तन्मे मन: शिवसंकल्पमस्तु।6।

drew ample strength from the practical philosophy of it and came out victorious facing many challenges in life.

There are only seventeen stanzas in it. The first stanza makes a statement of fact, which is the essence of the hymn. The following sixteen stanzas provide various explanatory notes and elaborate the theme.

According to the first *mantra*, thus, all that exists in this world of movement in the universal motion, whether big or small, whether sentient or insentient, God envelops it all. The innumerable forms and names seemingly real al around, in essence are one and the same. There is a commandment following this – you should enjoy after renunciation (40.1). It suggests that one sided enjoyment or renunciation, both are not proper. One should not keep his eye centered on the corpse like a vulture flying high in the heaven. This is being all greedy. You should not wish to acquire other's money. Does one really own it? That which can neither be owned nor possessed better need to be renounced. Thus even when you use and enjoy it, you can be very well free from that possessive spirit which binds you with an unreal object.

It may be concluded that if we can neither posses nor enjoy in this world, what is the use of living and acquiring things and property here? The Vedic seer, however, suggests that living for hundred years in this manner alone has to be our aspiration. It is certainly not any action, which binds human beings. It is the attachment with an action or the fruit thereof that binds.

Those who are famous for their physical strength and strive only for that are shrouded in the darkness of ignorance. They virtually kill themselves and join the ranks of these ignorant ones after they die. Killing him self here is not suicide literally. If we have confined our ever blissful and eternal real form into a pitiable lamenting human being, we are our own killers. If the body has become a reality and the soul unreal, we are the slayers of or souls.

The supreme godhead is one. It is unmoving but swifter than the mind. It makes others move, but it does not move itself. It is very far and yet it is certainly very near. It is present in everything and it is also outside everything. One, who visualizes this God inside and outside every element, never doubts this truth. One who attains this special knowledge, how shall he be deluded, whence shall he have grief who sees everywhere oneness?

The Omniscient God has no body nor does He have any senses. He is pure and energetic, untouched by sin. He sees everything and He knows everything. He has preordained the destiny of all in the prescribed path.

A person who is striving for the independence of individual entity, *Avidya*, is sure to get shrouded in the darkness of ignorance. But he plunges into a greater darkness, who devotes himself to the knowledge, *Vidya* alone. It means that even after understanding the true nature of self, if one continues to ignore the out side world of action, he will be shrouded by a greater darkness. Still the fruits of pursuing spiritual knowledge are certainly distinct and that verily is the message we have received from the wise men of past.

The terms *Vidyâ* and *Avidyâ* used here have been interpreted in various ways. Ordinarily, *Vidyâ* is the knowledge of the true self and the opposite of it is *Avidyâ*. What has been stressed in it is the fact that the mere knowledge is not the right course. One should be capable of applying his knowledge into actions.

There are two terms *Sambhuti* and *Asambhuti* used in the *Mantra* twelve again. According to the interpretation of *Shankrâchârya* they stand for the action and cause respectively. Sri Aurobindo interprets them as birth and non-birth. It has been stressed while concluding in *Mantra* fourteen that the real learned is one who has the proper knowledge of the self as well as of the world. It is through the right knowledge of the world that he can overcome death and through the knowledge of the self he is sure to attain immortality.

Thus from *Mantra* nine to fourteen it has been advised that the right way of living on earth is to live a life of activity following the true path of knowledge. The last three *Mantras* are virtually prayers. The seer is not an ordinary devotee in it. He is a realized soul. He is offering his prayers on behalf of us all.

The fifteenth stanza is the prayer for living up a complete life. The seer prays that his soul, which is like air should get merged in the collective air. The self should get merged in the higher self. We have to think about the deeds we have performed. It is also suggested by some interpreters that the deeds of God are worth remembrance.

In the sixteenth *Mantra*, God has been invoked in the form of fire. Fire lights everything up. 'Show us the path along which we may be able to elevate ourselves. Remove the sins that may be resulting from our evil acts. We bow down in obeisance before you and chant your praise.'

'The face of Truth is covered with a brilliant golden lid; you remove it, O God, for us to have the right vision of the Truth.' (40.17)

The very next stanza is indicative of the fact that the lid has been removed and the seer is having complete vision of the Truth affluent like Sun –

'The luster which is the most blessed form of all, I am beholding in you. The Purush (Lord) there and there, That I am.'[8]

---

8 ईशावास्यमिदं सर्व यत्किं च जगत्यां जगत्
तेन त्यक्तेन भुंजीथा मा गृधा कस्य स्वद्धिनम् ।
कुर्वन्नेवेह कर्माणि जिजीविषेच्छतं समा:
एवं त्वयि नान्यथेतोऽस्ति न कर्म लिप्यते नरे
असुर्या नाम ते लोका अन्धेन तमसावृता:
तांस्ते प्रेत्यापि गच्छन्ति ये के चात्महनो जना:
अनेजदेकं मनसो जवीयो आप्नुवन् पूर्वमर्शत्
तद्भवतोऽन्यानत्येति तिष्ठत्तस्मिन्नपो मातरिश्वा दधाति
तदेजति तन्नैजति तद्दूरे तद्वन्तिके
तदन्तरस्य सर्वस्य तदु सर्वस्यास्य बाह्यत:
यस्तु सर्वाणि भूतान्यात्मन्नेवानुपश्यति
सर्व भूतेषु चात्मानं ततो न वि चिकित्सति
यस्मिन्सर्वाणि भूतान्यात्मैवाभूद्द्विजानत:
तत्र को मोहा क: शोक एकत्वमनुपश्यत:
स पर्यगाच्छुक्रमकायमव्रणमस्नाविरं शुद्धंपापविद्धम्
कर्विमनीषी परिभू: स्वम्भूर्याथातथ्यतोऽर्थान् व्यदधाच्छाश्वतीभ्य: समाभ्य:।8।
अन्ध: तम: प्रविशन्ति येऽसंभूतिमुपासते
ततो भूय इ वते तमो य उ संभूत्यां रता: ।9।

अन्येदवाहु: सम्भवादन्यदाहुरसम्भवात्
इति षुश्रुम धीराणां यं नस्तद्विचचक्षिरे ।10 ।
सम्भूर्तिं च विनाशं च यस्तदवेदोभयं सह
विनाशेन मृर्त्यं तीर्त्वा सम्भूत्यामृतमश्नुते ।11 ।
अन्ध: तम: प्र विशन्ति ये ऽविद्यामुपासते
ततो भूय इ वते तमो य उ विद्यायां रता: ।12 ।
अन्यदेवाहुर्विद्याया अन्यदाहुरविद्याया:
इति श्रुश्रुम धीराणां ये नस्तद्विचचक्षिरे ।13 ।
विद्या चाविद्यां च यस्तद्वेदोभयं सह
अविद्यया मृत्यं तीर्त्वा विद्ययाऽमृतमश्नुते ।14 ।
वायुरनिलममृतमथेदं भस्मान्तं शरीरं
ओऽम् क्रतो स्मर क्लबे स्मरं कृतं स्मर । 15 ।
अग्ने नय सुपथा राये अस्मान्विश्वानि देव वयुनानि विद्वान्
युयोध्यस्मज्जुह्राणमेनो भूयिष्ठां तेनम उक्तिं विधेम ।16 ।
हिरण्यमयेन पात्रेण सत्यस्यापिहतं मुखम्
योऽसावादित्ये पुरुष: सोऽसावाहम् ।

ओऽम् खं ब्रह्म । 17 ।

7

Sâmaveda

Lord Krishna in *Bhagavad-Gîta* characteristically points out that he is *Sâmaveda* the Vedas.[1] According to *Manu, Sâmaveda* is related to the Sun in its origin. In other words, this Veda is as important as the Sun in its brightness. It is suggestive of its prominent place in the original Vedas, i.e. *Rik, Sâm* and *Yajush.*

Rigveda is in the form of verse, *Yajurveda* predominantly in prose but *Sâmaveda* is all-lyrical. Again, *Rigveda* is related to knowledge, *Yajurveda* to action and the *Sâmaveda* to devotion. *Rigveda* itself makes a mention of *Sâmaveda* at various spots. At one place it advises *Brahaspati* to be invoked with the prayers from *Sâmaveda.*[2] It has been emphasized at other place that one who keeps awake, he attains '*Sâma.*[3] In *Atharvaveda,* further, it is stated that the *mantras* of *Sâma* are the hair of the Almighty God.[4] *Chhândogyoupanishad* describes *Yajurveda* to be such a flower, which is full of nectar and is surrounded by the singing bees. (3.3.1-2)

Historically speaking, there are some scholars who believe that at a time when *Yajnas* were being performed continuously for long, the rhythmical singing inspired by *Samâveda* was a great source of respite and inspiration. It could well be compared with cultural programmes of present times which are scheduled to supplement the long staggered exercises of routine and compulsion.

---

1 वेदानां सामवेदोऽस्मि । (गीता 10.22)
2 बृहस्पति सामभिऋक्वो अर्चतु (ऋ.10.36.5)
3 यो जागार तमु सामानि यान्ति (ऋ.5.44.14)
4 सामानि यस्य लोमानि (अ. 9.6.2)

According to the *Sâma* scheme of music, the melody in it starts in a very high pitch. It is then gradually brought down to a lower pitch. This process helps mind attain the state of tranquillity very fast. Modern music has many up and down movements and is not therefore well suited for the rest of the mind. The melody apart, the singer of the *Sâma* also keeps the track of the meaning. That is why *Brahaddevta*[5] states that one who understands *Sâma* also understands *Vedas* (8.130). *Yâgyavalkya* in this context further points out that a person singing hymns from *Sâma* in a proper manner and cautiously practicing them attains God.[6] It has traditionally come to be believed that the hymns of *Sâma* sung in the prescribed rhythmical order please gods much and the singer attains the fruit of his prayer fast.

As pointed out, *Sâmaveda Samhitâ* is composed entirely in metrical form. It borrows considerably from the *Rigveda*. It consists of 1875 *mantras* in all out of which 1504 have been borrowed from the *Rigveda*.

Sâma, the Meaning

In the performance of the *Yajna*, the priest called *Udgâta* sings from the *Sâmaveda*. 'Sa', the first letter stands for *richa* or the stanza. 'Am', the later part of the term stands for the high pitch of the sound. This relationship of the *richa* and the sound has been ornamentally pointed out in the *Atharvaveda* stating that the pair of these man and woman is the basis of all creation. *Chhândogyopnishad* further explains this relationship suggesting that the voice and the *Prana* are *Rik* and *Sâma* respectively.[8]

Sâma stands for equilibrium and peace. The divinity can only be attained when a devotee sings in praise of his revered deity. This helps him attain concentration through absorption and brings about a state of union, *Yoga*.

---

5 सामानि यो वेत्ति स वेद तत्वम् (ब५.8.130)

6 यथाधिानेन पठन् सामगानमविच्युतम्
   सवधानस्तदभ्यासात् परं ब्रह्माधिगच्छति (या.3.4.11.2)

7 अमोऽहमस्मि सा त्वं सामाहमस्मि ऋक् त्वम्
   द्यौरहं पृथिवी त्वं ताविह संभवाय प्रजामजनयावहै ।(अ.14.2.71)

8 वाक् च प्राणश्च ऋक् च साम च (छा।.1.1.5)

Branches of Sâmaveda

In his commentary *Patanjali* mentions that there are as many as one thousand branches of *Sâmaveda*. It seems that because *Sâmaveda* is somehow related to the Sun and the Sun is supposed to be having one thousand rays, *Sâmaveda* has come to be known as having one thousand branches. Moreover, *Sâma* being a text to be sung there could very well exist thousand ways of singing it. Thirteen branches are, however, specifically mentioned in ancient books, which are following-

1. Rânâyanîya, 2. Asurâyaniya, 3. Vasurâyaniya, 4. Vartantareya, 5.Prânjala, 6. Shatyâyniya, 7. Satyamudgala, 8. Khalwala, 9. Mahâkhalwala, 10. Langla, 11. Kauthum, 12. Gautama and 13.Jeminîîya.

There are only *Rânâynîya*, *Kauthuma* and *Jeminîîya* branches available at present. The first two out of these have no difference in the order of *Mantras*. The division of these branches runs into *Adhyaya*, *Khanda* and *Mantras*. In case of the *Jerminiya Shakha*, the division consists of *Prapâthaka*, *Ardhaprapâthaka* and *Dashati*. *Kauthuma Shakha* has been popular in the north of *Vindhyâchala* Mountain whereas *Ranâyaniya* got spread over south of it. The other name of *Kauthuma* is *Chhandosgama, which* is popular in the Indian states of Tamilnadu and Karnataka. The ancient name of the *Jeminîîya Shâkha* is *Talavakâra*. The parts of this branch known as *Samhitâ*, *Brâmana*, *Srotsutra*, and *Grahyasutra* are available at present. It is important to note that distinction of the branches is to be marked because of the difference of pronunciation.

The Form of the Sâmaveda

The *Mantras* of the *Sâmaveda* are divided into two main categories called *Archikâ* (prayers) and *Gâna* (songs). The former is further divided into two called *Purvarrchika* and *Uttararchikâ*. All the two parts consist of 1810 stanzas. Some of them get crepitated again and again. Taking out these repetitions, the total number gets reduced to 1549. However, barring just 15 *Richas*, the rest have been borrowed from the eighth and ninth *Mandala of the Rigveda* only. Further, the *richas* are composed in the meter *Gayatri* or Paragatha, the mixed form of *Gâyatri* and *Jagati*.

Pûrvârchikâ is also known as *Chhanda Archikâ*. It consists of six *Prapâthaka;* chapters, which are further, divided each into two categories called *Ardhakahnda* with one more subdivision called *Dashati. Dashati* generally consists of ten *Richâs.*

In the first *Prapâthaka* of *Purvârchikâ,* there are *Richas* from *Rigveda* pertaining to *Agni.* This has been called *Âgneyakânda.* The *Prapâthaka* from the second to the four has been called *Yendra Parva* implying that the *Mantras* of it belong to *Indra.* The fifth one consists of the prayers of *Soma* and therefore called *Pavamâna Parva.* The sixth *Prapâthaka* is known as *Âranya Parva.* It comprises of a number of gods and meters. The last part of it is known as *Mahanamny Ârchikâ,* which consists of only ten *Richâs.* It is taken to be the appendix as such. That is the analysis of 650 *Richâs* of *Purvârchikâ.*

Uttrârchikâ consists of nine *Prapâthakas* the first five of which have two subdivisions called *Prapâthkârdha.* The last four *Prapâthakas* have three such subdivisions. The number of the *Mantras of Uttrârchik* is 1225. Adding 650 of *Pûrvârchikâ* the number goes upto 1875. 267 *Mantras* find repetition. Union of three Richâs has composed a song. These songs go into the making of hymns sung during the performance of the *Yajna.* As against the order of *Richâs* in sequence of the meter or god in *Pûrvrâchikâ, Uttarârchikâ* sets it in order of the *Yajna.*

Jemini,[9] the disciple of *Vedavyâsa* stated that *Sâma* is just singing. The rhythm is the essence of all music. *Sâmaveda* therefore makes suitable modifications in the *Richâs* for them to conform to the musical requirement. There are, for instance, some sounds called *Stobha* added accordingly. They are more or less in the lines a musician converts songs while performing a vocal presentation.

Sound is the spirit of the *Sâma. Udâtta* (stressed), *Anudâtta* (unstressed), and *Swarit* are three sounds finding place right from the period of *Rigveda. Udâtta* sound is well suited for the high pitch song whereas *Anudâtta* is appropriate for the low pitch voice and *Swarit* for the moderate. These three basic sounds later became

---

9 गीतिषु सामाख्या

the source of seven *Shadaj Swaras* of the modern music. *Nârdiya Samhitâ* [10] points out that *Udâtta* is to be compared with *Gândhâr* or its (*Samvâdi*) matching *Swar Nishâd*, *Anudâtta* with *Rishabh* or its *Samvâdi Dhaivat* and *Swarit* with *Shadaj* or its *Samvâdi* either *Madhyam* or *Pancham*.

The seven sound cycle of *Sâmgan* has been described as follows in *Sâm-Vidhân Brâmana*

1. *Atikrusht,* the sound in which gods sing- *Pa*

2. *Prathama,* sound used by human beings- *Ma*

3. *Dwitiya,* sound used by *Gândharva* and *Apsarâs*- *Ga*

4. *Tritiya,* Sound used by animals- *Re*

5. *Chaturtha,* Sound in use of birds- *Sa*

6. *Panchama,* Nishad Sound in use of demons- *Ni*

7. *Shashtha,* Sound made by herbs, plants and other creatures- *dha*

It has been suggested in this way that every matter or spirit of universe has a voice. When these are used in a prescribed combination, the harmonious music is produced. *Sâmaveda* is the scripture of such harmony intended to be attained in life with the help of a celestial scheme of manifold sounds.

The *Sâm Vidhân Brâhmana* further points out six *Vikârs,* which are the modifications of letters and syllables in accordance with the metrical requirement of the *Veda*. These modifications are sometimes brought about by addition and sometimes by deletions. These are as follows-

1. *Vikâr:* The suitable modification of a syllable such as *ognayi* for *Agni*.

2. *Vishleshana:* Breaking up a word.

3. *Vikarshana:* Prolonged stresses of sounds.

4. *Abhyâsa:* Repetition of a syllable or its part again and again.

---

5. *Virâma:* Observing silence and gaps in between.

6. *Stobh:* Adding up new sounds

In view of the specific sound arrangement of the *Sâmaveda,* some of the western commentator such as Winternitz has gone to suggest that they have much to do with magic. In India, likewise, with the start of *Sâmgan,* the chanting of *Rigveda* and *Yajurveda* had to be stopped.

As a matter of fact, *Sâmveda* represents and is suggestive of the significance of sound in the origin and development of the world. Right from the 'Big Bang' knock in the beginning, the world is undergoing through the process of evolution through the harmony of cosmic rhythm. This process may be expedited when the planned metrical setting of *Sâmaveda* is employed. Modern scientific researches have also proved that there are electromagnetic waves created by music affecting nervous order of living beings. This brings about a better harmony for faster evolution of the world.

Vedic music also helps human beings strike better coordination among human beings and gods. *Rigveda* states, 'the way a thirsty deer, drinks water from a pond, you (god) enjoy my songs sung in your praise.[11] The origin of the word *'Sâma'* as pointed out by some grammarians, is a technique by which gods are pleased.[12]

Brâmanas of Sâmaveda - There are seven *Brâmanas* of *Sâmaveda* namely, *Tândya, Shadvinsha, Sâma Vidhana, Arsheya, Devtadhyaya, Samhitopnishad* and *Vansh Brâman.* The second *Shadvinsha Brâmana* is the 26th part of *Tândya* therefore the first part is also known as *Panch Vinsha Brâmana.* These two parts apart, *Chhândogyopnishad* added to them, constitute *Tândya Mahâ Brâmana.* Because *Shadvinsh Brâman* contains some strange stories, it is also called *Adbhût Brâmana.* As regards *Aranyaks, Talavkaranyaka* and *Chhandogyaranyaka* are the names. Similarly, it has three *Upnishads* namely, *Kenopnishad, chhandogyonishad*

---

11 सेम न स्तोमम् आगाहि
   उपेदं सवन सुतम्
   गौरो न तृषितृ पिब । (ऋ. 1.16.5)
12 संतोषयति देवान् अनेन्

and *maitrayaniyopnishad*. *Chhandgyopnishad* is a highly philosophical book which also throws enough light on the cultural history of the Vedic times. *Shri Hajâri Prasad Dwivedi* has written a classical novel in Hindi called *Anâmdâs Kâ Potha* on the story of one seer *Raikwa* who is said to be a realised soul. Likewise, *Kenopnishad* deals with important philosophical matters with the help of deep questions. *Sâmaveda* also has some *Sûtra Granths* known as *Prâtishakhya* which are following-

1.*Mashak Kalp Sutra* 2. *Kshudra Sûtra* 3. *Latyâyan Shrot Sutra* and 4. *Gobhiliya Grihya Sutra*. As regards *Rânâynîya* branch, its books are- 1. *Drahyayan Shrot Sutra* 2. *Khadir Grahya Sutra* and 3. *Pushp Sutra*

Pûrvârchikâ

As stated earlier, this first out of the two main parts of *Sâmaveda*, has important *Kânds*, subdivisions called *Âgneya*, *Yendra*, *Pavamâna* and *Aranya*. They are basically predominated by *Agni, Indra, Soma* and a composite of various gods respectively. These are further divided into various chapters. The gods have been invoked and glorified in highly poetic style in them. Incidentally there are several notes and utterances of a universal order, which recurrently find places. Some of these important key-notes have been therefore reproduced separately for bringing home the eternal truth imbibed in them.

Important Key-notes from Sâmaveda

Pûrvârchikâ

1. (*Agni!* You have been produced after churning by *Atharva*

2. I seek protection from *Richâs*

3. *Indra!* All others operate under your command

4. I invoke *Indra* for assistance in every action every time

5. *Indra!* No one excels you

6. Bestow on us the intellect superior

7. One who has died today, shall begin a fresh journey tomorrow

8. Do not use tough words

9. Cows are always sacred

Uttarârchikâ

1. Reach the centre of the truth

2. Witness the cosmic poetry of creation

3. A poet becomes sacred by expression

4. Produce nutritious grain on earth

5. One who is awake to him *Richa* opts

6. One who is awake, he realizes equanimity

7. One who keeps awake to him this *Soma* reaching states 'I will stay with you as your friend'

8. Knowledge is my armour inside

9. May we hear good from our ears, o gods!

1   अथर्वा त्वां निरमन्थत (मंत्र 9)

2   ऋचा वरेएयं अव: यामि (48)

3   इन्द्र तत् सर्व ते वशे (126)

4   योगे योगे वाजे वाजे ऊतये तवस्तरं इन्द्रं हवामहे (163)

5   इन्द्र त्वां न अतिरिच्यते (197)

6   न: कतुं आ भर (259)

7   अद्य ममार सह्य: समान (325)

8   उग्रं वच: अपावधी: (353)

9   गाव: सदा शुचय: (442)

10 ऋतस्य योनिं आ अग्मन् (659)

11 विश्वानि काव्या अभि (775)

12 कवि: गीर्भि: पवित्रं अत्येति (1175)

13 पृथिव्या: अधि द्युम्नं (1186)

14 यो जागार तं ऋच: कामयन्ते (1826)

15 यो जागार तं उ सामानि यन्ति (1826)

16 य: जागार तं अयं सोम: आह, तव सख्ये अहं अस्मि (1826)

17 ब्रह्म मम अन्तर वर्म (1872)

18 भद्रं कर्णेभि: शृणुयाम देवा: (1874)

8

Atharva Veda

There is a reference to three *Vedas* and three *Vidyâs* (three paths of attainment- knowledge, action and worship) at various places in most of the original and ancient *Sanskrit* literature. *Atharva Veda* is thus said to have attained the status and recognition of a *Veda* historically much later. The contents, the language, the much evolved forms of the gods and goddesses as well as some superstitious charms and spells finding expression in this book are suggestive of its having been compiled much later. Thus although fourth in order, this *Veda* is no less important as one of its name is 'Brahmveda' as such which is indicative of its all encompassing significance. It does not confine itself to the happiness of the other world alone like earlier three *Vedas*, but assures both the material as well spiritual success. There are four types of gains worth attaining in the world i.e. *Dharma*, (religious) *Artha*, (financial) *Kâma* (worldly desires) and *Moksh* (salvation). *Atharvaveda* ensures that all these attainments are available for a person living in this world.

Traditionally looking, there were four classes of priests necessary for the performance of a *Yajna*. The first class of acolytes was called *Hotrî*. They used to invoke gods by reciting *mantras* from the *Rigveda*. The second was that of the choristers, *udgata* singing hymns from the *Samaveda*. The third category consisted of reciters, *adhwaryu*, chanting *mantras* from *Yajurveda* for the performance of the *yajna*. The last category belonged to the supervisor, *Brahmâ*, who was to be the scholar of *Atharvaveda*.

Atharvaveda owes its origin basically to one seer called *Atharvan*. Literally *Atharvan* stands for a seer who is capable of controlling his senses and remain calm. Another seer that finds long mentions is *Angira*. *Angira* is closely related to *Agni,* the fire. This is just opposite of *Atharva* in the meaning, which indicates that this *Veda* stands for both, the calm and the fierce aspect of human life.

The Form and the Contents

There are twenty books or *Kândas* in the *Atharvaveda*. In the first thirteen *Kândas,* the hymns are not arranged according to their contents. There is a heterogeneous mix of prayers, charms, spells, benedictions and invocations. *Kânda* fourteen confines to marriages, *Kânda* fifteen to wandering mendicants, *Kânda* fifteen and sixteen with conjuring and *Kânda* eighteen with funeral rites. *Kânda* 19 is a mixed bag of hymns, while *Kânda* twenty is basically culled from the *Rigveda* and consists of hymns addressed to *Indra*

As regards, the form, the first seven *Kândas* seem to be having some arrangement in terms of the number of the verses of the hymns. For instance, the hymns of *Kânda* one have four verses and those of *Kânda* two five. *Kânda* three similarly has six, *Kânda* four seven and *Kânda* five eight to eighteen verses. Further, *Kânda* six has three and *Kânda* seven from one to eleven verses. In subsequent *Kândas,* the number of verse extends even up to eighty verses. The entire *Atharvaveda* thus consisting of 740 hymns has 5962 verses in the following order-

Kânda	Number of hymns	Number of verses
1	35	153
2	36	207
3	31	230
4	40	324
5	31	376
6	142	454
7	118	286

8	10	259
9	10	302
10	10	350
11	10	373
12	5	304
13	4	188
14	2	139
15	28	220
16	8	103
17	1	30
18	4	283
19	72	453
20	143	928
Total	740	5962

Contents

In the first and the second *Kânda* of *Atharvaveda,* there are *mantras* pertaining to various diseases, enemies, worms and long life. The third deals with the hypnotising of the enemy and his forces, the election of a king, farming and animal husbandry. In the fourth there are topics like Supreme knowledge, destruction of poison, coronation, purification from sins and rains etc. The fifth describes the significance of the *Brâhmanas* and how to destroy enemies. The sixth covers the removal of bad dreams; increase of grains and the seventh the knowledge about self and the verses about victory. Eighth *Kânda* contains the number of the letters of seven metres of the *Rigveda* and the ninth the details of the medicine *Madhukasha,* the hospitability of guests and the hymn for the removal of tuberculosis. The tenth talks about the knowledge of the Supreme and His Greatness and the eleventh about the significance of the celibacy. The twelfth contains the famous *'Prithvi Sûkta'* and the thirteenth that of spirituality. In the fourteenth *Kânda* the verses about matrimonial rites figure elaborately. The fifteenth describes Almighty Lord as *'Vrâtya'*. The sixteenth carries hymns for the removal of sorrows and seventeenth for charms and hypnosis. Eighteenth *Kânda* describes the funeral ceremony and the nineteenth contains knowledge about astrology. There are details about stars, time and the auspicious moments for coronation and sacrifices. The twentieth *Kânda* is about *Somyaga*. It also contains verses about *Indra* and *Kuntâp Sûkta*, which lauds about the charities of kings and their priests.

It has been thus concluded that *Atharvaveda* represents a very old saga of human history. It is more representative of its time than any other Veda. It may as well be said that as compared to *Rigveda*, which represents a specified class of scholars or the warriors, *Atharvaveda* depicts the life of the common man. Western commentators such as Whitney and Bloomfield associate the hymns of *Atharvaveda* with magic and the charms. Bloomfield even interprets some pure spiritual hymns to be carrying the meaning of the magical art. Indian commentators find a much deeper meaning indeed. Some medicinal herbs' prescription and a few faith healing suggestions cannot be discarded as simple superstitions. The art of making use of the power of mind is best exemplified in some of the techniques suggested in it.

Social Order

Various classes and casts of the society find a repeated mention in the book. Brahmans definitely occupy a distinct place in the society. He commands respect in the society because he is the storehouse of great knowledge. It has been advised that Brahmans should not be tortured.[1] *Kshatriyas,* the warrior class controls the people. It therefore deserves to rule.[2] Farming, animal husbandry and trade are important functions of the society. *Vaishya* and *Shudra* are the functionaries for them.

As regards four stages of life, the first part of celibacy is quite important. It virtually lays the foundation in life. In verse 17 of hymn 5 of *Kânda* 11 it has been suggested that celibacy

---

1 न ब्राह्मणो हिंसितव्य:

2 अयं विशां विश्पतिरस्तु राजा

keeps the nation integrated, it prepares teachers for teaching and it adds charms for a girl to get married.[3] The second phase of house holding is marked with the physical, mental and spiritual union of man and woman. The woman has a very high place in the family. The daughter in law immediately becomes the empress of all her in laws- the mother in law, the father in law, the brother in law and the sister in law.[4] She has a full sharing in the fortune of her husband. There appears to be no specific description of the third stage of forest living, *Vânprastha* and Renunciation, but some indications can be collected. The *Prithvi Sûkta* in *Kânda* 12 describes the forestland vividly. It is indicative of the fact that these seers had the direct experience of living in forests. In the fifteen *Kânda*, *Vrâtya* finds an elaborate depiction. As a matter of fact, he is a *Sanyâsi* who is always on the move for the welfare of others.

Atharvaveda teaches to lead a complete life of success, worldly and otherworldly both. It is necessary first of all that a human being is healthy and disease free. Therefore, if there is any attack of diseases, the precaution and the cure should first be available. For a man to live happily, he should have grain, money, animals and servants. Then there should be harmony in the society. There should be just and honest rulers who should not be exploiting his subjects. Finally, peace and tranquillity should prevail on earth with a sense of global brotherhood irrespective of a number of languages, faiths and the parts of land and water.[5]

Classification of Hymns

The hymns of *Atharvaveda* can broadly be classified into following categories-

1.   Medicinal Cures

2.   Longevity in Life

---

3   ब्रहमचर्येण तपसा राजा राष्ट्रं वि रक्षति
    आचार्यो ब्रहमचर्येण ब्रहमचारिणिमिच्छते
    ब्रह्मचर्येण कन्या युवानं विन्दते पतिम्
4   सम्राज्ञेधि श्वशुरेषु सम्राज्ञंयुत देवृषु
    ननान्दुः सम्राज्ञेधि सम्राज्ञंयुत श्वश्रवः (14.1.44)
5   जनं बिभ्रती बहुधा विवाचसं
    नाना धर्माणं पृथिवी यथौकसम्

3.   Prosperity

4.   Repentances

5.   Women

6.   Kingship

7.   Sacrifices

8.   Philosophy

9.   Nationality

10.   World Peace

11.   Miscellaneous

1. Medicinal Cures – These hymns pertain to various diseases and their cure by the application of prescribed medicinal herbs as well as by the level of the mind after chanting these hymns. There is some times the presiding deity of the particular disease or the evil force causing disease, which has been addressed. The symptoms of various diseases as well as bodily disorders caused by them have been dealt at length. There are 99 diseases finding mention such as fever, leprosy, fainting, cough, breathing trouble, eye diseases, baldness, weakness, boils, snake bite etc. An herb to cure leprosy has been described in verse 1.23.1[6] The various medicinal herbs and their attributes have been described minutely and in full scientific details. Chlorophyll, for instance, find a mention in the form of *'Avi'* in 10th chapter in verse 31 of hymn eighth.

2. Longevity- Health occupies a very important place in human life. There are a number of hymns devoted for expressing the need and desire to live long. The chanting of these hymns marked all social rites. It has been prayed at time and again that all human senses, i.e. eyes, ears etc. should keep working in their natural form for hundred years.[7]

---

6   नक्तं जातस्यौषधे रामे कृष्णे असिक्निन च
     दूरं रजनि रजय किलासं पलितञ्च यत् ॥
7   पश्येम शरद: शतम् । जीवेम् शरद: शतम् (19.67.1–2)

3. Prosperity- All communities of the society, shepherds, farmers, tradesmen pray for their prosperity. There are verses depicting the art of house construction, ploughing field, and sowing seed, fast increase of the crop and the destruction of sects spoiling the crop. The importance of rains becomes important at such time. The mother earth has been prayed in a highest poetry ever written in 66 verses of hymn first of the twelfth kanda. "Oh, earths, you who keep stored all kind of richness, give me gold, jewels, grains and prosperity."[8]

4. Repentances- *Atharvaveda* prescribes repentances for many types of sins and misdeeds. There are *mantras* prescribed for controlling evil deeds. It is to be acknowledged that the Christian faith does incorporate this concept at length. It is, however, worth mention that the *Atharvaveda* is not simply concerned with the confession as such but also provides for making good any default in the performance of sacrificial rituals and other deeds. The purifications process at the time of making lapses or getting impure in mind, word or deed is quite exhaustive. A sin committed whether in knowledge or otherwise and the non performance of prescribed duties —all have got to be complied with chanting of hymns prescribed for the purpose. There are also prescriptions for removing the evil effect of mal planets, bad dreams and bad omens.

5. Women- Women occupy a prominent and highly respectable place in the society depicted by the *Atharvaveda*. The marriage ceremony and the mutual obligations on the part of man and woman are specifically discussed and respectively assigned. The relationship of the bride with her in laws is also described and a complete harmony and orderliness in family as well as in the society has been determined.

There are hymns detailing some rituals at the arrival of the bride in the house for her to make free from evil effects. There are also some such prescriptions for the childbirth and for the welfare and the security of the baby in the womb. *Kânda* fourteen of this Veda is full of hymns of this kind. There are even prescriptions for the control of co-wife by way of charm and hypnosis.

---

8   निधिं विभ्रती बहुधा गुहा वसु मणिं हिरण्यं पृथिवी ददातु ये
    वसूनि नो वसुदा राम्माना देवी दधातु सुमनस्यमाना (12.1.44)

6. Kingship- Royal heritage, coronation ceremonies and the rights as well as the rights and responsibilities of kings find suitable mention in the book. There are prayers made for the victory of the king and the annihilation of his enemies. There are furious wars described. The royal priest occupied a special place since he employed and exercised some special techniques for the success of his mentor. The election of the king is also described. The role of *Varuna* used to be that of a supervisor in it. The king should keep his friends posted at various places and his kingdom should be surrounded by friendly states, has been stated. (6.8.3)

The subjects of a king should live in prosperity and have ample milk, gold, ghee, grains and animals. A king who got elected because of his own power and competence used to be called '*Swarâta*'. In another system called '*Virâta*', the subjects were free to elect a king of their choice. In still one more form of government called '*Samrâta*', there were people's representatives forming the government. Various section of the society exercised similar rights. It has been stressed that there should not be any discrimination among people and all sections of the society should live in peace and harmony (12.1.2). The people should be toiling together and even their thought waves should meet so that all differences are wiped out.

7. Sacrifices- Towards the end of the *Atharvaveda,* there are some hymns for sacrificial purposes. It may be primarily because it is an assimilation of the characteristics of all three basic books of *Vedas,* namely, *Rik, Yajush* and *Sama* and secondly because the compilers of it were concerned that this finds a place in the category of *Vedas.* There are obviously some similarities with other Veda books. Two *Apri Sûkta,* for instance, are characteristically from *Rigveda* and the prose part praising water of the sixteenth *Kânda* has similarities with that of *Yajurveda.* The hymns about *Yama* and the funeral rites of the eighteenth *Kânda* have many similarities with the hymns of the *Yama Sûkta* of *Rigveda.* Likewise the *mantras* about the drinking of *Soma* in the twentieth *Kânda* are also worth mentioning in this context.

8. Philosophy- *Skambha Sûkta (10.7), Jyestha Sûkta (10.8), Kâl Sûkta (19.53), Mahad Brahma (1.32), Vak (6.30)* and *Adhyâtma*

(9.10) are all those hymns, which dive deep into the depths of being and its origin. It explores in a much larger perspective how this world is managed and governed by a superior order set in motion by the Supreme Being, *Brahma*. It has been therefore rightly called *'Brahma Veda'.* The technique of depictions the scripture employs, is imaginative and interesting. There are various symbols and parables used to bring home quite deep and mystical values.

It has been stated time and again that there is one and only one God who may be having innumerable names and attributes. The scripture itself offers many such names such as *Skambha, Uchchhista, and Vrâtya* etc. Obviously, the depiction of *Virâta* or *Viswarûpa* of *Mahâbhârat* and *Purânas* do have their origin in the all-encompassing vision of the Vedic seers of these *mantras.*

9. Nationality- Motherland and the nation are at times synonyms. Subjects of the states of the *Atharvaveda* earnestly desire that the enemies of their country should get destroyed. There are warfares, charms, rituals, prayers, prowess, arms and strategies evolved to fight enemies of the nation and ruin them completely. These enemies are rather the enemies of peace and progress therefore due assistance is also sought from the divine forces who can very well overcome them. Seer *Vasishtha* in *Sûkta* twenty-nine of *Kânda* one prays gods to grant him that emerald which *Indra* possessed for defeating his enemies. The seer encourages warriors to get ready to defeat enemies who are agents of terror. He is confident in the end that after vanquishing these terrorists, the victorious forces will receive honours for their courage and sacrifice. The rulers and the subjects shall then live in peace and prosperity.

In the *Prithivi Sûkta* again, in verse fourteen, mother earth is prayed to help fight those intruders and enemies of the nation who attack on it with enmity and evil intentions, kill innocent people and try to make its subjects slaves.

10. World Peace – *Atharvaveda* speaks of equanimity and order everywhere, whether family, country and the human society at large. It wishes that human families should live in conformity, happiness and in good health.[9] Taking meals and drinks together is suggestive of healthy social system advocated. The Vedic seer desires that eating and drinking together human beings should live like a wheel whose spokes always remain united.[10] The famous *Prithivi Sûkta* takes into account every particle of it in high imaginative and scientific accuracy. However, the geographical unity of it is in itself suggestive of the oneness of whole human race. The way a cow's milk makes no discrimination among people belonging to any caste, creed or land, similarly mother earth is one integrated home for every one to live and be nourished abundantly.[11] The seer constantly keeps wishing that people should have conformity in their thoughts, minds and heart. Consultations, action plans and their execution should also take place in an orderly manner (6.64). Surely, the results of such an approach would always be concrete and rewarding. It teaches high moral principles like truth, non-violence, good conduct, friendly good behaviour, courage and sweet worded conversation. It advises people to give up enmity, lust, anger and greed. It has also been advised that gambling, harsh words, indebtedness, ego, laziness and anger should be given up. Even measures of internal as well as international security and relationship find mention whose significance is equally important till date. For instance, the honesty integrity and dutifulness of the servants of a state, the honour for democracy, good governance, powerful army, sophisticated weaponry and the strategic fighting skills have been emphasised. It is ultimately world peace and human brotherhood that is the central note as the seer prays for all to be secure and fearless. Let there be peace dawning on earth, heaven, waters, plants, herbs, worlds, and gods and on peace itself.[12] In this ideal society of the Veda, all directions are expected to be friendly alone.[13]

---

9 यत्रा सुहादा: सुकृती मदन्ति (6.120.3)

10 संजानीध्वं स पृच्यध्व...समन मन्त्र:..., समी व अकूत: (6.64.-3)

11 सहस्र धारा द्रविणस्य मे दुहां धुवेवं धेनुरनपस्फूरन्ती (12.1.45)

12 पृथिवी शान्तिरन्तरिक्षं शान्तिद्यौ: शान्तिराप: शान्तिरोषधय: शान्तिर्वनस्पतय:
शान्तिर्विश्वे मे देवा: शान्ति: सर्वे मे देवा:शान्ति: शान्ति: शान्ति: शान्तिभि: (19.9.13)

13 अभयं मित्रादभयंमित्रादभयं ज्ञातादभयंपुरो य:
अभयं नक्तमभयं दिवा न: सर्वा आशा मम मित्रं भवन्तु । (19.15.6)

11. Miscellaneous- There are a number of various other topics covered, which throw adequate light on the life of the people living in the Vedic era as well as their interrelationship with society within and outside. There are ways suggested for animal husbandry, making livelihood through agriculture and trade and increasing cows, progenies, horses, health and long life. Modern and quite scientific as well as auspicious models of architectural designs about house construction have been provided. The houses, it has been suggested should have sufficient height. It should have a room to sit (*sadah*), a room to sleep (*patni sadan*), a part for cooking (*agnishalam*) and one allocated for god worship (*devanam sadah*). Its roof should be high enough to accommodate human conscience.[14] There are various kinds of crafts and crafts-man such as *twashta* (carpenter), blacksmith (*Karmar*), goldsmith (*Hiranyakar*), barber (*vapta*) and washer-man (*malag*).

Some Important Sûktas of Atharvaveda

As already pointed out, the subject matter of the *Atharvaveda* is manifold. It covers nearly all facets of the private and social life of an individual. But the most remarkable part of its contribution is its deep introvert approach towards understanding the creation, the creator and human relationship with it. Some such important Sûktas are briefly mentioned below.

Sûktas about the Creator- *Kânda* 10 is very important as it investigates in a unique way about the mysteries of life. Its approach is totally non-conventional and it has its original attributes to apply to the Creator. *Sûkta* 2 is *Ken Sûkta*. The seer investigates very closely about the unique nature of different organs of human body in it. The word *'Ken'* means from what. Many profound metaphysical and philosophical questions gradually suggest that the Creator of this unique world is beyond human comprehension. There is an *Upnishada* called *Kenopnishad*, which probably borrows its tone and texture from this *Sûkta*.

Enquiring about human body the seer asks, "Who created the structure of men? Who made the muscles and who made the

---

14 धरुण्यसि शाले बृहच्छन्द: पूतिधन्या (3.12.3)

calves? Who created the flesh and handsome fingers? Who created the senses? And who was it that stuck two legs at the base? Who gave forms to the central parts of the body?"

The mystery of dualities of the world is quite amusing. Moreover, the much deeper sense behind such creation suggests how superior in imaginative creativity did the Creator rest! "The world is full of sweet speech and harsh words." The seer goes on to elaborate," It has sleep, danger and impediments. But there is also happiness and bliss. Who is that great one who made all these? Why did he create the world?" About the perpetuity of life and the cosmic designing of the creation, the seer has to question and exclaim, "Who framed the concept of birth so that living beings may perpetuate their kind? Who gave living beings intelligence and the power to use their tongues? Who taught them how to dance?

"Who covered the ground? Who circumscribed heaven? Who made the mountains great? Who inspires men to action?"

The Vedic seer knows quite well that such a perfection and orderliness in various objects and experiences of life presuppose a creator assigning a definite and deeper meaning to life and the world. The attributes of such a creator (the seer calls him *Brahma*) are as manifold as those of his creation. "The Brahma is spread everywhere. It is known as the *Purush*. He is in all directions." The word *Purush* is suggestive of one who lives in a city, *Pur*. Ironically, however, this *Purush* is not confined to any particular limited city. The whole universe is the city in which he resides all over. This city has eight concrete circles, *Chakras* and nine invincible doors in it. It has been thus stated that one who knows this dwelling house of the Creator, he is sure 'not to be deserted by his sight or the vital force before the old age'.[15]

Skambha – *Sûkta* seven of this *Kânda* describes the cosmic character of the creator in the form of a column. It is like *Virata*

---

15 केनेयं भूमिर्विहिता केन द्यौरुत्तरा हिता
केनेदमूर्ध्वं तिर्यक्चान्तरिक्षं व्यचो हितम्
ब्रह्मणा भूमिर्विहिता ब्रह्म द्यौरुत्तरा हिता
ब्रह्मेदमूर्ध्वं तिर्यक् चानतरिक्षं व्यचो हितम् (10.2.24-25)

or *Vishwarupa* exhibited by Lord Krishna before *Arjuna* in the eleventh chapter of the *Bhagwadgita*. All exclamations and questioning about the unique world and its attributes lead the seer to the conclusion that everything rests and rises from *Skambha* only. The seer tries to find out how earth and heaven originated? How Sun shines everyday? What is the direction where Winds keep running? Where are days, months and years running for? Two women, one white and the other black (morning and evening) are constantly weaving cloth on the pegs of six seasons. These dancing girls yet all not suggest who is first among them. But the skilled craft man, the Creator in a beautiful manner, makes the weaving thread prepared by them. [16]

Jyeshtha- Seer *Kutsa* in *Sûkta* eight of *Kânda* ten invokes and prays *Jyestha Brahma,* Almighty Superior. This Lord is all-pervasive and is equally present in present, past and future. He is subtler than the hair for any one to witness. He is a woman, a man, a boy and a girl, all at one time. He is the one who walks with a stick when got old and when manifested becomes cosmic faced. [17] This Lord is so close that he cannot be forgiven but he cannot simply seen. The world this superior Lord has created is mysterious in many ways. It is like a poetry, which does not banish and never becomes old. [18]

Uchchhisstha- One more unique name, which the Creator of the world is given here, is *Uchchhishtha*. It implies that the God always remains available after partaking his being in the making of this world. In the famous *Purush Sûkta* the Vedic seer talks of four parts of the creator. He employs just one fourth in creating the world. Three fourth which remains intact with him in balance is *Uchchhishtha* which finds depiction in this seventh *Sûkta* of *Kânda* nineteen. This is again a description of the cosmic form of the

---

16 तन्त्रमेके युवती विरूपे अीयाक्रामं वयत: षण्मयूखम्
प्रान्या तन्तूस्तिरते ध्त्ते अन्या नाप वृजान्ते न गमातो अन्तम्
तयोरहं परिनृत्योरिव न वि जानामि यतरा परस्तात्
पुमानेन्द्वयत्युद्गृणत्ति पुमानेनद्वि जभराधि नाके
इमे मयूखा उप तस्त भुर्दिवं सामानि चक्रुस्तसराणि वातवे। (10.42–45)
17 त्वं स्त्री त्वं पुमानसि त्वं कुमार उत वा कुमारी
त्वं जीर्णो दण्डेन वंचसि त्वं जातो भवसि विश्वतोमुख: । (10.27)
18 पश्य देवस्य काव्यं न ममार न जीर्यति (10.32)

creator. He is like the centre of the wheel of creation and all the gods are like spokes attached to it. He is a form and a name in one representing the basic character of the creation. All that exists and that which is non-existing are present in him. The earth, the heaven, waters, winds, air and all living beings are present in him.[19] All knowledge, the storehouse of great knowledge, Vedas has have their origin in him.[20]

Prithivi Sûkta- Sixty-three *mantras* of *Sûkta* one of *Kânda* twelve are a specimen of the first and foremost superb world poetry in praise of mother earth. Its contents are very rich from the point of view of philosophy, thoughts, emotions and objective perceptions. Moreover, the depiction of the wealth, resources and the movements of earth are all scientifically true facts for any modern investigator to carry forward the investigation. The *Sûkta* begins with the mention that truthfulness, true knowledge, martial prowess, righteousness, skill in performing deeds, performing sacrifices and giving alms are the qualities which are necessary for the protection of the motherland.

There are many oceans, rivers, streams, lakes, ponds and waterfall in it. It produces all sorts of grains, vegetables and fruit. There are a numerous kinds of beings living in it. In it we find hard working farmers and artisans. The famous warriors of yore performed valorous deeds here. Gold, silver, diamonds, emeralds and other gems are found in it.

In the beginning, this great land was immersed in the water of the ocean. There is abundant milk and clarified butter provided by cows in it. Brave warriors have measured the length and breadth of this earth in the past. Learned and powerful ones freed it from enemies. The righteous ones are worshipped in it and sacrifices are important for its elevation.

Seer *Atharva* has many deep emotional touches felt and expressed while invoking mother earth in this *Sûkta*. "O my

---

19 उच्छिष्टे द्यावा पृथिवी विश्वं भूतं समाहितं
   आप: समुद्र उच्दिष्टे चन्द्रमा वात अर्हित: (19.7.1)
20 ऋचा सामानि छन्दान्सि पुराणं यजुषा सह
   उच्छिष्टा जज्ञिरे सर्वे दिवि देवा दिविश्रत: (19.7.24)

motherland", the seer says, " We your children want to serve you. We are all your subjects. May all of us be gifted with sweet speech! May we live together in harmony!"

Earth is the source of all fragrance. This fragrance best manifests in herbs. it enters into the lotuses. Gods use it when they go for attending the marriage of the dawn. This fragrance is equally present in a man, a woman, a girl, an elephant, a horse, and a deer and is the actual identity of each one of them.

The seer prays the earth to display the happy rays of the sun for its vast expanse." May I enjoy a long life in this great expanse! May my eyesight and other senses never become dull. May you protect me when I turn my sleep to the right or to the left! May the seeds I sow grow fast! May you grant us all that we desire!"

The forty-fifth verse of this hymn is one of those eternal notes, which stand for the universal brotherhood of Indian utterances. It points out very vividly that there are a number of religions, languages and creed followed here. There are towns and cities and localities developed in various parts of it. But truly speaking, this one earth is the only home of us all. It is one such cow, which is most simple and allows milking for everyone. It is a cow that has milk constantly flowing from its breasts in thousand streams.[21]

The seer is aware that this land will make flourish all the villages and the cities. The forests, the courts, the assemblies will all be flourishing. He then wishes lastly that those who are born here 'be free from diseases like tuberculosis.' They should live long. They should become learned and get enlightenment. They should be able to make supreme sacrifice whenever necessary. They should ultimately attain fulfilment in life.

Sûrya Vivâh- *Sûkta* one of *Kânda* fourteen is a dramatic presentation of the marriage of *Sûrya,* the daughter of Sun with *Ashwini Kumârs.* There are, however, many mystical references occurring in it which ultimately suggest that the Vedic seer has

---

21 जनं विभ्रती बहुधा विवाचसं ननाधर्माणं पृथिवी यथौकसम्
सहस्रं धारा द्रविणस्य मे दुहां ध्रुवेवं धेनुरनपस्फुरन्ती (12.1.45)

indirectly explained the significance of marriage and prescribed some important rites to keep the custom carry on human society live in discipline on a delicate issue like man and woman relationship. This *Sûkta* is more or less a reproduction of *Sûkta* eighty-five of *Mandala* ten of the *Rigveda*. It, however, represents the society of its time more vividly and provides opportunity for an in depth look into it.

The mind of *Sûrya*, the bride was a chariot on which she travelled while accompanying her husbands his home. The vast sky was like an umbrella, sun and the moon the wheels of his chariot and the wind god himself was driving it in the right direction. The bride is received with great honour amidst glittering celebrations. Her husband's house is no longer foreign to her as she is immediately given the authority to exercise full command on her in laws- She is just not the queen of her husband but the empress of her father, mother, sisters and brother-in-laws![22]

The groom accepts the bride's hand the way the fire accepts the earth. He accepts it for the sake of good fortune. It is under gods' design that they got married. May the husband and wife thus live for hundred years! There is no case of divorce or separation in such a divinely ordained marriage. The seer wishes, " May the husband and the wife always stay united and never be separated. May they have children to play with them! May they live their appointed lifespan in full and help each other complete it when old age has approached!

Brâhmans and Upanishads- *Atharvaveda* has one *Brahman* attached to it which is *Gopatha*. As regards *Aranyaks*, unlike all other three Vedas it has no *Aranyaka* connected to it. However, there are three important *Upanishads, Prashnopnishad, Mundakopnishad* and *Mandukyopnishad* written in the great tradition of *Vedânt* philosophy. *Mundakonishad* borrows its name from the *Mundaka Shâkha* as such. *Prashnopnishad* deals with high philosophical questions through various questions. *Mândukyopnishad* is very small in size and contains only twelve *mantras* but from the point of view of its contents it is quite important.

---

22 साम्राज्ञ्येधि श्वशुरेषु   साम्राज्ञ्युत देवृषु
ननान्दुः सम्राज्ञेधि सम्राज्ञ्युत श्वश्रवः (14.1.44)